WHERE WE LIVE

A
Social History
of
American Housing

Irving Welfeld

SIMON AND SCHUSTER
New York
London
Toronto
Sydney
Tokyo

Simon and Schuster
Simon & Schuster Building
Rockefeller Center
1230 Avenue of the Americas
New York, New York 10020

SIMON AND SCHUSTER and colophon are registered trademarks
of Simon & Schuster Inc.

Designed by Irving Perkins Associates
Manufactured in the United States of America

1   3   5   7   9   10   8   6   4   2

Library of Congress Cataloging in Publication Data
Welfeld, Irving H.
Where we live: a social history of American housing / Irving Welfeld.
p.   cm.
Bibliography: p.
Includes index.
1. Housing—United States.   2. Housing policy—United States.
I. Title.
HD7293.W373   1988
363.5′0973—dc19   88-13106
CIP

ISBN 0-671-63869-6

*The photograph on page 209 is courtesy of
Drexel, Burnham, Lambert, Inc.*

The line drawing on page 157 is by Alan H. Zwiebel.

I WOULD LIKE TO THANK:

Bob Asahina for suggesting the book and for requiring that it be written in the vernacular;

Andrew Carnegie for using a part of his ill-gotten gains to build a library in Williamsburg (where the bridge is falling down);

My father, whose success in America was, in large measure, achieved through the accomplishments of his children;

My mother for supplying me with my first home;

My sister for her generosity and concern for a brother she never quite figured out;

My brother for picking me up at the airport in Fort Lauderdale at 1 A.M.;

Renee for teaching our kids to be aware and care;

Wendy, Jeremy, Jonathan and **James** for learning their lessons well; and

God for exquisite timing and for silently denying some silly requests.

TO
OLD TIES
AND
NEW BEGINNINGS

CONTENTS

9

Introduction

"HOW GOODLY ARE THY . . . DWELLING PLACES! O AMERICA"

Once upon a time in America my family tree grew in Brooklyn. The family, consisting of two parents, a girl, and two boys, lived in a three-and-a-half-room apartment above the store. When it was time for bed, my sister would roll her roll-away into the living room. The boys would retire to their large sixty-square-foot closet. If nature should call, they would have to traipse through their parents' bedroom and trip over the bed in the living room to reach the bathroom.

A generation later, the mother, now a great-grandmother, lives in an apartment high in the sky in an area that a generation ago was considered country. Her daughter is an empty-nester who lives nearby in a house that has more bedrooms than she can use, except when the grandchildren come to visit. The sons have moved below the Mason-Dixon Line. The older lives in Washington with his three sons in a five-bedroom house. His divorced wife lives in a condominium in suburban Maryland. The younger brother lives in Miami, and although he has fewer bedrooms than his older brother, he does have a swimming pool.

This not atypical tale chronicles America's success in providing housing that accommodates the living arrangements of the vast majority of its citizens since the end of World War II. Yet when President Franklin Delano Roosevelt informed the nation in his

Second Inaugural Address that one-third of their fellow Americans were ill-housed, he was understating the problem. Half the nation's 35 million housing units in 1939 either had serious plumbing deficiencies or needed major repair.

If things were bad in 1939, they were even worse in the mid-forties. The war caused a massive migration and "the most drastic readjustment of the Nation's population since the gold rush." Some 4 million families pulled up stakes to move where the work was—in defense plants and related facilities located primarily in urban areas. And, having seen the city, most of the families had no desire to go back home, to paraphrase Otto Bettmann, to the good old places that were terrible. Others were eager to come home. In the first four months after the war ended, 5.25 million veterans returned from overseas or from military bases in the states. In the following year, an additional 7 million veterans were back as the nation demobilized at a breakneck pace.

In 1947, the Housing and Home Finance Agency (the predecessor of the Department of Housing and Urban Development) estimated that a total of between 17 and 18 million units had to be built or rehabilitated by 1960—an average of 1.3 million units a year. Based on past performance, this was a near-impossible goal. Housing at its zenith in the roaring twenties had peaked at 937,000 units. By 1933, in the depths of the Depression, the volume had dropped by 90 percent, to a paltry 93,000 units a year. By 1940, aided by a host of government programs, production had risen to 600,000 units a year. Had a group of experts gathered in Rome, the consensus would have been that the only solution to the housing problem was a Malthusian one. The country's population would have to be curbed if it were to be adequately housed.

Today, a generation later, the results have outstripped the projections of even the cockeyed optimist. The number of homes and apartments has tripled since 1940. There are 65 million more homes and apartments (over 60 percent of which have been built ever since 1960), and the number of housing units has now passed the 100 million mark.

In the process the landscape has been transformed, and new forms of housing have been created. *Condominium,* which in the fifties described the joint means of governing the Sudan worked out by the English and the Egyptians after the Mahdi's revolt failed (the only listing for the term in the Harvard Law School Library in 1961), entered the American lexicon as a home in the sky. America is now dotted with vertical homes and their counterparts, the horizontal apartments (of immobilized mobile homes)—in fact, 55 percent of all rental units in the country are in structures containing fewer than two units.

Quality has not been sacrificed in this quantitative leap. Over 97 percent of all units contain all plumbing facilities; in metropolitan areas, the figure is 99 percent. The key questions about bathrooms today is not whether but how many, and do they have a telephone. The average housing unit is not only heated in the winter but also air-conditioned in the summer—even on the farm.

For every homeless person, there are over ten vacant year-round units. At the end of 1987, there were 2.9 million vacant rental units in the United States. The amount of crowding has also been sharply reduced. Fewer than 4 percent of the dwellings today have more than one person per room. Notwithstanding the evening news, for every family that is "severely overcrowded" (more than 1.5 persons per room), 75 households have at least two rooms per person. The number of Americans in a housing unit has declined for over a century. In 1850, the average was 5.6 persons. By 1940 it had dropped to 4.1 persons. At present, it has dropped to 2.7 persons. And, as Bryant Robey has noted in his analysis of the 1980 census, two counties in the United States have shattered the two persons per unit mark—Manhattan and Kalawao, Hawaii (a leper colony).

Even more important, we have become a nation of homeowners. There are 20 million more homeowners today than there were housing units in 1940. Suburbia has been transformed from the enclave of the rich and famous, tied to the city by the train station, to the domain of the detached single-family house (home for 65 percent of American households) spread around the web of highway exits.

"Mass transit" in America, as B. Bruce-Briggs has noted, is the automobile. Two-thirds of the detached houses come with more than one car. For every 3 persons who leave these houses to go to work by subway or elevated train, 1,000 go to work by private vehicle. For every person on the train, there are 250 alone in their car or truck, 9 walking to work, and 2 biking or motorcycling. The long rush hour exists here and there. But for the average American, the journey to work consumes less than 25 minutes.

The road to riches has undergone a near-magical transformation. In the dimly remembered past, one achieved wealth and then bought a house. During the postwar period, one bought a house and then became wealthy. Young couples with almost no money to their name bought houses with a minimal down payment, and over the years, with the steady buildup of equity and a little inflation, before they knew it they were rich. The value of owner-occupied homes at the end of 1986 was $3.758 *trillion* and the net equity was $2.113 trillion—an average owner had an equity of over $50,000.

By looking at housing, we are looking at America. The lens, however, produces a kaleidoscopic view. Housing is one of America's largest industries, yet it is dominated by small entrepreneurs. It is both a product and a service; a necessity and a luxury; a nest and a nest egg. It is a consumer good that isn't consumed and a capital good that produces nothing tangible. It is a blend of private enterprise and government activity. And it is a service whose value is derived from factors that the house itself does not provide.

At rock bottom the house provides shelter. It has been defined as ''a nearly weathertight box with pipes in it.'' It is assumed that the pipes will not freeze in the winter, that there will be some lighting and ventilation, and that there will be cooking and plumbing facilities in working order. Yet, to quote Louis Winnick, ''The selection of a dwelling unit as a quantum of housing is unspoken testimony to our great material wealth.'' He cites the housing classification system established in St. Petersburg, Russia, in 1908—half bunk, bunk, corner, half room, room, apartment with roomers, individual apartments (this ultimate was achieved by 7 percent of the married workers). After the revolution and then some, Russian housing has improved. The average living space is now 100 square feet (3 persons per room). Twenty percent of urban households share apartments, 5 percent live in factory dormitories, and single-family houses are prohibited in towns of more than 100,000.

By world standards, American housing is virtually empty. The average home contains only 2½ persons (sons or daughters spend at least half of their time in the car), and the average apartment has two persons. In 65 percent of the homes and in 56 percent of the apartments each person can have two rooms to be sheltered from the outside world, and this does not take into account the bathrooms. In some countries, marriage raises the fearful prospect of close encounters of the most unpleasant kind—with in-laws. In the United States, marriage is the path to a crisis of another kind. If all the under-45 people in single-person households found themselves a partner who was similarly situated, they would reduce their heating bills and leave in their wake 3 million vacant housing units overnight.

The housing unit serves to protect the households from the elements—both climatic and social. While in some cases this may only mean barring or muffling the music of an alien culture, it may extend to the life and limb of the occupants. In areas in which yards are not equated with places in which to socialize with the neighbors, fear is often hovering and the house becomes a haven, to use Lee Rainwater's characterization. It is not surprising that double locks are so common and that the key words in the public housing design (more accurately redesign) vocabulary has become defensible space.

The protective aspect of the home also designates the freedom of the individual and the family. The Hebrew slaves, as one of their last acts before they left Egypt, were commanded to smear the blood of the Paschal lamb on their door posts and lintel. Samson Raphael Hirsch in his *Commentary on the Pentateuch,* more specifically the Book of Exodus, had the following to say on the significance of the act:

The door posts and the lintel represent the house, the home. The idea of a house is a double one, firstly to shut the inhabitants in against the human elements . . . and secondly, shutting the inhabitants in against the physical elements. . . . The two door posts represent shutting out the social element, the lintel . . . represents the protection against the physical elements. The slaves when elevated to free human beings with full human rights over their own family life, receive door posts and lintels, insurance by God of their protection against intrusion by the forces of man and nature.

Housing, however, is much more than walls and spaces. It is a bundle of delivered services. The walls, windows, and hardware of the house may keep the occupants dry and safe, but it is the fuel that heats and the water that is consumed that make the house livable. Residents are not interested in the pipes and faucets or the ranges and the refrigerators. They want the services that these products deliver.

No house is an island. The services that are being offered under the rubric of housing are usually performed outside of the house and are more often public than private. The house comes with a host of neighborhood services—from sewers to swimming pools. The quality and quantity of public services or the ambiance of the neighborhood are often far more determinative of the price of housing than the particular characteristic of the house. A bungalow in Santa Monica can be a hundred times more expensive than a bungalow in Rockaway.

There are also private activities that perform a public function. As Daniel Elazar has written:

[T]he impact of the private maintenance of lawns and gardens has generally been ignored . . . [T]he private expenditure for lawn and garden . . . far exceeds the public expenditure for parks, tree planting and other efforts of urban beautification. It represents an important contibution to the "public good" that would be prohibitively expensive if charged against the public purse and sorely missed if eliminated.[1]

Although not all neighborhoods offer amenities, they all perform a more important function. They define a person's place in society. The resident of public housing is not likely to get an invitation in the mail for a Gold American Express card. The person who moves into the latest of Trump's towers is not primarily seeking protection from the rain or snow, any more than a person buys a new BMW because he has somewhere to go. The move and the purchase are gold-plated announcements of arrival.

As a study of California suburbanites by Carl Werthman concluded, the facade of the house, like the clothes worn, tells a great deal about the occupant. The extroverted, self-made businessman chose the mock colonial display house. The helping professions opted for the quieter, inward-looking house. Who would mistake the palace of Tony Montana, the cocaine king in *Scarface,* for the brownstone of the Huxtables in "The Bill Cosby Show"?

The symbolic nature of the house was recognized by the master of symbols Carl Jung. In describing the building of his own house, he wrote, "From the beginning, I felt the Tower was in some ways a place of maturation—a maternal womb or a maternal figure in which I could become what I am and will be. It gives me the feeling as if I were reborn in stone. It is thus, a concretization of the individuation process."

It is but a short step from the work of the psychotherapist to the work of an interior decorator. Clare Cooper has written: "[T]he rise in popularity of the interior decorator is in some way linked to people's inability to make decisions for themselves, since they are not sure what their 'self' really is." In comparing the interior decoration of the urban commune with the traditional family home, Professor Cooper notes:

[T]he bedrooms [in the commune], the only private spaces . . . are decorated in an attractive and highly personal way symbolic of the "self" whose space it is. The living room, the communal territory of six or eight different personalities, however, is only sparsely decorated, since, presumably, the problem of getting agreement on taste from a number of disparate and highly individual "selves" is too great to overcome. . . . [T]he more normal family house may display an opposite arrangement, with bedrooms . . . uninterestingly decorated, and the living room where guests and relatives are entertained, containing the best furniture, family mementos, art . . . and photos, representing the collective family "self." Often the only

exception [is] the bedroom of a teenager . . . whose desire to establish his own personality is reflected in the very distinctive decoration
in his or her bedroom.[2]

Moving from matters of the mind to matters of the pocketbook,
housing is increasingly being viewed as an investment. Of course
the rental of property has been with us for millennia—at the very
least since the days when Joseph interpreted dreams and the starving Egyptians sold the land to Pharaoh, who in turn leased it back
for 20 percent of the crop. Even the vision of the American frontier
as the abode of hardy homesteaders needs some revision. As Paul
Gates pointed out in *Landlord and Tenant on the Prairie Frontier,*
even with free land the cost of settlement was quite expensive
(Conestogas didn't come cheap). The cost of farm implements and
oxen, plus funds to maintain the family until the first crop came in,
left many pioneering farmers "cherish[ing] the dream of owning a
farm while they worked for others."

In the twentieth century, rental housing dominated the housing scene until the end of World War II. At present, it represents
one-third of our housing inventory. Rental housing has provided a
double-barrel of shelter. It has provided shelter from the elements
for the tenants and, although recent changes in the tax law have
poked some holes in the roof, shelter from the tax collector for
the owners.

A new phenomenon is that the home is increasingly being
viewed by its occupants as an investment. Unlike the American
automobile, it is not consumed immediately after all the payments
are made. In Switzerland, where the belief is that a properly maintained house can last forever, many home loans do not require that
the principal be paid by a certain date. In America, where home
loans must be paid off in less than three decades, many older
Americans have a valuable asset. There are close to 24 million
households in the over-55 age group. Over 80 percent of all married
homeowners over 65 own their homes free and clear of all debt.
An even larger proportion of single elderly—87 percent of all men
and 91 percent of all women—are in the same category. A housing
problem for a substantial number of elderly households is having

too much housing and too little in the way of physical and fiscal resources to properly maintain it (a solution to this problem will be presented in the last part of this book.)

The home has another characteristic that makes it highly attractive as an investment, even when prices are rising at a moderate rate. In banker's terms, it is highly leveraged—a small dollar amount will gain control of a high-value item. To use a quaint example, a $50,000 house can be bought with a down payment of as little as $5,000. If housing prices rise at a rate of 5 percent a year, at the end of five years the house is worth $63,800. The owner's equity (putting aside the principal portion of his mortgage payment) has gone from $5,000 to $13,800—a return on the initial investment of over 55 percent a year.

It is a fine line that distinguishes the investor from the speculator, especially in times of sharp inflation. The late seventies were such a period for housing. In 1977, Alan Greenspan, before he became Chairman of the Federal Reserve Board, estimated that the market value of the nation's single-family owner-occupied homes was increasing at an annual rate of $62 billion. In 1978 and 1979 prices accelerated at better than a 15 percent per year pace.

From coast to coast and border to border there were tales of amazing "trade-ups." Thousands of owners sold their homes at double or triple their original cost (and many more times their original investment) and moved into more expensive new homes. Houses were resold for substantial profits even before they were finished. There were even advantages to those who stayed in their old homes. To paraphrase Alan Greenspan, people were able to live in more expensive neighborhoods without having to move.

This book will not show readers how to make a million dollars in real estate without investing any of their own money. Rather, it takes on the more challenging, if less lucrative, task of introducing those who live in the forest of housing to the complex ecology of their surroundings, and putting those who occupy themselves with specific aspects of the flora and fauna (and underbrush) in touch with the rest of their environment.

The first chapter will deal with the question of how the home-building industry, using craft methods, has been able to turn America into the best-housed nation in the history of the world. It will try to explain why, in spite of America's romance with technology and intensive efforts to industrialize the building process, the wave of the future turned out to be merely a tidal pool in the backwash of the sea of housing.

The second chapter will describe America's true romance with the single-family house, and explain the factors that made it possible for so many Americans to achieve their heart's desire. The third chapter will deal with rental housing and try to explain why people hate their landlords and why, in the face of hostility and lower profits than generally imagined, anyone of sound mind builds rental housing.

The fourth chapter will deal with the suburban boom. It will take the view that the unique event in modern history was not the rush to suburbia and the decline of the city, but rather the rise of the city in the first place. The fifth chapter will show how all those cities of the Northeast and Midwest acquired their population in the first place, where those people began moving once economic and technological changes gave them a choice, and where their future abode is likely to be.

The sixth chapter will deal with the segment of the population that has had the least choice in housing, namely blacks. One path of their housing history leads out to the suburbs and the mainstream of housing, the other into the federal government's urban reservations—subsidized housing projects. The seventh chapter will examine what has happened to tenants and landlords in the last approximately two decades, which has led many to believe that the nation is facing the worst housing crisis since the Depression.

The eighth chapter will trace the history of subsidized housing and try to explain why well-intentioned and on the whole intelligent and prudent people were able to produce such perverse results. The ninth chapter will examine why, for the longest time, the federal government didn't just give poor people money so that they could afford housing and why, now that they are beginning to do this, they are not doing it too well.

The tenth chapter deals with the near bankruptcy and reorganization of the savings-and-loan-association industry when it moved from the problem of having too little money to the problem of having too much. It will tell of the trials and travails of the institutions that provided money for housing in the past decades and how housing is increasingly being financed by money raised on Wall Street and in Europe and Asia rather than at the neighborhood bank.

The eleventh chapter will look at whether the American Dream of the Single Family Home is likely to be a reality for the next generation. The final chapter will deal with proposals that, if enacted, will result in a coming of age of housing policy. The proposals will include: programs for overhoused elderly households; production programs for a nation that may have, on the whole, more than enough housing; a housing assistance plan that takes as a premise that the government knows much less than it thinks it knows; and finally an approach to move public housing into the mainstream of American housing.

Chapter 1

FROM HANDICRAFT TO POWER CRAFT

According to an anonymous wit "If Jesus were to return to the Earth, the only thing he would recognize is the home-building industry." How did a home-building industry burdened with such obsolete craft methods manage to put a roof and four walls and then some over so many American families in so short a time?

The "then some" is a rather awesome list. The following materials are used in the construction of a 1,700-square-foot house:

- 9,726 board feet of lumber
- 4,614 square feet of roof, wall, and floor sheathing
- 243 square feet of plywood for sheathing
- 55 cubic yards of concrete, ¾ of which is poured concrete and the remainder concrete block
- 2,528 square feet of exterior finish either aluminum siding, brick, or wood
- 1,992 square feet of asphalt shingles for roofing
- 2,500 square feet of insulation
- 6,484 square feet of gypsum wallboard
- 90 feet of ducting
- 55 gallons of paint
- 302 pounds of nails
- 750 feet of copper wiring
- 280 feet of copper (water supply) piping, plus 100 fittings

- 170 feet of plastic pipe for drain, waste, and vent piping, plus 70 fittings
- 12 windows
- 10 interior doors and 4 exterior doors
- 2 tubs or 1 tub and shower stall
- 2 toilets
- 3 sinks
- 15 kitchen cabinets
- 1 range, 1 range hood, 1 refrigerator, 1 dishwasher, 1 disposal, smoke detectors

The basic reason for the success of the traditional building industry was its ability to learn the distinction between industrialization and appropriate technology. It was a distinction that its main competitor, the manufacturers of prefabricated houses, never learned.

WHY NOT INDUSTRIALIZATION?

Although there was no fanfare, the prefabrication of housing industry in the United States celebrated its 350th anniversary in 1974. In 1624, the English brought a panelized house of wood to Cape Ann for use by a fishing fleet. The house was subsequently disassembled, moved, and assembled many times. A more permanent house was erected when pioneer settlers, moving from the Plymouth Colony to the south shore of Connecticut, took along the cut and partially assembled parts of a house to provide them with shelter and protection from the hostile elements and Indians.[1]

Later the California Gold Rush of 1849 and the Civil War both provided lucrative markets for early prefabricators. Railroad freight rates for wooden portable homes date from 1870. Starting at the end of the nineteenth century, the modern home could be bought by mail. The Sears (when it was still Roebuck & Co.) mail-order catalog was the place to purchase not only everything to fill an American house but the home itself.

From Pleasantville, N.Y., to Coldwater, Kans., from Philadelphia, Pa., to Cowley, Wyoming, and beyond, 100,000 families turned to

Sears . . . for one of their most important purchases: their homes. Between 1908 and 1940, . . . it . . . manufactured and sold . . . houses—approximately 450 ready to assemble designs from mansions to bungalows and even summer cottages. Ordered by mail and sent by rail . . . these popular houses were meant to fill a need for sturdy, inexpensive and, especially *modern* homes, complete with such desirable conveniences as indoor plumbing and electricity.[2]

Wood was not the only product used. Between 1910 and 1918, several hundred homes were built out of precast concrete panels. In 1908, the ever inventive but not always successful Thomas Edison proposed to pour an entire two- or three-story house of concrete.[3]

It was during the 1930s, however, that the industry captured the imagination of the public and of serious businessmen. By 1930, Sears had sold 50,000 homes (25,000 in a single year—1925). The Chicago World's Fair in 1933 featured a twelve-sided structure of glass and steel sections bolted together and supported on a cantilevered frame, with an airplane hangar in the basement. Glowing visions of the "house of the future" were sandwiched in the popular magazines between visions of tear-drop automobiles and the heralded $700 airplane. In 1933, heavy industry was desperately looking for new markets, and the "house like a Ford" was put forward as an outlet for steel. The initial goal was to create a vast new industry, which, like the automobile industry, would turn out standard models that the public was expected to buy.

After years of intensive study, the leaders of the prefabrication industry (seemingly unaware of what Sears had been doing) had a better idea—the way to reduce construction costs was to deliver to the building site parts of the structure that could be assembled without cutting or alteration. Approximately 10,000 units were produced during the thirties. By 1940, when Sears left the home-building business because of insufficient profits, there were thirty firms manufacturing and selling prefabricated homes.

World War II provided the prefabricated industry with a great opportunity. If 71,000 naval ships, 300,000 aircraft, 100,000 tanks, 2.5 million trucks, 370,000 artillery pieces, 5.9 million bombs, and assorted other goods were to be built, housing would have to be provided for the builders. Early in 1942, the Defense Housing Division of the Federal Works Administration announced a program to build 70,000 prefabs in one year. Although the program got bogged down in red tape and these grandiose projections were not achieved, an estimated 200,000 factory prefabricated homes were built during the war years.

Once the war was over, many people, including government officials, believed that in the near future houses would be built on the assembly lines used for tanks, planes, and ships. A writer in a Sunday weekly magazine captured the spirit of the times:

> Thanks largely to lessons learned in constructing emergency wartime housing, it is no longer necessary to erect a home laboriously, stone by stone, board by board. . . . We have discovered how to effect enormous savings in labor, material and transport by manufacturing most of the essential elements of a house on machines in factories and merely assembling them on the building lot. We have arrived at the same stage in home construction which was reached when . . . Henry Ford came out with his Model T. As a result of mass production we will be able to turn out a completely modern 4 to 5 room basic house in the post-war era for from $2,000 to $3,000 [that] will be bought in much the same way that most Americans purchased cars in the past.[4]

A survey of prefabricators reported that they expected within ten years to be building 66 percent of all houses under $5,000 and 33 percent of all houses over $5,000.

The bubble was burst by the "Lustron house," the most ambitious attempt to mass produce factory-made homes in the postwar years. The Lustron house was a one-story, 1,025-square-foot structure framed in steel and faced with porcelain-enameled-steel panels. It was manufactured and totally assembled in a factory, then shipped and installed by franchised dealers. The cost was about $7,000. It was advertised as "the greatest single development in housing since one stone was placed on another." The Reconstruction Finance Corporation (RFC) loaned Lustron $37.5 million. After selling only 2,000 houses in its two-year existence, Lustron went bankrupt.

The autopsy revealed a number of reasons for Lustron's demise. Lustron had mastered the art of building a house but not the art of selling it. The home buyer is a conservative creature. Few wished to live in steel and plastic buildings that resembled the neighborhood Esso station. Constructing a house in a few hours or days is not a strong selling point to a family making the largest investment of its life. There are also large swings from year to year, and within a given year, in the total number of housing units, and the price class of the units. But with its large fixed investment, Lustron needed a regular annual volume of $65 million in sales (11,600 two-bedroom houses) in order to achieve a 10 percent return on its investment. Ironically, the quality of the house also played a crucial role in its undoing. As a result of its heavy use of steel, the house was fireproof, verminproof, rotproof, too strong and too expensive. The company had painted itself into a corner. As the management consultant firm of Booz, Allen & Hamilton reported to the RFC, "Lustron . . . has produced a house which is in a price class in which there is no real opportunity for large volume; yet the only hope for a profitable enterprise, against this large investment, is a large volume." [5]

Industrialized housing did not die with Lustron, however. But during the next two decades, many of the firms were on the brink of extinction. The National Commission on Urban Problems in 1968 would review the industry record:

> To date the profit record of the U.S. home manufacturers has not been inspiring. One of the largest companies . . . for example, had sales of 23,000 units in 1959; last year's sales were 15,000 . . . Earnings . . . were only one-tenth of 1 percent of investment. Many other companies, usually much smaller, have experienced similar or worse profit margins, and many have gone under. Those companies that have stayed in business . . . are often able to do so because of profits on land and home financing. [6]

Yet the old romance was rekindled, in the late 1960s, when the Douglas and Kaiser commissions issued reports that concluded that 26 million housing units would have to be built or rehabilitated in the next decade in order to meet the country's housing needs. The residential construction industry was perceived as lacking the capability, technology, and resources required to build an average of 2.6 million units a year without adding unduly to the price of housing. So the need for more efficient mass-production techniques designed to achieve significant economies of scale were viewed as essential.

In 1968, Congress proposed to test the hypothesis that industrialization was the way to lower the cost of housing. The Housing and Urban Development Act of 1968 (which wrote the 2.6-million-unit goal into law) authorized the use of five different systems to erect 1,000 units a year for five years.

At the tail end of the Great Society, when America was putting men on the moon, when HUD had George Romney, an auto man, in its driver's seat, when Russia was building 2 million industrialized housing units a year, this modest program became a crusade known as Operation Breakthrough. Headed up by a recruit from NASA, Harold Finger, the program was organized in three phases: system design and testing, prototype construction, and volume production and market aggregation, the Achilles' heel of the industry.

The government did not propose to be the buyer, as it had been in wartime (and was still in Russia). Instead, in a period in which Congress was authorizing annual production of hundreds of thousands of units, the aggregation was done by allocating subsidized housing to the program—eventually 26,000 units.

In the initial phase HUD received 989 applications, weeded out to five production systems, including the industrial giant General Electric and firms at the leading edge of space-age technology such as TRW. Although Operation Breakthrough led to substantial institutional change—building code reform, basic agreements with organized labor, and general acceptance and an improved understanding of the concept of manufactured housing by state and local government, it did not succeed in putting the industrialized house on a firm foundation.

As in so many other crusades, most of the participants, even if they returned alive, were more battered than ennobled from the experience. General Electric's experience is illustrative. During the late sixties NASA officials indicated to GE management that the space program was winding down. GE got the message and began to seek other areas for investment. Naively, they chose housing.

The primary innovation in GE's housing system was a way of casting plaster on steel studs and a paper honeycomb floor. In its factory, panels with this cast-plaster on one side and Sheetrock on the other were assembled into finished modules. But the paper floor was soon dropped as a result of high production costs. Eventually, GE realized that costs were getting out of hand. GE was paying high wages and using facilities intended for the space program in the low-cost-housing demonstration. It was applying a high-priced, high-technology, high-overhead (approximately 300 percent) structure to the down-to-earth job of producing housing.

GE did reduce costs, from $28 a square foot to $18 a square foot, by making a series of design changes. Unfortunately, GE's selling price for the units was only $13 a square foot, and the roofs of its units, covered by Du Pont's latest roof membrane, were leaking. So GE closed its plant, got out of the business in the United States, and began franchising its system in the friendlier environment of the Shah's Iran.

In large part, the government could not deliver on its promise of the large constant flow of business to the housing industry that was required to justify the initial investment and high overhead associated with factory construction. It was a matter of too little control and too much control. There was too little control over economic conditions, resulting in a tight credit market and increasing prices that depressed the housing industry. Even worse was the government's imposition of a moratorium on subsidized housing in 1973. These factors convinced producers of medium and large housing and industrial corporations that had participated in Operation Breakthrough that the housing industry would have to remain in its fragmented condition, unable to reach a plane of efficiency.

In the end, according to a research report delivered to HUD (and never published) by the Real Estate Research Corporation and Arthur D. Little, there was some evidence that industrialized construction could be competitive with conventional methods when it came to high-rise construction. But when it came to low buildings and especially single-family housing, industrialization simply was not competitive.

THE IMMOBILE HOME

Yet, one form of prefabricated dwelling has achieved an amazing success—the mobile home. In the 1940 Census, trailers occupied the same category as caves, uncounted housing. Beginning as a small, simple bedroom on wheels that could be attached to an automobile of vacationers, the trailer became a major source of housing in the postwar years. During the eighties, an average of 257,000 new mobile homes a year have been placed into residential use.[7] In 1983, there were 4 million occupied mobile homes representing 4.4 percent of the country's housing.

After World War II, builders of trailers recognized that their product had a market as year-around homes. The trailer not only lost its name but its wheels in spite of its Census definition ("a movable dwelling, 8 feet or more wide and 40 or more feet long, designed to be towed on its own chassis, with transportation gear integral to the unit when it leaves the factory, and without need of a permanent foundation"[8]), though others kept the wheels and added a motor, and went the motor-home route. The loosening of highway regulations has allowed the width of the trailer to grow to 14 feet and the length to over 100 feet in New Mexico and nineteen other states that have no length restriction. The average home has two bedrooms, at least one bathroom, is fully furnished, although the dishwasher, disposal, and air-conditioning are optional. And, then there is the double-wide mobile home (two factory-built units joined at the site) for the approximately one in three residents who want and can afford the space.

The major selling point of the mobile home is its cost. In 1986, the median price of a new mobile home (on the dealer's lot) was $19,900—$17,200 for a 990-square-foot-single-wide and $29,500 for a 1,375-square-foot-double-wide. In contrast, the median price of the new conventional 1,650-square-foot, 3-bedroom home on a 9,000-square-foot lot was $92,000.[9] It is not surprising that the average income of the trailer owner is $10,000 lower than that of a conventional home owner ($24,400 versus $14,300).[10]

Mobile homes are primarily a country and western phenomenon. Sixty percent of the units are located in rural areas and only six percent in central cities. The states in which mobile homes make up the largest portion of the housing inventory are in the West. Wyoming leads the nation with 18 percent, followed by Montana, Nevada, and Arizona at 13 percent, and Idaho at 12 percent (compared to less than 1 percent in Massachusetts, Rhode Island, Connecticut, and New Jersey).[11]

Eighty percent of the mobile homes are owner-occupied. Notwithstanding the common perception of mobile-home residents residing cheek by jowl, only 19 percent live in parks containing more than 100 units. The majority of the homes (54 percent) sit in areas of six or fewer units (why the Census has chosen six I know not). Unlike the conventional homeowner, two-thirds of the occupants do not own the site upon which the dwelling sits.[12]

The residents of mobile homes are quite happy with their accommodations. Eighty-three percent indicate that their house is an excellent or a good place to live and about three in four would recommend it to others.[13]

Mobile homes are unique in being covered by a national building code. Congress, concerned about their safety and durability, required that every mobile home built for single-family occupancy in the United States after June 15, 1976, comply with federal standards covering the entire design and manufacturing process. The effects of the federal standards are mixed. A study done for HUD concluded that homes built under the new standards have somewhat more durable outside and inside walls, roofs, and moisture-prevention systems and somewhat less durable foundations, joining of doublewides, windows and doors, and electrical, and plumbing systems.[14] Another HUD study, reporting on the transportation of mobile homes, concluded that "mobile homes when towed on road surfaces considered representative of typical towing conditions and when installed on home sites, are subjected to greater stresses than they are currently designed to withstand and that the homes degrade under these loads." [15]

Although (or because) the Federal Housing Administration is willing to insure twenty-year mortgages on mobile homes, there is reason for concern with their durability. Manufacturers have shipped 7.7 million units since 1950. The Annual Housing Survey in 1983 could only find 4 million housing units. Twenty-nine percent of the mobile homes that were occupied in 1973 were lost from the inventory by 1981 (compared to less than 5 percent of the conventionally constructed single-family homes). Only one in four of the owner-occupied mobile homes in 1983 was acquired before 1975. The Bureau of Census makes note of this short life span by not taking into its count unoccupied mobile housing.

The low purchase price of mobile homes is not necessarily translatable into lower occupancy costs. In 1968, the President's Committee on Urban Housing commissioned the McGraw-Hill Information Systems Division to study the comparative production and occupancy costs of different types of units. Among the types were a conventionally built 1,000-square-foot single-family home and a 660-square foot mobile home (the difference in size between the typical house in 1968 and 1986 is a measure of how far we've come in upgrading the quantity and quality of housing). The total development cost, namely the cost of construction plus the cost of land and site preparation, was twice as high for the conventionally constructed home. Nevertheless, the monthly occupancy cost of the mobile home was 90 percent of the more expensive house.[16] The reason was the high debt retirement costs of the mobile home, which was financed with a short-term loan at high interest rates, and the cost of site rent.

The Federal Housing Administration will now coinsure loans (share the risk with the lender in the case of default) for mobile homes, and the Veterans Administration will now guarantee longer-term loans. The FHA insurance was originally available only to finance the home and not the land (under Title I of the National Housing Act, which was traditionally used to finance home improvements). Since 1974, the cost of the lot has been included in the loan. The maximum amount of the loan is $40,500

($54,000 if two or more modules are being combined). The maximum term is twenty years. The down-payment requirements on mobile homes and the interest rates are higher than on conventional homes and the typical new mobile-home mortgage runs from twelve to fifteen years. In 1985, FHA insured approximately 30,000 loans.

Land for mobile homes also does not come cheap. Rents are in the $150–$200 per month range. The price is often not commensurate with the value of the location. Since mobile homes are considered personal property and do not contribute to the tax base of the community, their residents are viewed as second-class citizens when it comes to community services.

There are no good statistics regarding the appreciation or depreciation of mobile homes. But even the most ardent boosters of mobile homes would not argue that they compare to conventional housing, which increased in value from $17,100 in 1970 to $51,300 in 1980. The latter rise is primarily due to inflation. In terms of constant 1972 dollars the increase was from $18,874 to $23,468. It is, nevertheless, of interest that in gathering statistics on the nation's housing HUD and the Census Bureau ask the value of conventional homes only, but the purchase price of mobile homes.

Although the mobile home does provide serviceable housing to a significant portion of the population—in attempting to reach its 26 million housing goal, HUD began to count mobile homes—it is outside of the housing mainstream. Americans did not trek to suburbia in search of wheelless trailers. To the contrary, the mobile home is an ingenious alternative for households that never made it or moved away from the suburban heartland of the conventional construction industry—those who stayed down home near the farm or who left the hustle and bustle of metropolitan America for the wide-open spaces.

THE ASSEMBLY LINE IN THE FIELD

The mainstream of new homes flows from the conventional construction industry. Operation Breakthrough and its predecessors and its successors have made a number of assumptions about the conventional homebuilding industry—that the industry is technologically backward, that new methods will result in drastic improvements, and that technological improvements will be translated into lower costs. All of these assumptions are wrong.

The conventional homebuilding industry has been able to pull off a trick that eluded the great prophet Mohammed. It was able to bring the mountain to it—the assembly line was brought to the building site. As Martin Mayer describes the building operation of a large Dallas builder:

> The real factory . . . is out at the site. Each . . . tract, serviced by a crew of workers that may run to 300 men, is an assembly line on a piece of land, different from a usual assembly line only that its the people and the material rather than the product that moves. The delivery of parts to the work station is as precisely organized, the schedule is as exact . . . as anything in conventional industry.[17]

Homebuilding may still be a craft industry. However, it is a power-craft rather than a handicraft industry. The new tools range from mundane paint rollers to power tools of all sorts, including power guns that take nails from an unrolling paper strip the way World War I machine guns took bullets (as Mayer puts it). There is also a spate of new equipment and new materials. Bulldozers, backhoes, and forklifts dot construction sites and there is a host of laborsaving devices—ready-mix concrete, gypsum rather than plaster, precut lumber, prehung doors and windows, as well as factory- or shed-made panels and trusses. And perhaps most important, rising out of the industry's experience in World War II, there is an emphasis on the organization of the work force and the precise scheduling of the work.

Faced with the postwar challenge, the merchant builders who changed the American landscape with large subdivisions of similar-looking houses did not try to revolutionize the way the houses were built. They, however, did see the advantages of the assembly line in continuity and specialization. Their response was attention to the scheduling and the division of the work, so the site would not be cluttered with nonproductive highly paid workers. So a crew of, for example, doorhangers, rather than general carpenters moved from house to house, leaving no hand idle.[18]

In order to build at a pace where this precision paid off, sites large enough for large developments were needed and houses would have to be built by the hundreds and in the case of Bill Levitt by the thousands. In addition, the design of the house had to be simplified. And here, the teachings of Henry Ford were relevant. It was, however, in the area of marketing, rather than production that the builders paid heed. One of the first things that went was the basement. As Ned Eichler, son of a large postwar California builder, tells the story:

> Bill Levitt in 1947, and a host of builders . . . broke with tradition and built on a slab with no basement. Their marketing advisors— banks, real estate salesmen, wives, and just about every one— warned that people would not buy. "That's what they told Henry Ford about the Model T," replied merchant builders. They will buy if the value is there." And buy they did.
>
> . . . In the fifteen-year period following the war, most went after the low-end of the market. They were selling value not trying to win design awards. Though they resented the condemnation of aficionados of good architecture, they paid little attention.[19]

The prefabricated housing industry was unable to gain a foothold to support the large amount of capital required for facilities, inventories, accounts receivable, and transportation costs because of the increased cost-cutting that has resulted from the refinements in on-site fabrication. By moving toward subcontracting of large portions of the work and the increased use of on-site assembly methods, even the small builder can attain close control and lower costs. For example, he can replace a subcontractor who has not met either the cost or the time goals, while a builder tied to a prefabricator's system cannot take such corrective actions so readily or so promptly.

This matter of control was graphically contrasted by a builder who has built under both methods:

The worst thing economically is that you're under the thumb of the manufacturer. When he knows that your foundation is sitting out in the field . . . and his manufactured home is the only one that's going to fit on it, you're in a bit of a box as far as bargaining. Now, you can have contracts and the rest of it, but when it comes down to practical application, you're not in a good bargaining position. . . .

You have tremendous ability to bargain with conventional construction. Each piece of your home is bought and selected and negotiated with separate people. If the lumber supplier starts giving you noises about having to increase his prices, someone down the street has the same lumber and your supplier knows it. So, he tends to get along with you a little better.

The increased efficiency in the use of labor in the building industry also undercut the theory that increased costs entailed in industrialization and transportation would be more than offset by reduced labor costs. Contrary to popular conceptions, homebuilding is not an industry in which there is a high ratio between the labor cost and material cost. In spite of high hourly wages, on-site labor costs represent only a small portion—15 percent (as compared to the 30 percent level it was at immediately after World War II)—of the purchase price of the house.

The story of Billy and Spanky indicates how the high cost of labor is more than offset by the high level of production:

I spent a very cold morning watching two deft rockers [short for Sheetrockers] named Billy and Spanky put up ceilings and walls in a brand-new house. . . . First they stood around smoking cigarettes in front of a kerosene heater. Then, when they had warmed up, they cut about a foot off a twelve-foot panel, hoisted it to the ceiling of the dining room, and banged in enough nails to hold it up. Then Spanky "screwed off" the panel with an electric screw gun, putting in a screw roughly every foot along each joist. While he did this, Billy measured and cut the next panel. The entire ceiling took about ten minutes to finish.[20]

Most of the labor that goes into the cost of the house is performed in other industries. Thus, for every billion dollars—every 20,000

homes priced at $50,000 in 1980 dollars—spent for single-family
housing, 9,500 jobs are created in the construction industry (1,200
of which are off-site) and 12,500 in other industries, such as mining
or lumbering, to obtain the raw materials that will be fabricated
into products transported to the building site.[21] These products are
manufactured in highly efficient and heavily capitalized industrial
plants. USG, the manufacturer of the gypsum wallboard that Billy
and Spanky turned into walls and ceilings, produced 7 billion
square feet (160,700 acres) in 1986, and the second-largest manufacturer produced a mere 5 billion square feet. Material represents
approximately 30 percent of the cost of the house.

If discovered in recent years the materials would be considered
miracle materials. As Ralph Johnson, former head of the National
Association of Home Builders Research Foundation, wrote,
"Concrete, gypsum, wood, steel, aluminum and even plastics (in
the way in which they are used) are low-cost-per-pound-per-unit
of performance materials. My own experience in researching new
systems and trying to innovate has been that even a few cents per-
square-foot improvement is difficult to achieve when compared to
advanced practices."[22]

Another reason why so many prefabrication systems fell by the
wayside can be gleaned by examining the list on the first page of
this chapter. The purchase price of the average house was $9,500
in 1940 and $70,000 in 1982. The building envelope (the structural
frame and the basic enclosing material) makes up only one-sixth of
the total construction costs. The bulk of the cost is attributable to
the utility systems, plumbing, heating, ventilating and electrical—
and the provision of an attractive and functional interior.

If the construction costs add up to only 45 percent of the purchase price of the home, what are the other components of cost?
The largest is land and site preparation, which represent 24 percent
(compared to 11 percent in 1949) of the purchase price. The cost
of construction financing in 1982 comprised 15 percent (compared
to 5 percent in 1949). The only element that has remained more or
less the same is overhead and profit, 16 percent in 1982 and 15
percent in 1949.[23]

The efficiencies that have been achieved have been passed on in

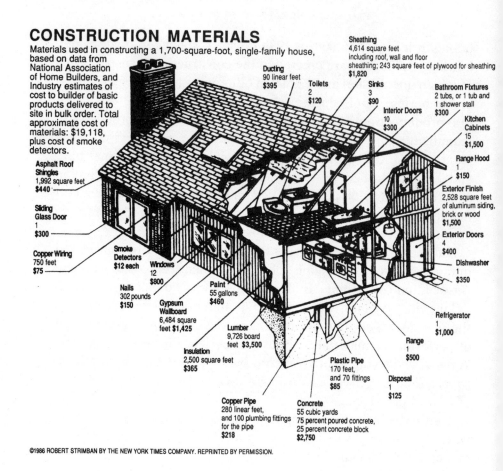

CONSTRUCTION MATERIALS

Materials used in constructing a 1,700-square-foot, single-family house, based on data from National Association of Home Builders, and Industry estimates of cost to builder of basic products delivered to site in bulk order. Total approximate cost of materials: $19,118, plus cost of smoke detectors.

Asphalt Roof Shingles
1,992 square feet
$440

Sliding Glass Door
1
$300

Copper Wiring
750 feet
$75

Smoke Detectors
$12 each

Windows
12
$800

Nails
302 pounds
$150

Gypsum Wallboard
6,484 square feet $1,425

Insulation
2,500 square feet
$365

Paint
55 gallons
$460

Lumber
9,726 board feet $3,500

Copper Pipe
280 linear feet, and 100 plumbing fittings for the pipe
$218

Concrete
55 cubic yards
75 percent poured concrete, 25 percent concrete block
$2,750

Plastic Pipe
170 feet, and 70 fittings
$85

Disposal
1
$125

Range
1
$500

Refrigerator
1
$1,000

Dishwasher
1
$350

Exterior Doors
4
$400

Exterior Finish
2,528 square feet of aluminum siding, brick or wood
$1,500

Range Hood
1
$150

Kitchen Cabinets
15
$1,500

Bathroom Fixtures
2 tubs, or 1 tub and 1 shower stall
$300

Interior Doors
10
$300

Sinks
3
$90

Toilets
2
$120

Ducting
90 linear feet
$395

Sheathing
4,614 square feet including roof, wall and floor sheathing; 243 square feet of plywood for sheathing
$1,820

©1986 ROBERT STRIMBAN BY THE NEW YORK TIMES COMPANY. REPRINTED BY PERMISSION.

an improved product rather than in lower costs. The present-day house not only is much larger but also contains features that would have been considered luxuries only a few decades ago.

THE STRUCTURE OF THE BUILDERS

The structure of the industry is a response to the uniqueness and the complexity of the process (See Table 1). The bond between the building and land and the fragmentation of local government has forced the industry to focus on small geographic areas. The histor-

Table 1. The Housing Process—
Major Participants and Influences [24]

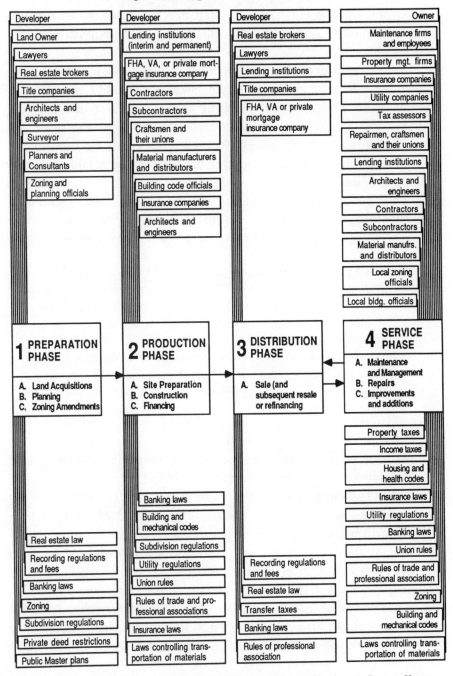

Preparation	Production	Distribution	Service
Developer	Developer	Developer	Owner
Land Owner	Lending institutions (interim and permanent)	Real estate brokers	Maintenance firms and employees
Lawyers	FHA, VA, or private mortgage insurance company	Lawyers	Property mgt. firms
Real estate brokers	Contractors	Lending institutions	Insurance companies
Title companies	Subcontractors	Title companies	Utility companies
Architects and engineers	Craftsmen and their unions	FHA, VA or private mortgage insurance company	Tax assessors
Surveyor	Material manufacturers and distributors		Repairmen, craftsmen and their unions
Planners and Consultants	Building code officials		Lending institutions
Zoning and planning officials	Insurance companies		Architects and engineers
	Architects and engineers		Contractors
			Subcontractors
			Material manufrs. and distributors
			Local zoning officials
			Local bldg. officials

1 PREPARATION PHASE
A. Land Acquisitions
B. Planning
C. Zoning Amendments

2 PRODUCTION PHASE
A. Site Preparation
B. Construction
C. Financing

3 DISTRIBUTION PHASE
A. Sale (and subsequent resale or refinancing)

4 SERVICE PHASE
A. Maintenance and Management
B. Repairs
C. Improvements and additions

Preparation	Production	Distribution	Service
			Property taxes
			Income taxes
			Housing and health codes
			Insurance laws
			Utility regulations
	Banking laws		Banking laws
	Building and mechanical codes		Union rules
	Subdivision regulations		Rules of trade and professional association
Real estate law	Utility regulations	Recording regulations and fees	Zoning
Recording regulations and fees	Union rules		Building and mechanical codes
Banking laws	Rules of trade and professional associations	Real estate law	
Zoning		Transfer taxes	
Subdivision regulations	Insurance laws	Banking laws	
Private deed restrictions	Laws controlling transportation of materials	Rules of professional association	Laws controlling transportation of materials
Public Master plans			

SOURCE: The Report of The President's Committee on Urban Housing, *A Decent Home* (1968).

ical regulation of land development by local governments means that builders must learn a new set of rules each time they venture from their home territory. As they move the battery of building and mechanical codes, zoning ordinances, and subdivision regulations change.

In each new area, the builder must face a buyer who has strong feelings not only about the style, size, and quality but also the location of what is likely to be the largest purchase of a lifetime. Since each location is unique, structurally identical houses on different sites may vary widely in their acceptance by consumers. The mass-produced cookie-cutter houses may be salable in countries with huge shortages or in countries in which the only game in town is government construction. In the United States those conditions are only a memory. As an executive of the firm that was synonymous with the building of suburbia has written:

> We believe that the production techniques we employed in building the post-war Levittowns result in the greatest possible construction economics, and we reluctantly modified our operation only because a changing marketplace dictated a change as a requisite for economic survival.
>
> Instead of building 5,000 identical houses at a single site in one year, we now build 5,000 homes in 150 varieties at 18 sites during the same time, houses whose designs are dictated by marketing, not production, disciplines.[25]

The industry is also characterized by wide swings in production both on a national and on a local market basis. For example, 1.45 million single-family houses were started in 1977, but only 663,000 in 1982. The basic cause of this instability is the combination of the industry's sensitivity to the availability and cost of credit (which will be discussed in greater detail in later chapters) and the dominance of the existing market. Rarely does a household have to move into a new house. New construction makes up little more than 2 percent of the total inventory. Builders, in the short run, are not essential to the housing market (although in the short run they may go bankrupt). Potential purchasers are usually able either to find an existing house into which to move or to fix up the one in which they are living. In 1986, over $90 billion was spent for remodeling.

Residential construction is a big business, typically accounting for 5 percent of the Gross National Product. In 1986, $218 billion was spent, and over 1¾ million new housing units were completed. Nevertheless, the building industry, like the fashion industry, is the domain of the small entrepreneur. It doesn't take much capital investment (only one of every six contractors has any inventory) to get into the business, and if times are tough many a builder moves into other construction-related activities. In 1982, only 15 percent of the builders limited their activities to new construction. Twenty-three percent did only alterations and repairs and the remaining 61 percent were involved with both old and new buildings.[26]

The *Census of the Construction Industry,* in 1977, counted 101,000 residential builders with a payroll and an additional 28,000 with no payroll. These builders were backed up by 300,000 subcontractors. During 1982, a bad year for the business, the number of residential builders with a payroll (about 10 percent of whom build only multifamily buildings) had declined to 94,000. The number of subcontractors had increased to 320,000.

Over two-thirds (69 percent) of all builders in 1986 were characterized by the National Association of Home Builders as small builders—building fewer than 25 homes (46 percent in 1982 built fewer than 10). Approximately one-fifth (22 percent) were characterized as medium-size builders (25 to 100 homes). The remainder were large builders. Less than 1 percent were building more than 500 units. Nevertheless, the large builders accounted for more than two-thirds of all units.[27]

The average firm in the business has only four workers. A description of the organizational structure of a prominent builder in the Washington metropolitan area, who builds 250 single-family homes a year, indicates that Mom and Pop have been replaced by Pop and the Boys:

Q: How large a staff do you have in your office and out in the field?
A: In the office we have a controller, an assistant controller, five

bookkeepers, a receptionist and a secretary and this year, we'll do about $15 million worth of business.

[I]n the field I have my two sons and son-in-law who, you might say are project managers, and on each job we'll have two or three foremen and we'll have three, four, five laborers, whatever there needs to be on the job.

When we deal with the share of the market among builders, we're not talking of the top 3 or top 10 or top 100. The *Long Range Planning Report* of the National Association of Home Builders contains a pie chart entitled "Share of the Market of Top *2,614* Builders, 1983." The top 20 had 8 percent (led by the U.S. Home Corporation with 14,000 units). The next eighty had 7 percent of the market. Number 101 through 2,614 had 26 percent of the business and the remaining builders had 59 percent.

The Planning Report, looking toward the future, sees the brightest outlook for those that have the advantage of scale—be it large or small:

With the advent of the new home financing system of the early 1980s, . . . the big builders' greatest advantage has been their access to the credit markets. Several large building firms, such as U.S. Homes, Ryan Homes and Pulte Homes, have their own mortgage companies and enjoy direct access to the secondary mortgage market. They are thus able to issue builder bonds and raise capital through public offerings.

Small builders, whose strength has traditionally been . . . at the high end of the market, have successfully adapted to changing economic and financial conditions because they have low overhead and carrying costs. . . . The nation's housing industry remains the domain of the small independent home builder. Small builders increased from 57.6 of NAHB's builder membership in 1969 to 72.6 percent in 1982. . . .

In general, the battle between smaller . . . builders and the corporate giants of the industry may be overstated. While larger corporate firms will gain a stronger hold over the starter housing market during the balance of the century, it is yet to be seen whether the housing giants can significantly increase their share of the trade-up market . . . a segment of the marketplace . . . that will be strengthened by changing demographic characteristics of the population.[28]

Chapter 2

OF RUSSIAN DREAMS AND AMERICAN REALITY

Yelena Bonner, in bidding farewell to America to return to her husband, Andrei Sakharov, in the Soviet Union, wrote:

> My dream, my own house, is unattainable for me and my family—that is, for my husband and myself, as unattainable as heaven on earth. But I want a house. If not for me, then for my son and his family. My son and I plan to buy one. And I am learning many new things. The house should be near good schools, my granddaughter is three and schooling is not far off in the future. It should be in the suburbs—vacations are short and a child should not have to grow up in a polluted city. It should be close to their work—both parents have jobs and there is only one car. . . . It should have three bedrooms so that my mother can be with them, or at least visit. . . . But the cost is . . . oh! I want, I want, I want. . . . But it's time for me to pack my bags.[1]

The Russian dream is the American reality. The difference explains the explosion of homeownership in the postwar years. Like Russia, this country is blessed with an abundance of land. But there the likeness ends. Russia lacks a legal system in which the private home receives anywhere near the protection it receives in a country where the home is in large measure what the pursuit of happiness is all about; financial institutions that encourage home-

ownership; a highly developed highway system; an efficient construction industry; and prosperity.

ACCESSIBLE LAND

There are 2.3 billion acres of land in the continental United States,
as the geographer measures. There is not even a measure of the
amount of land for housing the way lawyers, condominium dwellers, and survivalists would define the concept—ownership of the
land includes the space above to the heavens (subject to right of
flight) and the space beneath. Were it not for the fact that the
American masses are huddled together in cities and suburbs, they
would be lost in the American landscape; 70 percent of the population resides on about 35 million acres—1.5 percent of the land.
Add to this roads, highways, airports, and state institutions and
the percentage jumps to a measly 3 percent.[2]

With close to 70 percent of the population living in metropolitan
areas, there is much talk of urban sprawl and of the Megalopolis.
Nevertheless, there is plenty of room. Even if we use a low thresh-
hold to define an urban environment—1,000 persons per square
mile (which can be visualized as 1½ persons per football playing
field, not counting the end zones), only a small portion of America
is urbanized. New York City has approximately 25,000 persons
per square mile. But seventeen states do not have a single county
with a population density of even 500 persons per square mile.
Contrary to the impression gathered from driving the Turnpike,
New Jersey, the most densely populated state, is 75 percent rural
(it is, after all, the Garden State). If all Americans would move to
the states of Texas and Oklahoma, a distinct fear of residents of
those states when oil was thirty-five dollars a barrel, their population density would then be comparable to West Germany or the
United Kingdom.

In contrast, Japan—with a population half that of the United
States, packed into an area (much of which is mountainous and
unsuitable for construction) smaller than California, and a government policy of being self-sufficient in rice production, has made

land so scarce as to make it incredibly costly and the price of housing prohibitive. The value of all the land is equal to the value of all the land in the United States, which is twenty-five times larger. Put another way, the cost of Japanese land is twenty-five times more expensive than U.S. land. James Fallows has noted the quality (or lack thereof) of the housing may be related to Japan's troublesome trade surplus:

> . . . Because land is so expensive, people cannot afford to buy more than a tiny plot on which to build a house. Real estate ads do not say "house on an acre" or even "half an acre"; they say "124.93 sq. meters.". . .
>
> Perhaps the Japanese would still be intent on exports, rather than domestic consumption, if they had bigger houses and more money left after paying for land. But I think that the spartan nature of Japanese home life encourages salary-men to spend more time at the (comparatively) plush office, dreaming up new export plans, and at bars, cementing those crucial work-group relationships. What's more, it reinforces the export-or-die mentality that helped Japan recover after the war but is now making problems for it and the rest of the world.[3]

In the 1945–1960 period, years that are synonymous with the suburbanization of America, the availability of land was never a problem. One of the worries, in fact, was that the forests were growing. Thus, Jean Gottmann, in his massive study of the urbanized Northeastern Seaboard, *Megalopolis,* wrote:

> For the whole region the forested area increased . . . in the years 1946–1956 [and there was] a further advance in the total wooded area during the late 1950's. . . . [I]t would be unwise to conclude that . . . there is no cause to worry. Having 16 million acres of forest . . . means only half an acre per inhabitant in Megalopolis.[4]

Alas, poor Tarzan.

It took more than land to make Americans a nation of homeowners. In the nineteenth century, we had just as much land but fewer people, and these fewer people were huddled in congested cities

near their places of work. The crucial additional factor was improved transportation which vastly increased the accessibility of
cheap residential land. As Homer Hoyt wrote in 1939:

> The revolutionary change in transportation that affected nearly all
> American cities and enabled them to spread out in far-flung lines
> was the advent of the electric surface lines about 1890. . . . The
> last great revolutionary change . . . was . . . the automobile. . . .
> Neighborhoods built along street car lines were supplemented by
> neighborhoods reached largely by automobile. . . . Since the area
> on the periphery increased with the square of the distance from the
> city, the automobile opened up extensive areas because it had a
> speed on open highways several times greater than that of electric
> street cars.[5]

This increase in accessible land was translated into reduced relative land prices. In 1949, the estimated market value for an FHA
home site was the same as in 1936. In contrast, the average value
of the structure and other improvements increased about 40 percent, and residential construction costs increased by over 100 percent. Between 1900 and 1950 the ratio of site cost to the total price
of a single-family house declined from about 30 to 12 percent.[6]

THE MORTGAGE FINANCE REVOLUTION

America in the late forties was especially lucky in having in place
a mortgage finance system. Housing is a creation that lives on
credit. It is an "OPM" (other people's money) business par excel-
lence. The builder's most important talent may be his ability to
borrow. He may use some of his own money to start the work, but
the work won't be completed unless he is able to borrow. In like
manner, the buyer may have saved some money to make a down
payment on the property, but he is dependent on a lender for the
bulk of his funds. What keeps the whole business humming is a
medieval piece of legal wizardry called a mortgage.

The mortgage predates the Domesday Book of William the Conqueror, the precursor of the present-day recording systems. The "gage" part of the word derived from the French word for pledge. In the context of land ownership, it would be the handing over (a pledge) of some of the incidents of ownership as security for the repayment of a debt. The gage came in two varieties, live and dead. In the live variety, the land was transferred to the creditor, who retained the crops and fruits of the land until the loan was repaid —an utterly impractical solution in the case of a one family house. In the dead gage, which in French becomes a "mort"'gage, the creditor is willing to play dead. Although as a legal matter the creditor owns the land, the owner is allowed to have all the benefits (the equity), including possession. The creditor comes to life if the debtor fails to live up to his agreement (by failing to pay his debt, to give his sovereign his due, to maintain and insure the property), at which time the creditor can foreclose the equity of the debtor (the part of the bundle of legal rights that confers on the holder the right of possession and the right to sell or rent), take possession, and sell the property in order to have his loan repaid.

The mortgage was, nevertheless, in many ways an unattractive instrument from the point of view of the lender. The mortgage has a long term, and the lender is unable to require the borrower to prepay the loan, even if the lender needs the money or if the cost of the money has become greater to the lender than what he is charging the borrower. The lender is also lending his money in bulk and getting it returned in small payments. The lender has also traditionally not had a market to sell his loan. With the laws of every state differing on such crucial items as the length of time of the foreclosure process and the owner's rights to cure the default and regain the property, the lender who had to sell a mortgage quickly would have to take a substantial loss.

The home mortgage is also a unique type of capital investment. The usual capital investment in factory or farm machinery is contributing to the production of wealth. The debtor is, therefore, being made more able to repay the loan. The home mortgage contributes only to the satisfaction of its user.

With these negative characteristics, it should not be a surprise that for the longest time, lenders charged higher interest on mortgage loans, were unwilling to grant long-term mortgages, required bulk repayments, and would further limit their risk by granting loans that represented only a small percentage of the value of the property. In the 1920s, most of the notes that were secured by mortgages did not provide for the full repayment of the debt by periodic payments (amortization). The entire principal or large balances often fell due in only five or six years. It was also customary for home buyers to obtain two or three separate home mortgage loans, with the first mortgage being limited to one-half or two-thirds of the value of the property, and the second and third mortgages bearing progressively steeper interest rates that reflected the greater risk of their being junior liens (the first mortgagee got his money out first in the case of a foreclosure, and in like manner the second came before the third).

The system of short-term multiple mortgages that had to be renewed or renegotiated at considerable trouble and expense created a structure fraught with the danger of collapse. And collapse it did, in 1929. Banks faced a shortage of credit, and buyers faced a shortage of income. A wave of defaults swept the nation, and both banks and owners went under.

Herbert Hoover began the process of putting the Humpty Dumpty mortgage finance system back together again, and Franklin Roosevelt got it back up on the wall, where it would sit quite securely for over four decades. Successive initiatives between 1932 and 1934 laid the structural foundations for a complete overhaul of what is now called the "conventional" mortgage lending industry in the United States.

President Hoover's intervention sought to shore up the surviving mortgage lending institutions, stimulate construction (which had dropped below 200,000 units), prevent a repetition of the mortgage industry's collapse, and create a structure for the promotion of homeownership.

The Federal Home Loan Bank Act of 1932 authorized a specialized form of reserve banking tailored to the needs of housing and designed to maintain a flow of funds in times of shortage. Being nationwide in scope, it would also channel funds from regions with surpluses to those where funds were in short supply. It created a system of regional Federal Home Loan Banks roughly parallel to the Federal Reserve system. Initially, the banks were to be capitalized by federal funds that would be replaced by the investment of member institutions—savings and loan associations, mutual savings banks, and other home mortgage lenders. The regional banks were to provide guidelines and supervision to their members and, perhaps most important, expand the source of credit by making advances on the security of mortgages held by them.

The approach attempted to encourage long-term saving and habits of thrift, not only because they promoted the economic stability and mobility of the savers but also because such savings are a peculiarly appropriate source of funds for home mortgage investment, as distinguished from the more volatile flow of funds in the general investment market.

A great effort was made to distinguish the institutions under the wing of the Federal Home Loan Bank Board from ordinary "banks." The funds of individuals were viewed as investments and the account holder was deemed a shareholder rather than a depositor. Consistent with the investment terminology, the account holders had no right to demand withdrawal. Instead, the associations had the power to impose a waiting period. Checking privileges and other general banking services were considered outside the general range of operations. The appropriate scope of these institutions was rather narrowly limited to the making of first mortgage loans on residential property.

The Federal Home Loan Bank Act was long-term legislation. In the short run, families were losing their homes and banks were collapsing. The Home Owners' Loan Corporation (HOLC), authorized in 1933, addressed this problem. It provided a new loan in cases where the owner had defaulted on his existing mortgage debt but had reasonable prospects of paying off the new loan. This consisted of a single mortgage loan, large enough to pay off the old debt and fully amortized over a long term through equal monthly payments. The HOLC invested nearly $3.5 billion in refinancing more than a million home loans from 1933 to 1936 and in subsequent advances to borrowers.

The same act that created the HOLC also provided for the chart-ering and regulation of savings and loan associations by the Federal Home Loan Bank Board. In order for savers to have confidence in savings and loans, Congress extended deposit insurance to the shareholders.

HOLC showed the way to create a more rational mortgage lending pattern. The National Housing Act of 1934 created the Federal Housing Administration and granted it the power to insure the loans of lenders that were secured by mortgages with high loan-to-property-value ratios and long terms. The borrowers were indirect beneficiaries of the system, since the high loan-to-value ratio meant lower down payments were required and the longer terms meant lower monthly payments were needed to amortize the mortgage. A subsequent amendment in 1938 extended coverage to mortgages on rental housing built by profit-motivated sponsors. The reform accomplished a conservative revolution. As Hilbert Fefferman, a HUD attorney whose career spanned four decades, wrote in a report to Congress:

1. The volume of local housing credit was increased because of the Federal insurance, and savings banks and other conservative institutions increased their participation in residential financing;

2. The . . . uniformity of the Federal guarantee . . . encouraged the flow of credit across state lines as insurance companies and other non-local lenders—primarily relying on the Federal insurance—made mortgage funds available . . . ;

3. Many small families with small savings, particularly younger families, were brought into the housing market because of the lower downpayment made possible by FHA insurance;

4. Families of moderate income were brought into the house buying market, particularly as general economic conditions improved, by the lower monthly payment which resulted from lower interest because the level repayment plan, having first eased the burden of payment in early low income years, provided for steady and complete amortization over the life of the mortgage;

5. The FHA insurance provided a steadier flow of credit for rental housing [added in 1938]; and

6. The increasing size of the housing market and the increasing flow of mortgage funds . . . made more efficient housing construction possible.[7]

It is important to note that it takes two loans for a house to be built and sold. The first is an interim short-term loan (usually made by commercial banks) to cover the costs of construction of the building and the second is the long-term loan to the buyer of the house (usually made by a savings and loan association). The construction loans are especially risky loans for a bank, since the builder usually has little or no net worth, and there is always the possibility that because of misjudgment about costs or market, the house won't sell.

FHA* came to the rescue. It could insure both the construction and the long-term loan. Builders could apply to FHA, which would issue commitments to insure both the interim and permanent loan. Since FHA was now assuming the risk, the builder had to show it that he had correctly judged the market and the value of the house. In addition the buildings had to meet FHA's minimum property standards—an important consideration, since many of the localities in which potato fields were being turned into subdivisions had neither building nor subdivision controls. The construction loan could only be drawn after completion of defined stages of the building process. Before FHA would insure the bank's advance it would inspect the work to confirm it was done and met specifications.

Since the builder had to be the owner of the land before it could begin to obtain money, and since there were engineering costs and fees and deposits required before the necessary permits would be granted, the builder had to have the timing of a juggler (to pay for the land almost simultaneously with the drawdown of the money) and the skills of a pitchman (to have design professionals "carry" the developer until his first drawdown) to limit his actual cash investment. Since the construction loan was usually limited to 85

* And the Veterans Administration (VA), which ran a similar and somewhat more liberal program of home guarantees for veterans.

percent of the appraised value of the house, these skills were necessary throughout the entire process—to obtain the highest possible appraisal and to convince subcontractors that their check really was in the mail.

Most of the potential home buyers were like the builder—dream rich and money poor. Before they could even consider the long term, they needed some money to make a down payment. In this regard, the FHA and the VA came to the rescue. The FHA down payment requirement, which had in 1934 stood at 20 percent, was down to 3 percent in the fifties. The VA guaranty program in 1954 offered the ultimate—the no-down-payment loan.

All that was needed was a lender who had the money to loan. This posed a problem in areas of the country such as Florida, California, and the Southwest, where the dreamers outnumbered the savers. The savings and loans were of no assistance, since their lending resources were limited. What saved the situation was the eastern mutual savings banks and life insurance companies, relying on the FHA and VA to limit their risk.

The great distance between the lenders and the borrowers created the need for middlemen—mortgage bankers. Mortgage bankers identified the money sources and negotiated commitment of funds from the far-off cities where the sun rises. Although they sometimes lent their own money, the basic profit in the business came from loan-originating fees (payment by the borrower for the processing of the loan application) at the front end of the house purchase, and servicing of the loans (collection of the loan payments and dealing with the borrower for the lender) at the end of the deal.

The Federal National Mortgage Association (Fannie Mae), a government entity that was founded in 1938 but came into its own in the late forties, was also a key player. Its purpose was to create a "secondary market" for home mortgages and thereby turn the mortgage into a liquid asset. It would buy mortgage loans insured by FHA or VA from lenders or mortgage bankers. Although FNMA never dealt directly with home buyers, its activities were crucial to them when money was short or when they happened to live in an area bypassed by larger lenders.

Favorable mortgage terms, made possible by the federal guarantee and insurance programs, plus the shortage of decent housing in cities made the suburban house an offer too good to refuse. In the mid-fifties, with mortgage interest rates at about 5.5 percent and the average new home price at $12,000, the monthly payment on a thirty-year self-amortizing loan, assuming no down payment, was $68.13. The economic terms are translated into human terms, in a memoir, *Man in Metropolis*[8] by Louis Schlivek:

> We could find nothing that could meet our needs in any neighborhood we cared to live in at a price we could afford. Instead, what we did find, poring over the real estate pages of the paper, was ad after ad urging us to buy a house in the suburbs. We weren't interested in living in the suburbs, and had not planned on buying a home, but the terms made us rub our eyes in disbelief. It was impossible to resist at least going out to look. Imagine, a six-room house with a yard of its own which could be "carried"—amortization, taxes, insurance—for a monthly payment lower than the rent on our one-room apartment.*

The added ingredient of the baby boom and economic prosperity turned the move to the suburbs into a mass exodus. The prolonged baby boom from 1946 to 1963 came as a surprise to most demographers. Coming into the forties, most believed that the future would bring a leveling off of total population and perhaps a decline. The birth rate during and after the war rose dramatically. Between 1946 and 1951 the increase amounted to more than 1 million births per year. Although there were fewer women in the prime childbearing years (20 to 29) thereafter the boom continued. They were producing more.

A significant change had occurred in the attitude of women. In 1940, most American married women saw the ideal family as a foursome—a father, mother, and 2 children. In 1945 the number

---

* Note the similarity to Juvenal's exhortation to the Roman populace in the second century, "If you can tear yourself away from the games of the Circus, you can buy an excellent house at Sora, at Prusino, for what you now pay in Rome to rent a dark garret for one year. And there you will have a little garden."

had grown to a quintet with 3 children. In 1955 and 1960 it had grown into a band with 4 children. The previous generation of "depression wives" born between 1906 and 1915 bore the lowest number of children, 2.4 to 2.5. Those born in the thirties averaged 3.1 to 3.6.

The size of the family was a prime mover in the search for the home during the postwar period. The size of the family and the willingness to assume a large debt load in the form of a home mortgage was to a large extent dependent on the family's confidence in the future. And there was much reason for the confidence. The country was going through an unparalleled period of prosperity and a major shift in income distribution that vastly increased the number of moderate-income families—the market the homebuilders were aiming at. Between 1945 and 1955 consumer prices increased by 20 percent while hourly earnings in manufacturing rose by 84 percent and per capita disposable personal income by 52 percent.[9] The income distribution curve had shifted sharply to the right.

Table 2. Income Distribution (in constant 1963 dollars) [10]

Income Level	1929	1963
Under $2,000	30%	11%
$2,000 to $4,000	38%	18%
$4,000 to $6,000	16%	20%
$6,000 to $8,000	7%	18%
$8,000 to $10,000	3%	12%
Over $10,000	6%	21%

When the economic conditions changed, when prosperity came to America, when the suburbs became accessible, the consumer preference for homeownership made itself felt. The dam of economic barriers burst. Surveys during the thirties and early forties indicated that seven out of ten families preferred to own, while only one in five preferred to rent. Ownership was preferred by nine out of ten owners and by more than half the renters.[11]

THE DRIVE TOWARD HOMEOWNERSHIP

The changes in financing and economic conditions made home-ownership achievable. However, the preference was primarily driven by deeper emotions. The United States Savings and Loan League during the late sixties found that the dominant reason was noneconomic by a margin of 62 percent to 38 percent. The economic motive fell into two main categories—32 percent were building an equity in real estate or wanted something more than rent receipts to show for their money, and 6 percent thought that owning was cheaper than renting. The remainder mentioned a better environment for their children, privacy, freedom to improve the property and the need for more space. When Herb Gans asked his neighbors in Levittown the same question, the primary reasons given were house-related (need for more space, desire for home-ownership, and desire for a free-standing house), community-related (inadequacy of schools, racial change in neighborhood), and job-related (transfer by employer).[12]

What is amazing about these various reasons for the desire for homeownership is that none of the surveys found a reason that is conventionally viewed as a major factor, namely the tax breaks, the homeowner's ability to deduct from his income taxes the cost of interest and real estate taxes, if he itemizes his deductions. I would venture to say that the reason it wasn't mentioned was that it wasn't there. The families that left the cities for the suburbs in the decades after the war were not upper-income families for whom the benefit would have been valuable. In fact, even in the eighties, three-fourths of all homeowners took the standard deduction and, therefore, receive no benefit from the tax break.

The high tax bracket for whom the itemized deduction is valuable would have been homeowners (although their homes might not be as costly) even if taxes were to take only a negligible portion of their income—a condition that held true in the thirties. Table 3 compares the percentage of homeowners by income level in the mid-thirties (when the effective tax rate for a household with a net income of $10,000 was 3.4 percent) and 1980:

Table 3. Percentage of Owners by Income Level

| 1935–1936[13] | | 1980 | |
Income Level	Owners	Income Level	Owners
Under $500	21	Under $3,000	44
$500–$1,000	21	$3,000–$7,000	47
$1,000–$1,250	28	$7,000–$10,000	53
$1,250–$1,500	31	$10,000–$15,000	57
$1,500–$1,750	34	$15,000–$20,000	66
$1,750–$2,000	37	$20,000–$25,000	75
$2,000–$2,500	44	$25,000–$35,000	83
$2,500–$3,000	51	$35,000–$50,000	90
$3,000–$4,000	54	$50,000+	92
$4,000–$5,000	59		
$5,000–$10,000	64		

A perfect match.

A look at the international scene also brings into question the importance of "tax subsidies." Canada's homeownership rate is comparable to that of the United States (64 percent in 1981). Nevertheless, it does not have comparable homeownership deduction provisions in its tax laws. Australia does not permit the deduction of home mortgage interest and has a higher homeownership rate than the United States. Prosperity is not a sufficient explanation. West Germany had a homeownership rate in 1978 of only 36 percent. Prosperity may be necessary, but the key seems to be much lower price for land in North America and Australia, an advanced mortgage finance system, and an efficient homebuilding industry.

Sweden offers an interesting case study of homeownership thriving in the face of government opposition. To alleviate a postwar shortage of housing, the Swedish government followed the policy of building and subsidizing multifamily structures in suburban and new-town locations. The housing was not limited to low-income families and the quality was equal to the best American rental housing. The Swedish thesis was that good housing and good services in the form of schools, day nurseries, sports facilities, shopping, and transportation would attract households with high standards.

The people disappointed the planners. After a decade of building multifamily housing, the Swedes discovered that many suburban multifamily units were vacant. From the mid-seventies, 75 percent of all new dwellings were constructed in the form of small houses.

As Ake Daun, Professor of European Ethnology at the University of Stockholm, put the matter:

> The desire to live in one's own house, in "close contact with the earth," with a garden and control over one's own form of living in the spirit of "a joy and a pride, one's own fireside," turned out to be a much more common dream than many had perhaps suspected. . . . [T]he very impetus of the intensified construction of private houses that prevailed during this period must have further increased the need. It became fashionable to live in a house, especially among families with children, to a degree that had been formerly unknown. . . .
>
> The desire to move depends to a great extent upon the attractiveness of living in some particular one-family-house area that friends and acquaintances have talked about. *Only to a certain degree can the large-scale moving be explained by dissatisfaction with the rented apartment areas that so many moved away from.* [emphasis added] [14]

This lusting after ownership is a near universal and ancient attribute of mankind. Louis Winnick has noted, "It's like the sex drive, to own my own home on my piece of land." Dr. Winnick is only seconding the opinion of a higher authority. The "Ten Commandments" prohibit the lusting after a neighbor's house before the lusting after a neighbor's wife.*

Most Americans have had their desires satisfied. At present the homeownership rate in the United States stands at 64 percent, the highest in the industrialized world, except for Australia. The gross

---

* When Moses reviews the commandments in Deuteronomy he reverses the order. An explanation may be that the Hebrews at the time of Exodus remembered the houses of Egypt. The review was given after forty years of wandering in the desert in which they were tent-dwellers. Alternatively, when they were slaves they had neither the time nor the strength to lust for their neighbor's wife. In the Sinai, however, there were many rest stops, no work, and plenty of time.

rate actually understates the consumer preference for homeownership since we are considering all households, which includes many young households who do not have the desire to settle down or the wherewithall to afford a house. If we look at the homeownership rate by age group we discover that for all age groups over 35 the rate is above 65 percent. It peaks at over 80 percent in the 55–64 age group and remains at a high plateau—72 percent of all households in the 75-and-over age group are homeowners.[15]

Chapter 3

THE INDUSTRY THAT RODE ON ITS LOSSES

THE UNPOPULAR IMAGE OF THE LANDLORD

The poem "Kill My Landlord," soulfully recited by Eddie Murphy, playing a convicted murderer in a poignant "Saturday Night Live" vignette, tells us more about the uneasy role of rental housing on the American scene than reams of statistics (which we will get to soon enough).

The owner of rental property operates in a hostile environment. In spite of mercenary motives no worse than those of other providers of goods and services, the landlord occupies an almost unique place as a bad guy in American culture, the fat cat taking unfair advantage of the little mice. However, he is constantly harassed and often bruised and battered.

In spite of such abuse, the landlord plays an absolutely essential role in a nation's housing system. There are always a substantial number of people who choose not to own or for whom ownership may not be a good idea. In the era before the condominium (which arrived on the shores of America from Puerto Rico in 1960 and received the blessing of FHA mortgage insurance in 1961), when apartment living and renting were synonymous, the rental sector could count on the newly married, the singles, and those who would not give up the cosmopolitan life for all the fresh air in the world. At all times, it would include the highly mobile, the poor, and the financially insecure.

In a country in which the right to homeownership is on every politician's lips, it is important to note that the need for a rental alternative is felt quite strongly in many European countries. In England, the Conservative Party's policy of selling off council housing (public housing and the major source of rental housing) has led to fears that it will lead to hardship for those unwilling or unable to buy, and the opposition Labour Party has adopted a "Right to Rent" policy as part of its political platform.[1]

The bad rap landlords receive may be attributable to the rent-gouging attributes of the breed or the high profitability in real estate investment. The popular perception is unfortunately not supported by the facts. Reviewing rent increases and the change in the value of rental property in the decades of the sixties and seventies, Anthony Downs of the Brookings Institute concluded:

> [R]esidential rents did not increase as fast as consumer income, operating costs, or construction costs. . . . The best available estimate is that real rent levels *fell* about 8.4 percent from 1960 to 1980. . . .
>
> . . . In 1980 rents would have had to be 77 percent higher than they actually were to support real market values equivalent to those in 1960. . . .
>
> Putting the conclusion another way, the real value of rental housing properties in the United States *sustainable from rents alone* appears to have fallen substantially since 1960—perhaps by 50 percent or more. The enormous drop results from much faster increases in operating costs and rates than rents.[2]

The phenomenon is not a new one. As Louis Winnick wrote in the fifties:

> . . . [T]here is little doubt that the present generation of investors as a group has lived through a long period of relatively poor earnings as owners of rental property. On the basis of historical records of operating experience, the free and clear return on residential real estate, related to original acquisition cost, was quite unfavorable from the end of the 1920s to the 1950s.[3]

The bad reputation of landlords may have to do more with consumer psychology and the nature of the product and service sold than with economics. As Roger Starr noted in an article entitled "The End of Rental Housing":

> The major difference between landlords and other kinds of entrepreneurs is that the landlords are involved in a long, continuing relationship with their customers, one in which the customer pays over and over again for what he already has—i.e., access to an apartment that in the very nature of things is a little bit older and worse each month. . . .
> . . . The tenant cannot truly understand why he should be asked to pay again for something the landlord already made. Renewing a lease on an apartment is not like buying a new suit or a steak. . . . Perhaps they cost more than the previous suit or steak—but they are new, and the purchaser is thrilled at the prospect of eating a fresh sirloin, or wearing a new suit for the first time. An economic relationship in which the supplier cannot increase his volume except by raising his unit prices, and the customer has no psychological satisfaction to show for each new expenditure of money, inevitably produces severe tension. . .[4]

WHY DOES ANYONE BUILD RENTAL UNITS?

The title of Mr. Starr's article is typical of a genre in the housing economics literature since World War II, which has continually seen private rental housing in a state of crisis or near its demise. With the ownership always rising in the seesaw, it is not surprising that the rental sector has been viewed as depressed. When the 1940s started it was sitting pretty—56 percent of all the units were occupied by tenants. By the late forties, owner-occupancy was the dominant form of tenure in the United States. During the next three decades rental housing continued down the slippery slope. At present, it houses approximately one-third of America's population.

The postwar years were not halcyon years for rental housing. Production was far behind that of the first decade of the twentieth century—50,000 more units were built in 1905 than in 1955. And it fizzled compared to the Roaring Twenties. In 1925, 360,000 apartments were built, three times as many as in 1955 (for a population one-third larger).[5]

Rental housing, nevertheless, has not lost all of its productive punch. The stock of rental housing continues to grow. The 28.5 million rental units in 1980 represented a 5-million-unit growth during the seventies, and there are now 9 million more rental units than there were before World War II. Its growth rate has been puny only in comparison with the phenomenal growth of the ownership sector, which reached 40 million in 1970 and 52 million in 1980—more than tripling the number of homes in 1940.

Rental housing may be in perennial crisis because in good times it faces competition for occupants from the homeownership sector while in bad times the occupants lack sufficient income to provide a reasonable rate of return. So who has been building the units in the postwar years and why?

Immediately after the war, large life insurance companies looked as though they were going to dominate the field. But times changed and FHA accidently became a "sugar daddy," first in the unsubsidized field and a decade later in the subsidized field—as private producers were called on to do a better job than public housing. And in a sharp shift from tradition, in part by accident, the shelter industry rode on losses, as it found it was more profitable to depend on tax shelters than on cash flow of the building. The Internal Revenue Code also provided a backdrop for the landlord's ultimate revenge, the condominium, in which the tenants pay dearly for the privilege of being their own landlords.

THE INSURANCE INDUSTRY

The distinguishing feature of rental housing is that the owner is not the occupant. The twosome of developer and lender becomes a foursome to include the manager and the investor. There was a short interlude when the money provider, the developer, and the investor were one. Metropolitan Life had dipped its feet into the rental waters in the 1920s with the development of a 2,200-unit project in Queens, New York—Sunnyside Gardens. The initial experience was good. However, the project was swamped with losses as a result of the Depression and the collapse of the real estate industry.

By 1939, conditions had improved in the country, and returns were up at Sunnyside (a 6.7 percent return on its depreciated book value). Metropolitan, Equitable, and Prudential saw an opportunity to expand their profit margins and polish their image. Rental housing seemed a way for insurance companies to double-dip in the rapidly growing pool of newly married couples, by providing for their short-term housing needs and for insurance to protect their families over the long term.

The profit margins on alternative investments were very low— yields on high grade corporate bonds were 2.7 percent per annum, and mortgage interest rates were continuing to decline. Metropolitan took the plunge again and built Parkchester in New York, Park Fairfax in Virginia, and Parklabrea and Parkmerced in California —some of the largest rental projects ever built in America.

When the war ended, these projects were highly profitable by the standards of the past—Parkchester was returning 7.6 percent of original cost. Lemminglike, the other insurance companies followed in Metropolitan's path. New projects were launched and existing ones expanded.

By the fifties, however, the lead lemming went over the cliff. The projects were making neither friends nor money. By 1952, the net yield of all insurance company housing projects was a meager 1.7 percent, substantially below the return on U.S. bonds. And it is a rare landlord who finds himself an object of affection when rents have to be raised to meet rapidly rising operating costs. Instead of receiving public adulation for meeting the housing shortage, the projects were criticized as poor planning (except for Fresh Meadows, which won the plaudits of Louis Mumford) and the companies were attacked for practicing racial discrimination.[6]

The baton was handed back to the more traditional team, which had a cast of characters all belonging to the Buck family—Quick, Safe, and Easy. The developer supplies his wits and his time and as little money as possible. The lender (often two—one short-term and one long-term) supplies the money. The investor, or group of

investors, supplies the patience. The developer is primarily interested in the quick buck. He rarely has an abiding interest in the
property. He wants to part with his project as quickly as possible
at a price that will reward him for his services and enable him to
go on to another [ad]venture.

The lender is primarily interested in the safe and steady buck.
His profit is the spread between his cost of money and the price at
which he sells it to the developer. The spread must also represent
the risk he bears of never being repaid, because the developer
made a mistake about the housing market or the lender made a
mistake about the integrity or ability of the borrower.

The investors are interested in the easy buck. They want to sit
back and get a check every month, and being in a leveraged situation, they hope that rising prices will provide them with a big
payoff.

Developing a new rental project is not a job for amateurs. The
planning, building, and leasing of a new apartment building is a
long-drawn-out process in which every step is fraught with the
possibility of disaster. It requires some, but not too much, smarts
(many projects would never start if the developer knew what was
in store for him), guts (and the lower part of the anatomy), as well
as technical and financial skills. It requires assembling and acquiring a site, designing plans, obtaining the necessary government
approvals, arranging the requisite financing, supervising a long
construction project, and merchandising the new units to prospective tenants.

The successful developer and the unsuccessful developer both
can do well when they build a successful project, but when failure
occurs the successful developer doesn't go down with the project.
There is always a risk that something will go wrong somewhere
between the formulation of the plan and final occupancy. There
are many factors over which the developer has no control—the
terrain he traverses is often ruled by Murphy's Law. In the three
to four years the process is likely to take, the market for apartments can soften as other developers have also come to the conclusion that the times are ripe for new projects or as potential
customers have found more attractive alternatives; interest costs
can escalate because the government is having trouble balancing

its books; local laws can change because a new party is in office; building costs can change because the Teamsters went on strike. There is no end to the items that can interfere with the developer's sleep.

The conventional view is that the federal government mortgage insurance and guarantee programs have favored homeownership at the expense of rental housing. In the mid-fifties, at the peak of the government's involvement, 50 percent of the mortgages on new homes were either insured by the FHA or guaranteed by the Veterans Administration,[7] and between 1946 and 1955 the FHA and VA programs accounted for approximately one-third of single-family starts.[8] There is, nevertheless, compelling evidence that single-family housing prevailed *in spite* of the support the federal government gave to rental housing.

The FHA was needed because of the hesitancy of all the parties concerned—the developer, investor, and mortgage lender—to put too much of their own money at risk in a rental development. A new project would have to face competition from single-family housing and the low rents of existing housing. The low rents represented not only the lingering effects of rent control but also the check on rents provided by these alternatives. By the late forties, notwithstanding higher construction costs and operating costs, the price increases renters faced in moving out of the old rental units would have put them into their own home. During the rental boom in the twenties the rents in new buildings were only 40 to 50 percent above the rents in existing units. In 1950 the rents in new buildings were 130 percent higher.

If a high return were going to be made, it would require landlords to be highly leveraged, with the loan representing a high percentage of the value of the building. This was something most institutional investors (commercial and savings banks and life insurance companies) could not provide their borrowers—since most states limited the amount of the loan to approximately two-thirds of the value. And, even if they could, they wouldn't. The Depression experience was still fresh in their minds—35 percent of the mortgage loans made by life insurance companies between 1925 and 1929 were foreclosed. The lenders would need government insurance to move into rental housing.

THE ROLE OF THE FHA—HIGHRISES IN THE DESERT

Between 1935 and 1957, 733,000 units were built under the FHA program,[9] and during the decade immediately following the war approximately one-half of all private rental units were built with FHA-insured mortgages. As Louis Winnick concluded, "[T]he evidence suggests that government aid has resulted in a relatively greater expansion in private rental construction than in single-family construction."[10]

There was a brief period when the country was in danger of being engulfed by a sea of garden apartments. In 1942, Congress added a Section 608 to the National Housing Act. The section did not have a real impact until a technical change was made in the valuation formula in 1948. Change of the maximum loan amount from 90 percent of the "reasonable replacement cost" to 90 percent of the "necessary current costs" of the proposed project, virtually eliminated the equity requirement. A high loan-to-value ratio plus a liberal valuation of the land and a high estimate of development costs translates into a profit for a competent developer even if he builds in the middle of the Sahara Desert. The developer has all of his money and profit out—"mortgaged out" in the jargon—before the first tenant moves in or even if a tenant never moves in.

The program succeeded beyond all expectations. Four hundred sixty thousand units were built (half in four metropolitan areas: New York City, Chicago, Washington, and Los Angeles). Of these approximately 400,000 were built by the end of 1951.[11] More units were built under the "608" program in 1950 and 1951 than had been built by all the life insurance companies, limited dividend corporations, semiphilanthropic organizations, and consumer cooperatives.

Then the ax fell. The administrators of the program had to explain to congressional committees why so many projects were so sparsely populated; why over four hundred projects were in financial distress; and why FHA had become the landlord in so many buildings.

The program was subsequently cleaned up and the Golden

Goose was sterilized. Developers were forced to make money the old-fashioned way—they had to build buildings whose tenants would pay high enough rents to cover operating costs and produce a profit. Given the high risk and the unpleasant task of having to be a landlord, high returns were required, in the 15–20 percent range. There were many fewer takers.

In the post-tax-shelter age following the Tax Reform Act of 1986, there are few who remember that there was a pre-tax-shelter age in which the dominant form of ownership of new rental housing was the corporation rather than the limited partnership. In 1950, corporations owned about one-quarter of the nation's mortgaged units and over three out of every four units in large projects. In the late fifties, investments in new apartment projects were made almost entirely by private corporations.[12]

The FHA insurance program for rental housing required that the mortgagor be a corporation. Unlike the single-family program, in which the FHA assumed that its interest and the homeowner's coincided, the FHA operated on the assumption that there was a basic conflict of interest between it and the owner of a rental project. Given its experience in the "608" program, the attitude of many of the participants in the FHA program was that the rules and regulations were there to challenge their entrepreneurial instincts, and the fact that most developers were smarter than the FHA field staff (and if they weren't they could hire the staff away with offers they couldn't refuse), the only way to keep the program from sinking was red tape.

FHA required that the mortgagor be a corporation formed for the sole purpose of developing, owning, and managing a particular rental project and that it adopted a certificate of incorporation dictated by FHA (the Model Form, to use the euphemism). FHA held the purse strings of the project quite tightly—restricting both the inflow of money through rent increases and the outflow through cash distributions. At one point in the mid-1950s, the Model Form had a provision that "No increase in charges from the approved rental schedule shall be made except with the consent of the Preferred Stockholders." The FHA held all the preferred shares. Congress mandated that the rents of insured projects be "reasonable."

FHA read the mandate as authority to protect the tenants of the project by means of rent control. Rents were set to provide sufficient income (allowing for a 7 percent vacancy loss) to cover all operating costs and debt service and provide for a fund to replace structural parts and to yield 11 to 12 percent on the book equity. For a project run at full occupancy the return could be 20 percent. Since the cash equity was usually less than 50 percent of book equity, there were profits to be made.

FHA wanted to make sure some money was invested and stayed invested in the project, so it required that 30 percent of the total book equity investment had to be in nonredeemable common stock paid for in cash. The remaining 70 percent could be paid for in notes and in redeemable stock that could be paid off if the project had surplus cash. Although the investor could get the cash invested through distributing surplus cash by means of a dividend (if the developer was lucky enough not to be in a state that required net earnings before a dividend could be issued and expenses for the "cost" of depreciation included), the receipt of a dividend was a mixed blessing since the typical investor was in a high tax bracket (up to 70 percent of his income). If the project was successful, it made much more sense to sell the stock to another investor and pay the much smaller capital gains tax. Given this hassle, why would an investor even consider rental ownership, when the corporate tax rate was 52 percent of income?

DEPRECIATION AND TAX SHELTERS

It is time to follow the rabbit into the Wonderland of taxes to meet the Queen—depreciation, which is based on the metaphysical notion that nothing corporeal lasts forever. Ever since the Revenue Law of 1913, the wear and tear on property used in a trade or a business that will necessitate its replacement has been recognized as a legitimate cost of doing business. The classical method of depreciation is "straight line"—in which the amount to be deducted is calculated by dividing the cost of the property by its "useful life" (determined by the Internal Revenue Service). In the case of FHA-insured projects during the 1950s, this deduction was sufficient to offset any net income, so that the corporation was not only limiting the shareholder's liability but also limiting the shareholder's liability to the tax collector.

What the tax laws allow should not be confused with either business or economic reality. As Paul Taubman, a Professor of Economics at the University of Pennsylvania, has noted in regard to rental real estate, "[F]or each of the first 40 years of useful life —the average tax life of shell and equipment—the true loss in annual loss in value of the building is less than that allowed by the straight line formula with a 40 year useful life." In addition, the value of a building rarely depreciates in value in inflationary times. Taking these two factors into account, Taubman concludes, "[I]t seems that not only are the permissible tax depreciation rules . . . a subsidy, but so is straight line depreciation." [13]

What are these more liberal rules, and when and why were they enacted? The rules permit the owners of new rental housing to adopt extremely liberal depreciation formulas: the declining-balance method at up to twice the straight-line rate in the initial years of life, the sum of the years digits. Although the amount that can be depreciated remains the same, the methods accelerate the deductions in the early years. The following table and chart illustrate the different results over the first ten years:

Table 4. Comparison of Annual Depreciation Allowances (First 10 years)

Cost of Building—$1 million; Life—40 years

End of Year	Straight line (2.5%)	Declining balance (5%)	Sum-of-the Years'-digits
1	$25,000	50,000	48,780
2	25,000	47,500	47,561
3	25,000	45,125	46,341
4	25,000	42,869	45,122
5	25,000	40,725	43,902
6	25,000	38,685	42,683
7	25,000	36,755	41,463
8	25,000	34,917	40,244
9	25,000	33,171	39,024
10	25,000	31,513	37,805

The depreciation methods were further accelerated by the carving up of the building. While the average person might see a building with a useful life of forty years, a tax lawyer or accountant sees components that have shorter lives. Their actuarial table might look like this:

Component	Life
Land	Forever
Building Envelope	45 years
Landscaping & Land Improvements	20 years
Fixed Equipment	15 years
Portable Equipment	10 years
Painting	5 years

The rapid depreciation provisions were enacted in 1954. Its application to real estate was an accident. As Stanley Surrey, a former Assistant Secretary of the Treasury for Tax Policy and Professor of Tax Law at Harvard Law School, explained it:

> The present accelerated methods were initially adopted in 1954 with industrial machinery and equipment primarily in mind. Acceleration of depreciation in buildings in 1954 appears to have been a happenstance, coming along as an inadvertent appendage to the liberalization directed at machinery and equipment. No conscious decision was made to adopt the present system as a useful device to stimulate building or to provide us with more or better housing, let alone lower-income housing. The present tax system for building just happened.[14]

The tax system that was created broke the bond between cash flow and profits. The real estate industry moved from double-entry bookkeeping to double sets of books. With two sources of income, the investor could not only keep all the real estate cookies away from the taxman but also retrieve some of the cookies the taxman thought were his. The name of the game was "tax avoidance," a game played by and for professionals and not to be confused with the amateur and illegal game of "tax evasion."

A simple example shows the double benefit available to the investor. In the example below, he not only gets the cash flow of $37,000 tax free but he can also use the $10,300 "loss" as an offset against other earned income. If he is in a 70 percent tax bracket, the savings are over $7,000.

Table 5. Sample Statement of Taxable Income (Loss) and Cash Flow [15]

	Tax Pro Forma	Cash Pro Forma
Income	$230,000	$230,000
Less: Operating Expenses	86,300	86,300
Interest on Mortgage	89,500	89,500
Amortization of Mortgage	—	11,200
Replacement Reserve	—	5,700
Depreciation	64,500	—
Taxable Income (Loss)	(10,300)	
Cash Flow		37,300

Depreciation is not the only denizen in the Tax Wonderland. Leveraging of expensive buildings with meager amounts of cash is encouraged by the tax fact that the deduction is not limited to the investment. An investor who has put in $100,000 in a building with a mortgage of $900,000 can claim the depreciation deduction for the full million dollars—even when the investor has assumed no personal liability for the payment of the mortgage. For an investor in the 70 percent bracket, this can result in a near riskless situation. If the building breaks even and has no cash flow, accelerated depreciation during the first three years provides over $140,000 in tax losses, producing a tax savings of over $99,000. He has all his money out and he owns a building.

There are tax benefits available even while a building is under construction. Part of the development cost is the interest and taxes being paid during construction, which are part of the capital cost (like architect's fees), included in the building loan. For tax purposes, however, rather than requiring these costs to be depreciated over the life of the building, these items were treated as "expenses" in the years they were paid. Since there was little or no income during the period, these expenses could be used to shelter other income.

But, eventually accelerated depreciation crosses over the line and becomes less than straight-line depreciation. A high-bracket investor is then faced with the prospect of a negative cash flow, the tax exceeding the cash distributions. The investor may even have to pay a substantial capital gains tax, since the use of accelerated depreciation has eroded the cost base of the property.

The capital gains provision was rarely more than 25 percent of the gain. If the sale price were large enough, the investor would still have a profit. There was also the possibility of a gift to a charity in which the taxable gain might be offset by the deduction of the property at its fair market value. Death and taxes are inevitable. However, in the tax-shelter world, death could be in lieu of taxes: "Death of the partner, surely the most favorable of all the solutions, gives his interest a stepped up market basis thereby substantially eliminating the otherwise substantial capital gains tax on the subsequent sale." [16]

A more dangerous creature was the "recapture provision," which transformed the difference between accelerated depreciation and straight-line depreciation from capital gains into ordinary income if the investor's stay in the project was too brief—originally ten years and subsequently extended (in 1969) to close to seventeen years. Nevertheless, this was an avoidable hindrance except when the project was so poorly located or managed that the mortgage was foreclosed in the initial years.

To gain these tax goodies a new form of organization was needed. The answer was the limited partnership, which retained the advantages of the corporation without surrendering tax advantages. The owner of the property is a limited partnership that engages in no other business. None of the parties is liable for the mortgage. The lender depends on the real estate (and mortgage insurance). The developer, assuming some responsibility to those who invested their money in his venture, stays on as the general partner (and remains personally liable). However, the outside investors, as limited partners, trade their voice in management for the absence of liability for the debts of the partnership beyond their initial contribution to the capital of the partnership. They pay their money and wait for the losses. Unlike the corporation, the partnership form allows the losses to be passed through to the partners, who can deduct these losses against income from other sources for income-tax purposes.

The operation was quite profitable for the developer. As a result of the tax laws, the property that was worth a million dollars was now worth from $1.1 to $1.2 million, in a typical case. The 10 percent equity had doubled or tripled in value. It was worth the sleepless nights putting the project together. And there was no shortage of limited partners, even when cash flow was strictly limited. In the case of subsidized privately owned projects whose occupancy was limited to lower-income households as soon as the "limited dividend corporations" (the language in the original act) were transformed into "limited *distribution entities*," the supply of investors was almost unlimited. Doctors, dentists, actors, ballplayers, and lawyers lined up to get a chance at "doing well by doing good."

CONDOMINIUMS

The lure of tax breaks was so strong for high-income households that it permitted landlords to turn disgruntled tenants into proud homeowners of their apartments—the condominium conversion boom.

The condominium was imported from Puerto Rico (which had inherited the system from the Latin countries, where it dates back at least to Roman times). The most striking feature of the condominium besides its exotic name is that the occupant of an apartment can have ownership (dominion) over the space therein and share the common space with his neighbors (con.) It was the sharing that made it unique, since the ownership of air space has a hoary history under common law. The Temple legal societies at the Inns of Court at the end of the sixteenth century allowed members to build new chambers over existing buildings. For their efforts, they were given legal ownership of the space. In a case of breaking-and-entering, a court in 1638 concluded, "[A] chamber of any Inns of Court or Chancery broken open may be *domus mansionalis* of him who is the owner of said chamber. . . ." By the twentieth century, the ownership of air space made possible the creation of Park Avenue over the tracks of the New York Central Railroad.

The condominium is a cousin of the cooperative. The difference is that a cooperative corporation owns all of the apartments and all the common space. The shareholders of the cooperative have a right to lease a specific unit as long as they remain shareholders.

Since the late 1800s there has been a modest cooperative housing movement in the United States—in fact, cooperative housing was an American export to the Scandinavian countries. As a result of a middle-income subsidy program ("Mitchell-Lama") it was fairly widespread in New York State—producing 50,000 units a year in the early 1960s. But, it was merely a blip on the national scene. Federal mortgage insurance had been extended to cooperatives in 1950, but in its first decade, fewer than 36,000 units had been insured.

The Housing Act of 1961 extended mortgage insurance to condominiums, and state legislatures legalized the format in short order. In the initial years, the main promoters of the idea were title insurance companies which saw the opportunity to sell title insurance to the multiple owners of a multifamily building rather than to a single landlord of a rental building.

The condominium took off in the early 1970s and accounted in 1973 and 1974 for one-fourth of all new for-sale housing starts. To many young married couples and empty-nesters (couples between 45–64 whose children were no longer living at home) the condominium offered the ease of maintenance of apartment living and the preferred ownership qualities of single-family homes—the chance for equity appreciation and tax shelter. This latter point came to the attention of converters, who saw a ready market. For landlords, caught between rising fuel prices and lagging rent increases, the converter offered a profitable sale and the advantage of capital gain treatment (whereas if the landlord sells the individual units, he would be considered a "dealer," and the profits would be treated as ordinary income). For high-income tenants they could provide a wonderful deal—to buy their unit for nearly twice its value as a rental unit at a discount of perhaps 30 percent (to buy good will and avoid the loss of income during the conversion process).

The process and arithmetic is as follows. The landlord owns a unit that is worth about $75,000. He has a $60,000 twenty-year mortgage at 8 percent requiring a monthly payment of $418. He has operating expenses of $250 and charges a rent of $700. Deciding that his $32 a month is insufficient, he has the alternative of raising rent by $25 and hearing his tenants grumble or selling to a converter who offers $85,000.

The converter offers the tenants the opportunity to buy their apartments (which he will paint in any color they desire) for the measly sum of $140,000 each. The rich and wise tenant sits down with his calculator and tax accountant and concludes this is not a bad deal—if he puts down $20,000 in cash and obtains a $120,000 mortgage at 8 percent for twenty years, his monthly debt service is $963 and with the $250 in operating expenses his monthly bill is $1,113. However, since most of his mortgage payment is interest and he is in a 70 percent tax bracket his net monthly payment is only $693. He will also be able to deduct his share of the property tax. Then there is the probability of equity appreciation. On top of this the kindly converter offers a $20,000 discount if he signs by next Wednesday. And so the boom started on the windy shores of Lake Michigan at the end of the 1970s and rocketed to the golden sands of Florida.

In truth there were three faces to the condominium boom. The category described above covered the quality units in the quality locations—the "gold coasts" of large urban areas, often nonreplicable areas such as the lake shore in Chicago or Central Park in New York City. The buildings were usually high rise. However, in new cities such as Phoenix it was in low-rise townhouses in the resort shopping area surrounding downtown Scottsdale.

The market for these units tended to be empty-nesters and retirees (not to be confused with the "elderly"). Many of the households were beyond the stage either financially or chronologically where ownership of a home is an important status symbol. They were drawn to the location and to the low maintenance. For those who were prior occupants, the inconvenience of moving, the fact that the move will not improve the location, and the likelihood that a substantial investment has been made in decorating the apartment are all features that made them amenable to conversion.

This was the rich mother lode of the gold mine. There was the most profit to be made, while the investment needed to upgrade the common elements of the building and refurbish the individual apartments was negligible. The bite taken from the upper crust did little harm to the housing market or for that matter even to those being bitten.

The second category, young urban professionals, also seeks a quality location. However, they lack the wealth to afford the most affluent areas. They are willing to take a chance on transitional neighborhoods with cultural or architectural values and vintage buildings. In Chicago, the areas are near but not on the lake. These are often areas that are being revitalized where conversion "tended to lag behind rather than serve as a catalyst for other reinvestment."[17]

In these areas, conversions are risky. The work needed to bring the building up to modern standards is often substantial, involving new wiring and plumbing, window replacement, roof work, and boiler replacement. There is a sharp difference in expectations between a tenant and an owner in this market. The former is willing to live with the old kitchen; the latter demands the newest appliances. Conversions in these buildings usually involve a complete turnover in tenancy, rising cash-flow problems to a converter borrowing money at a close to 20 percent interest rate in the early 1980s (the prime rate plus 4 or 5), and political problems. A number of the tenants are elderly who resided in the neighborhood through its unfashionable period and who are likely because of the length of their residency to be paying substantially below-market rents.

The impetus to convert these buildings came from owners desiring to sell as a result of marginal profits and the need for substantial new investment. The competition among converters causes a sharp rise in the prices of existing buildings—profits breed competition, obscene profits breed cutthroat competition. The higher initial cost, the problems in rehabbing older structures, the greater sensitivity of less affluent buyers to price, the greater difficulty in

qualifying buyers for loans, and the higher interest rates transformed the condo market almost overnight into a high-risk market.
If the first-tier market was characterized by easy profits, the second tier saw some hard losses.

The third category of conversion is primarily a suburban phenomenon. It involves garden apartments whose low profile kept
them hidden from the media. The prime market for these are young
households who cannot afford a detached single-family home. The
condominium is a means of amassing a sufficient down payment to
afford a larger home in the future. In this sense it can be viewed as
the "basic home" families were exhorted to buy in the mid-
seventies as an answer to the inflation of housing prices. Instead
of heeding the advice of housing economists and giving up the
"dream," these families joined the inflationary trend—hoping to
get on the rising equity bandwagon and ride it to the single-family
detached home.

The conversion of garden-type apartments involves a good deal
of displacement. However, rapid turnover is the norm. The price
increase to occupants has been far more moderate than in other
categories of condominium conversions. The young nonprofes-
sional household is likely to be much more price-sensitive. The
multitude of garden apartments in the suburbs, the lesser variance
of ambiance among the various developments, and the shorter time
frame for residence makes the prospective occupant less prone to
panic buying than yuppie sophisticates.

One of the major fears was that the conversion process would
seriously weaken and in the long run lead to the disappearance of
private rental housing in the United States and raise prices in the
rental market. But in spite of its geographic spread, the depth of
its penetration in any market has been thin. The rule seems to be
that conversions occur only in exceptional rental areas. In Chicago, which was the most active condominium area in the country,
the market was concentrated adjacent to the lake shore. In the vast
sea of rental housing that stretches to the west, the main danger is
abandonment rather than conversion. During the 1970–1980 decade, less than 1.4 percent of the nation's rental units were converted to condominiums.

The condominium's strongest selling point was the general opinion that real estate prices could only go up and that the ownership provided substantial tax breaks. The eighties proved for the umpteenth time that the law of gravity is a principle of prices as well as physics, and that the average renter household had neither the money with which to speculate in the housing game nor the income level at which the tax break would be beneficial (the increase in the amount of the standard deduction dropped the proportion of *all* taxpayers itemizing their deductions to approximatley 25 percent by the end of the decade). In 1983, the income of the average tenant was $12,400, approximately one-half of the income of the average homeowner ($24,400). Seventy percent of renters had incomes below $20,000.[18]

The condominium has a place in the scheme of things. However, it is a very small place and it certainly will not now or in the future sweep the nation clean of rental housing.

Chapter 4

FROM RURAL TO SUBURB WITH A STOP IN BETWEEN

The suburban boom and the expression of consumer preferences were not greeted with glee by most urbanists or those concerned with the state of culture. The decline of the relative importance of the city has been viewed as a peculiar American aberration, and a temporary one at that. There is still much talk about the comeback of the city, of the "Brownstone revival," and of the gentrification of neighborhoods. Yet, the plain truth is that the heyday of the city is long past. The new neighborhoods and the revived harbor and marketplaces that are springing up in downtowns are merely quaint tourist attractions. The main streets of America are in the shopping malls, and the future is likely to bring us, in Irving Kristol's phrase, "an urban civilization without cities."

The headlong rush that created the great cities was a result of economic necessity rather than the lure of libraries and museums. Indeed, the wave of urbanization that hit Victorian England in the nineteenth century was viewed as a threat to civilization. As Eric Lampard has written:

> During the third quarter of the century, when the census classified more than half the population as urban, the loss of rural character could no longer imply a passage to urbanity. . . . A growing segment of the town population was thought to be dangerously uncivilized

and the prospect of "rural depopulation" as a social disaster. "Civilized man," de Tocqueville said, "is turned back almost to a savage." The social philosopher J. S. Mackenzie was uttering a commonplace by the 1890's in stigmatizing the growth of large cities as "perhaps the greatest of all problems of modern civilization."[1]

The people ignored the experts and voted with their feet. What to the cosmopolite was a quaint and merrie Old England was anything but a happy place for the rural folk. In like manner, the dazzling city of the twentieth century was usually quite dirty and a lousy place to raise kids—open fire hydrants are picturesque but few would choose them over public, let alone private, swimming pools.

THE ABSENCE OF CITIES

Cain, of biblical fame, is credited with building the first city (which should provide a clue about the Book's attitude toward the city). Jericho was a 5,000-year-old city by the time Joshua arrived.[2] Twenty walls had been downed by invaders before Joshua's trumpets and the people's shouts downed the walls over 3,000 years ago. Nevertheless, until the recent past city dwelling was the exception rather than the rule. People worked and lived in rural areas.

Rome housed over a million people prior to the visits of the Goths and the Huns. By the ninth century its population had declined to approximately 17,000 inhabitants.[3] In the rest of the West, for over a millennium, urban places were basically towns. The word "urbanize" was scarcely used in English before the end of the nineteenth century. People commonly spoke of the growth of towns. The verb "to urbanize" had the connotation to render urbane, courteous, refined in manner, elegant, suave.[4]

In the early 1700s, cities remained medieval right down to their fortified walls. They were generally a place for the ruling class and the urbane, who lived there to escape the isolation of the countryside and partake in the pleasures of the town. The rest of the

townspeople knew their place or lack thereof. As Oscar Handlin
described the social structure:

> The basic elements were corporate and communal organizations.
> Whether they were formally embodied in guilds . . . or more loosely
> structured as in America, each was an entity that comprehended a
> complex of functions. Knit together by kinship, localized in a defin-
> able residential district, and possessed of both an occupational and
> a religious nexus, each group enjoyed a status defined by custom
> and law. . . . Outside the accepted order were a multitude of inferior
> men. The Jews lived in ghettoes or outside the walls. . . . In addi-
> tion, a floating population of seamen and strangers and of servants
> and journeymen without masters were grudgingly permitted to lodge
> in town.[5]

THE RISE OF THE CITY

The development of New York State[6] telescopes the European
experience and provides a microcosm of the urbanization of the
United States. New York State's initial development was attributable to the assets of its geography—its valleys and its harbor. The
valleys created natural trade routes, running eastward, connecting
New England with western Pennsylvania and the Great Lakes, and
north-south, connecting Canada to the Atlantic Ocean. One valley
runs along Lake Ontario and then eastward across the center of
the state to the Hudson River, which runs north by way of Lake
Champlain to the St. Lawrence River and Canada. At the southern
terminus of the Hudson lies a great natural harbor that is unaf-
fected by the tides and turmoil of the ocean or the vicissitudes of
weather.

The early development of the state was based on the fur trade,
centering on the junction of the two routes at Albany. In 1720, furs
represented 15 percent of Manhattan's exports. The trapper was
followed by the lumberman, who was even more dependent upon
the natural water routes. The establishment of lumber camps and
sawmills determined the sites of the earliest settlements. By 1810

there were nearly five hundred of these settlements. Lumbering overtook fur trading in value and retained first place until the middle of the nineteenth century.

The farmers followed the lumbermen and generally stayed within the river valleys. Once the laborers in town saw the land that was available, there was no keeping them in town. The farms were basically self-sufficient. Homespun clothes and handmade shoes and the use of wooden pegs instead of nails made these farmers, if not rich, at least economically independent. As the British Governor complained to the Lord of Trades in 1767:

> The custom of making coarse clothes in private families prevails throughout the entire province and in almost every house a sufficient quantity is manufactured for the use of every family, without the least design of sending it to market. . . . The price of labor is so great in this part of the world . . . where every one can have land to work upon leads them so naturally to agriculture that it prevails over every other occupation.[7]

The industries that served these farmers were small and village-based. In 1825 there were 2,264 mills grinding grain into flour or meal, 1,584 carding machines, and 1,222 local fulling machines preparing wool for home looms or finished products. The factories depended on waterwheels for power, and the medium of exchange was barter. Both the farm and the factory lived in their own small world.

In 1790, the Hudson Valley and Long Island contained all but 17,000 of the state's 343,000 inhabitants. The Hudson Valley was a more important population center than New York City or Long Island. The upper Hudson contained 139,000 persons, the lower valley 118,000, and the city and island only 69,000.

Although the population increased more than sevenfold between 1790 and 1840, from 350,000 to 2.4 million, it was more evenly distributed at the end of the period than at the beginning; 80 percent lived on farms, 5–10 percent lived in villages of less than 2,500, and a few percent in larger towns, with the remainder living in and about New York City.

Although farm acreage and farm population continued to grow after 1840 (peaking in 1880), the most significant movement was to the cities. The movement was, literally and figuratively, powered by steam. The building of the railroads (and the Erie Canal) made it possible to market the agricultural products of the more fertile West and, even more important, opened up markets for the manufactured goods of the city. It turned cities into factories for the entire country. The state changed from a group of self-sufficient units into a specialized part of a highly complicated national economic mechanism. Before 1850, the Erie Canal was primarily an intrastate carrier. After 1850, it became a national waterway to and from the West.

Before steam, the factories had to find energy. Now the fuel came to the factories, which were located where the transportation facilities were the best, along the railroads or the docks. Steam increased the scale of production, forcing industry to search farther for both raw materials and untapped markets.

New York was both the gateway and the terminus of America. It was the best American port—closer to Europe by sea and better connected to the West. Between 1820 and 1869, its population increased tenfold. It changed from a city of 120,000 (containing 16 percent of the state's population) to a metropolis of 1.2 million (containing 38 percent of the state's population).

The next stage was one of abandonment, specialization, and concentration. Improved farmland was being abandoned at the rate of 100,000 acres a year between 1880 and 1920. By 1920, there were fewer people living on farms than in 1810. Unable to compete with the western farms in grain and beef production, the remaining farmers of the state specialized in dairy and fruit products.

The demise of the general-purpose farm was accompanied by the demise of local industries that catered to their needs. The sawmills, woolen factories (the sheep population of the state declined from 5 million in 1840 to half a million in 1920), gristmills, tanneries, and their accompanying water mills were left idle.

The drift from the rural areas was accompanied by the growth and concentration of the state's population in its largest cities—Buffalo, Rochester, Syracuse, Albany, Utica, Schenectady, Yonkers, Troy, Niagara Falls, and last and foremost, New York City. In 1925, New York City (Manhattan during this period having merged with the suburban counties of Brooklyn, the Bronx, Queens, and Staten Island) had a population of 6 million, accounting for more than half the population of the state.

New York City in its heyday was a city of dreams. It was also a nightmare. In an essay entitled "Dinosaur City" Clarence Stein described the situation in 1925:

> Look at the great city in its entirety: the turbid mass of traffic blocking the streets . . . , the slow moving crowd clambering into street cars, elevateds, subways, their arms pinioned to their sides, pushed and packed like cattle in ill smelling cars. . . . Look at the dingy slums of the East Side, Long Island City, the stockyard neighborhoods. . . . What part does art, literature, culture, financial opportunity play in the lives of millions of men and women who go through the daily routine of life in our great urban districts? The city of dreams is as far away from them as it is from the denizens of Winesburg, Ohio.
>
> To the few the great city gives all: to the millions it gives annually less and less.[8]

Although the dominance of the great industrial cities was to continue for another two decades (New York City emerged from World War II as the leading manufacturing city in the country), the end was in sight. Electricity had passed steam in importance, and cars and trucks were rolling off the assembly line and onto the roadways. By 1925, New York State was the home for 2 million cars, and half of the families in the United States owned their own cars.[9]

The city as a form of urban settlement came of age and became obsolete in less than a century. It can be viewed as a transitional stage between rural and suburban. The housing choices made by urban dwellers in the century between 1850 and 1950 were dictated by technological limitations, the shortage of accessible land, and economic necessities. The coastal towns that were to grow into major cities—Boston, New York, Philadelphia, Baltimore, New Orleans, San Francisco—were located at the mouth of a river emptying into a well-protected harbor. Likewise, the confluence of waters was decisive for the location of such inland centers as St. Louis, Cincinnati, Pittsburgh, Cleveland, and Chicago.[10]

The focal points of these cities were waterfronts and their employment centers—the location of warehouses, factories, counting houses, and government offices. By necessity, in the pre-trolley-car age, the homes of those who could not afford carriages were close to these centers.

The railroads initially reinforced this tight pattern of settlement. But new technology eventually broke the tie between foul and noisome steel mills and stockyards and center-city neighborhoods, freeing the middle class from the foul downtown slums. In Boston, the street-car route became the avenue of escape.

> [T]he new transportation allowed the wide diffusion of the residential area. Most of the extension of the metropolis that took place with the establishment of street railways benefitted middle-income families. Though they still had to seek their livelihood in the central city, their homes spread over an unprecedented area of suburban land. During the last fifty years of the nineteenth century Greater Boston tripled its population but the houses of the new suburbs generally had two or often three times the land of their predecessors.[11]

More than a century ago, in 1872, there was fear in New York City among the farsighted that its middle class would soon disappear.

> Every man of moderate income saw . . . that he could house his family more decently in any one of the suburban towns of New Jersey . . . even if twenty miles away. . . . Therefore, an exodus began to these towns, which has continued for several years, to the detriment of the city that is hardly yet realized . . . its middle class in large part self-exiled and its laboring population being brutalized in the tenements . . .[12]

H. G. Wells in 1902 foresaw the next stage:

> Many of our rail begotten giant cities are destined for such a process of dissection and diffusion as to amount almost to obliteration within

the further space of years. These cities will present a new and entirely different phase of human distribution. The social history of the middle and later third of the nineteenth century . . . has been the history of a giganticrush of population into a magic radius of—for most people—four miles, to suffer there physical and moral disaster . . . But new forces bring with them the distinct promise of a centrifugal application that may be equal to the complete reduction of all present congestion.[13]

THE OBSOLESCENCE OF THE CITY

Wells saw the instrument of dispersal as the passion for nature and the craving for the "little private *imperium*." The instruments were actually more mechanical. The city that grew as a result of the technological innovations of the nineteenth century was to be brought to its knees by improvements in the twentieth century. The long-distance transmission of electricity broke the tie between the energy provider and the location of the manufacturing plant. And the coming of the internal combustion engine meant that the factory could be supplied with materials and workers even if it wasn't in the city.

By the forties, it became clear that the in-town plant was both old and obsolete. Manufacturing and warehousing could be more efficient in the suburbs. Where speed was directly related to the profitability of the enterprise, the old loft that had to rely on freight elevators for material handling and trucks inching through congested streets for shipping could not compete with a suburban site that relied on conveyer belts and fork lifts and had acres of parking and access to highways. For manufacturing plants that did not have a decade in which to find a site for expansion and for firms in which low-cost distribution was crucial, the city was the wrong place—even for items that had to be sold there. Breweries, bakeries, newspaper plants, and wholesale food markets moved to outlying sites. The American experience was no different from the European experience. In New York, the artists replaced the wholesale markets in SoHo, and in Paris, the Pompidou art museum replaced Les Halles.

Technology eventually even repealed the geographic assets of the city. The need for space to accommodate modern unloading facilities and for quick access by trucks to and from the piers eroded the advantage that Manhattan had over other ports. The coming of the transatlantic flying machine doomed passenger-ship travel. Even the diesel liners were no match for Pan American's clippers. The focus of long-distance travel moved to the once idle wilds of Queens. For the piers on the Hudson, a long boat ride is a round trip to Bear Mountain. The piers on the East River became landing strips for helicopters. Los Angeles with a largely man-made harbor is now the leading port in the United States in terms of value of goods.

Much of the cities' residential stock was also functionally obsolete. The plumbing couldn't handle the washing machines and the wiring couldn't handle air-conditioners and televisions. Kiddie transportation was difficult, with the lack of parking for carriages and bicycles. And in many buildings the only things that moved around freely were the rats and roaches.

The lure of the suburbs was not limited to the tenement dwellers. It extended to the second-generation middle class (the children of Willy Loman's neighbors)—who had moved out of the slums to tree-shaded suburbs. It was the desire for the new and the cost of rejuvenating the old that led people to trade neighborhoods with old trees for developments with saplings. "To steam the ancient paper off the crumbling plaster a third-of-a-century old, to patch, size, and repaint walls cost more than the pristine decorations of the newly built home." [14] The handcrafted piecemeal rehabilitation of old city homes could not compete with the power-crafted assembly-line methods used to construct the new housing in the suburbs.

People were also moving to a less fragile environment. The high level of density and the complexity of the infrastructure of the city often puts the steering wheel of life into the hands of strangers. As B. Bruce-Briggs has written:

> . . . America has the best mass transportation system in the world. . . .
>
> The . . . system consists of three principal elements. First, part

of the land area of the nation is dedicated as rights-of-way for the system. . . .

The second element . . . is the hundred million individually operated vehicles. Almost all of these vehicles have four wheels and synthetic rubber tires, and are powered by mechanisms that mix air and liquid hydrocarbons carried in the vehicle to produce kinetic energy. . . .

The third element . . . is . . . [the] owner-operators. Approximately 125 million Americans have varying degrees of competence in negotiating . . . vehicles on thoroughfares. . . .

Of course this is the auto-highway system . . . with benefits so manifold that they are often forgotten . . . Every rider sits in a nicely padded seat . . . with plenty of leg room. The internal temperature can be controlled. . . . The vehicle is almost always provided with entertainment—a radio with dozens of stations to choose from or a tape . . . deck with thousands of cassettes available.

Perhaps more important, the rider has privacy. He is not bothered by the presence of other people. [H]e can even talk to himself. For many . . . the time spent driving is the only extended opportunity for contemplation. Moreover the driver has the opportunity for pleasure in the act of operating the vehicle. It is a form of athletics, requiring coordination of man and machine and offering the satisfaction of doing things well. . . .

There are other advantages . . . [A] driver is working for himself . . . and does not go on strike. . . . The highway is such a simple mechanism that a total failure is very rare and can be made good by alternative routes. . . .

Another advantage . . . is personal security. A moving vehicle is usually protected from attack. . . . An auto is a private place locked from the inside. Pedestrians and riders on public transit are mugged; drivers hardly ever.[15]

The outward spread of both jobs and people was mutually reinforcing. Many jobs in the urban labor force automatically followed the population drift. The butcher, the baker, the candlestick maker, the supermarket and department store will follow their customers. The pediatrician, insurance salesmen, and lawyers will follow their clients. Throw in jobs in the construction industry, local utilities, local government, schools, and you have half the urban labor force.

THE FEDERAL ROLE

Just as King Canute and his knights could not stem the tide, so neither could the federal government nor all of the elites stem the flow to the suburbs. The turn of the century was the best of times for the latter group. As Raymond Vernon, the co-author of a massive study of the New York region, told a Harvard University audience in 1961:

> [T]he well-to-do urban dweller has a number of satisfactory living choices. One possibility was to take a mansion on Fifth Avenue. . . . Here one could have the propinquity to the office and the theatre, easy use of city streets in the evening or on weekends, and only a minimum of exposure to the relatively localized and compact slums. Alternatively—or in addition—one could maintain a home in an exclusive suburb, barely thirty or forty minutes from an office in the central city by way of the new suburban train.[16]

By 1960, their mansions had been swallowed up by apartment houses, the central business district was being ringed by slums, their exclusive suburbs were being encroached on by the development of suburbs for the masses, and both the service and the scenery on their train ride into the city had deteriorated. Nevertheless, they were economically and culturally tied to the city. To return to Raymond Vernon:

> [T]he compulsion of executives to remain . . . has been very strong. The delicate problems of face to face communications . . . prevented them from moving very far away from the tight-woven mass of which they are a part. Typically, therefore the executive suites of the large manufacturing enterprises, the advertising agencies, the banks and the law firms remained firmly anchored to the central business district.
>
> [I]n every major city, there is a group of substantial business interests which are immobilized in the city. . . . [D]epartment stores with heavy investments sunk in central city locations are eyeing with concern the need to make new investments in the growing suburban areas. . . . [N]ewspapers fear an irretrievable loss of circulation and

advertising from the drift . . . to outside locations. One can safely predict, therefore, how the articulate and influential elite is likely to react. . . .

   [T]he attachment derives from sentiment, tradition, and avocation. . . . Few urban areas can support more than one Harvard Club, one Council on Foreign Relations. . . . No list of sponsors for the leading orchestra or leading art museum . . . fails to include a generous sampling of the leading families.[17]

Things were getting worse for the rich and famous, and terrible for those with rich tastes but moderate incomes (those who had to take the subway to the symphony), but Vernon continues:

To most Americans, the personal experience of urban living seems not one of urban retrogression but of continuous improvement. By moving out of the slag heap of a worked-out city, they have improved their surroundings sufficient for a generation. . . . Let the central city weep, let the sociologists fume, except for such intractable problems as death, war, and taxes, things are getting slightly better all the time.[18]

URBAN RENEWAL

There was very little the federal government could do (or had political support to do) for the central city. After four years of debate Congress, in Title I of the Housing Act of 1949, authorized federal financial aid to local public agencies for slum clearance and urban development. The immediate purpose of the legislation was to replace slums and blighted areas and to provide for their redevelopment by private enterprise in accordance with a publicly adopted plan.

   Title I was a partnership between the local and federal government. The former would acquire the land either by purchase or eminent domain for the purpose of clearing slums or blighted areas. The latter would pay two-thirds of the difference between the cost of acquiring the site (which included clearing the buildings, relocating the residents, and preparing the site) and the site's fair market value for the use specified in the development plan.

The program received a great deal of criticism for destroying older neighborhoods and for displacing the poor. Even an almost establishment critic such as Roger Starr can write:

> [T]he city took some of its Federal slum clearance subsidy and used them to create Lincoln Center, a wholly tax-exempt cultural center into which they moved the Metropolitan Opera House, along with the New York Philharmonic orchestra, the Juilliard School of Music and a new noncommercial theatre. Out went thousands of poor families. In a city with New York's long history of concern for housing problems, Lincoln Center was a dramatic example of the new importance attached to culture by the elite and consequently by municipal government itself." [19]

It's a bum rap.* The city was in an impossible box. It needed money to cover the increasing costs of servicing an area that was getting poorer by the day. In order to do this, it had to retain its economic base and its upper-income residents. Urban-renewal money had to be used to "level the field" in its competition with suburban areas. The central business district had to be redesigned to offer multilevel and underground parking and pedestrian malls if it was to retain the stores and specialty shops that would attract suburbanites, at least for their nonroutine shopping. If it was to be healthy enough to support the poor, it had to be attractive enough to entice the rich with luxury hotels and apartments. And, it certainly had to do everything within its powers to enhance its most valuable assets—major medical centers, museums, concert halls, and theatres that serve the entire metropolitan area.

But urban renewal was too little too late. Raymond Vernon told some Cambridge professors who were much impressed by urban renewal:

> Well, I suggest that urban renewal . . . is an insignificant program. Try the helicopter approach. . . . In New York I spent the equiva-

---

* Starr's subsequent observation may be more to the point, "When in the late 60's, the museum [Metropolitan] sought to use more of the site [Central Park] many New Yorkers objected. . . . Trees, they pointed out, were God's cultural artifacts, raising a point that had not been made about people in the Lincoln Center site." [20]

lent of 10 full days just sitting over the city and the eye-impression
you come away with is that you can't find the urban renewal projects
in the city mass. And when you do find them, with a few isolated
exceptions, they're terribly close to the central business district.
Why this location? [B]ecause the whole leadership of the urban
renewal program see the problem the same way that a New Yorker
sees the United States. Nine-tenths of it is east of the Mississippi,
and from this point of view nine-tenths of the problem lies fairly
close to the central business district.[21]

THE INTERSTATE HIGHWAY SYSTEM

The usual charge against the federal government is not that it aided
the cities through urban renewal, but rather it did much to destroy
them by its massive support of federal highways. While no one
would deny that the highways made some major tears in the urban
fabric, the federal government was a latecomer to the wake.[22] The
building of the New York parkway system began in 1907 with the
Bronx River Parkway, which helped open up Scarsdale. By 1939
—when all roads led to the New York World's Fair and the Highways and Horizons exhibit at General Motor's Futurama, with its
grand vision of new superhighways (based on the design of Hitler's
autobahns) that would be available to the motorist in 1960—Robert
Moses had just about completed the New York parkway system.
The Pennsylvania Turnpike, a superhighway (distinguished from a
parkway in that it permitted trucks) was ready to open without a
speed limit, and construction was beginning on Los Angeles's first
freeway—the Pasadena Freeway.

At least as far back as Woodrow Wilson, American presidents
supported the building of highways (Wilson even contributed five
dollars toward the attempt to build a transcontinental highway). It
was not until the days of Franklin Roosevelt, however, that substantial federal sums were appropriated for the building of roads.
Taking a cue from Huey Long, who had turned a road program
into a relief program that employed 22,000 men (more men than
even New York), Roosevelt used federal funds for the construction of the Blue Ridge Parkway and Skyline Drive.

Roosevelt envisioned a national land authority with the right of eminent domain to acquire the land to build superhighways. It didn't get very far. The Reconstruction Finance Corporation had bought $35 million of Pennsylvania Turnpike Authority bonds, and the Public Works Administration provided a $29 million job-creation grant, but the notion of direct federal funding of highways still smacked of socialism in the thirties, and Congress rejected every road plan. In 1940, the Bureau of Public Roads (BPR) issued a plan for a 29,300-mile superhighway system that would cost $6 billion. In 1944, Congress, with an eye to providing employment and giving the GIs one more thing to fight for, approved a plan (but not dollars) for interregional highways based on the BPR Scheme.

After World War II, Pennsylvania soon found imitators in New York, Ohio, West Virginia, and New Jersey. However, federal money had to wait for the second Eisenhower administration. Ike had learned in World War I that the railroads were inadequate to supply the troops in Europe. Unfortunately, the highways were also far from adequate. After the war, at the direction of General Pershing, he participated in a motorized convoy of seventy-nine military vehicles that traveled from Washington, D.C., to San Francisco over the Lincoln Highway (partially paid for by Wilson's contribution and only partially paved). The trip took a mere fifty-six days.

World War II and the sight of the autobahn also convinced Ike of the importance of a national road system. The legislation, although it carried the name "National Defense Interstate Highway System Act," had plenty of peace-loving supporters in the major industrial sectors, such as automobiles, steel, rubber, plastics, and construction. Better highways meant greater convenience and ultimately greater happiness.

Ironically, the legislation received the strong support of the representatives of the cities—the U.S. Conference of Mayors. They saw the new superhighways as major urban renewers. They saw the problem as one of congestion, and if they could unclog the arteries, people would want to return to the cities.

As a matter of fact, by 1960 the majority of the urban residents were already in the suburbs. The federally funded interstate sys-

tem was but a small part of the country's system of roads. It
represented only 20 percent of road spending in the twenty years
after the legislation's enactment and only 2 percent of the mile-
age.[23]

The growth of the urban area has gone not only beyond city
limits but also beyond "metropolitan" limits. The standard definition of the metropolis (the U.S. Census's Standard Metropolitan
Statistical Area or SMSA) takes a pre-Copernican view of the
urban universe—that the city is at the center. The metropolitan
area is viewed as stopping at the boundary of the city's commuter
shed. However as Hans Blumenfeld has noted in an article "Metropolis Extended," "That model no longer corresponds to reality
. . . as more and more places of employment locate at the periphery. Consequently, many workers who live beyond commuting
distance to the center do commute to those suburban jobs. . . ."[24]
Greater Los Angeles is at present the nation's largest manufacturing location (in terms of the value of goods produced). Nevertheless, the city constitutes only 11 percent of the metropolitan area
(4,100-square-mile area). Its 4½-square-mile downtown area accounts for only 4 percent of the jobs in the area.[25]

Moving from Los Angeles, which can be considered as a series
of "constellations" forming an urban "galaxy" to the more traditional East, we find the city is one among equals of the metropolitan constellations. And, increasingly, it is even losing its status as
the "first among equals." Washington, D.C., the tenth-largest
metropolitan area in 1985, is an example of this phenomenon. In
1970, with a population of 756,668, it had 100,000 more people than
its closest suburban rival. By 1985, its population had declined to
626,000 and it ranked fourth in the area, trailing the suburban counties of Fairfax, Prince George's, and Montgomery.[26]

The primary pattern is for people not only to live in the suburbs
but to work there as well. This is true even in New York City,
whose skyline is dominated by skyscrapers and whose underground is crisscrossed with thousands of miles of rails. In the second half of 1986, New York City reached its highest level of
employment in sixteen years—3.6 million people. Nevertheless,
there are still more jobs in the suburbs. Northern New Jersey had

Washington Metropolitan Area

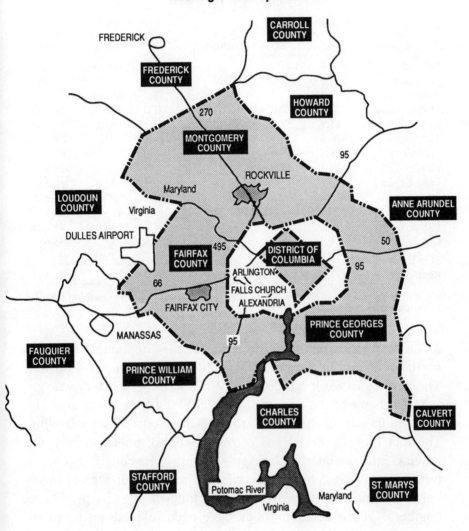

Population and Jobs Forecast

Numbers in Thousands

Jurisdiction	Population			Jobs		
	1985	*2010*	*% Change*	*1985*	*2010*	*% Change*
District	627.4	627.7	.05	686.1	886.0	29.14
Arlington	157.8	178.8	13.31	170.8	261.8	53.28
Alexandria	108.5	113.7	4.78	75.3	167.6	122.56
Montgomery	628.0	820.0	30.57	371.0	670.0	80.59
Rockville	45.1	52.5	16.42	44.3	86.6	95.51
Pr. George's	676.9	841.7	24.34	274.5	473.0	72.31
Fairfax	668.3	936.8	40.18	265.8	547.3	105.91
Fairfax City	20.3	21.0	3.45	20.5	25.0	21.95
Falls Church	9.5	11.0	15.79	9.2	12.0	30.15
Loudoun	65.8	210.8	220.51	23.3	97.4	317.87
Pr. William	176.1	342.8	94.64	40.9	119.6	192.65
Indep. Cities	26.2	35.0	33.59	11.0	16.0	45.45
Charles	84.8	136.8	61.32	23.6	32.0	35.68
Frederick	127.7	182.9	43.23	45.7	55.0	20.40
Region Totals	3,377.3	4,459.0	32.03	2,017.7	3,362.7	66.66

SOURCE: Maryland Department of State Planning and Metropolitan Washington Council of Governments.

2.7 million jobs, and six surburban counties on Long Island and north of the city had another 1.7 million, for a total of 4.4 million. The journey to work is increasingly a suburb-to-suburb drive.

The rumors of the "return to the city" and the reversal of the outward flow is, alas, untrue—the popular media notwithstanding. The fact that all the friends of the makers of public opinion are moving into quaint townhouses or overpriced condominiums in trendy areas and thereby "gentrifying" and revitalizing old neighborhoods, may have improved the fortunes of the city but not its numbers. These neighborhoods have been revived not by immigrants from the suburbs but rather primarily by prior residents of the city or newcomers. These neighborhoods are doing a better job of stemming the flow of their people to the suburbs, but they are still losing population as the former resident families move to the suburbs in search of better schools, adequate play space, and greater safety.[27]

As *The New York Times* recently reported, the life of a juvenile and his keeper leaves much to be desired in a rejuvenating neighborhood:

> Life for Mary and her 3-year old son in their high-rise apartment was like living in a prison. "He was like a confined animal. . . . He broke every appliance we had; he tore the wallpaper from the walls of his room. He would run out into the hall and it would take me a half-hour to coax him back in. . . . "
>
> Mary and her husband eventually moved from the Upper West Side to a house in Westchester County, where their son, Adam, has easy access to the outdoors.[28]

THE MALL AS MAIN STREET

These gentrified neighborhoods are parochial enclaves compared to the cosmopolitan areas found in the suburbs around the enclosed shopping mall. The mall has become "the signature structure of the age" in the words of William Kowinski.[29] The separation of the auto from pedestrian shopping areas dates back to before World War I to Roland Park in Baltimore. The enclosed mall, however, is barely thirty years old. Victor Gruen, given the job of designing a mall for a location that experienced frigid, Minnesota-type winters and torrid summers, enclosed the entire area and provided climate control. The change resulted in an entirely new retail environment.

The mall has become America's downtown. Seventy-eight percent of all Americans—some 185 million—went to a large enclosed mall at least once a month in 1985. It is a place for teenagers to roam and a safe haven for the elderly. An architectural critic recently returned from a trip to the exotic world of the giant malls of the outer suburbs with the following report:

> To visit Potomac Mills is to experience the quintessential suburban phenomenon, urbanism turned inside out. People like me have driven for miles . . . and entered a hermetic streetscape whose appeal is undeniably urban, both in form and function.

Droves of people promenade. . . . Eateries seem to be concentrated in one location. . . . And . . . there are the movie theatres—ultimately 10 of them.

Potomac Mills' atmosphere . . . is festive and frenetic. Colorful merchandise and graphically arresting signs are displayed everywhere and vigorously compete for your attention.

Coming to malls is a compelling utilitarian social event, a recurring communal activity. . . . Where else can people of every social and economic strata come together and engage in orgies of either real or imagined consumption.[30]

And, we ain't seen anything yet. The future is again taking shape in a northerly clime. In West Edmonton, Canada, the mall has been taken to its penultimate state of development—the combination of mall and amusement park. The mall, the size of 108 football fields, has 11 major department stores, 110 eating places, 200 women's clothing stores, 50 shoe stores, over 800 stores in all. In addition to having the world's largest indoor amusement park, indoor waterpark, and outdoor parking lot, it has room for a Spanish galleon in its own lake, 4 submarines, 37 animal displays, a petting zoo with Siberian tiger cubs and miniature Arabian horses, reindeer and moose, a baby elephant and for good luck a fortune teller.[31]

All of this is coming to the United States. The developers—the Ghermazian brothers—have agreed to build the ultimate mall, not far from the first enclosed mall in Minneapolis–St. Paul, which will add offices and educational facilities to its shopping and amusement mall.

This growth of metropolitan areas has been, by and large, a result of myriad decisions by the private sector. Economic development attempts by the federal government to help depressed rural areas or to develop new towns in order to avoid some of the unfavorable conditions of city life have been a failure. Although intuitively appealing and achieving some success during the Depression (Greenbelt, Maryland, is now engulfed by the Washington suburbs) they ran against the tide of economic and geographic processes and failed. As Brian Berry testified in a hearing on urban growth:

[T]o have a reasonable chance of success, a new town must be part of the growing concentration and scale of society today. It must take advantage of the processes that are operating rather than running against them. There are new zones of growth that are emerging . . . [in] the confluence zones between metropolitan areas. Into these . . . zones we find the decentralizing of population, of industry, of activity, from the central cities converging . . . from more than one metropolitan center . . . This is the kind of location in which the necessary natural base for development of the new town exists. . . .[32]

One need only compare the growth of the privately sponsored new towns of Columbia, Maryland, and Reston, Virginia,* and the federally sponsored and now defunct Soul City, North Carolina, and Gananda, New York.

AN URBAN CIVILIZATION WITHOUT CITIES

What has developed on the American landscape is thus very new and very old. The core city has been enlarged into the core metropolis. Hans Blumenfeld has written about the four factors that have determined human settlement patterns—rural, urban, production techniques, and transportation and communication techniques.[33] The precursor of the first two factors—dominion over the earth and the need for human relationships—are to be found in the two creation stories in the Bible—the first[34] dealing with the former and the second dealing with the latter.[35] It is not an accident that Cain was the farmer and the first city builder. After the expulsion from the Garden of Eden, civilization required an agricultural base and a surplus for its development. Cain's dominion over Abel, the nomadic animal herder (the classic conflict between the farmer and the rancher) was a necessary condition for the growth of the city. Jericho needed walls only after the discovery that wheat could be

* Although both areas have grown quite rapidly, because of the high carrying costs of the developing infrastructure, the profits of the initial developers were only psychic.

cultivated. The early Mesopotamian* and Egyptian cities were both economically based on the exploitation of the earth.

Through most of history cities were limited in size by technology (unless the city, militarily or administratively, could expropriate the wealth of vast areas), and the labor force needed to exploit the natural resources of the earth represented 80 percent of the population. As the percentage dropped because of improved technology and the opening up of new farm areas, the urban place became the source of jobs and a livelihood. The new products now were dependent on man's exploitation of his mental resources. The movement to the city, resulting from the development of long-distance communication on the sea (steamships), on the land (railroads), and through the air (telegraph), made possible a previously unknown level of concentration. Further development of technology and communication, on the other hand, resulted in a previously unknown amount of urban deconcentration.

The two stages can be seen in the locus of activity of the characteristic sports at each stage. Baseball is played by the Boston Red Sox in the middle of the city—Fenway Park. Football is played by the New England Patriots in Foxboro, Massachusetts, on the periphery of the metropolitan areas of Boston and Providence. The movement of the metropolis is continually outward. As the urban planner put it:

> [T]heir orbits may extend so far as to leave no genuinely nonmetropolitan area and population in the northeastern United States. . . . [W]ithin the next century the entire ecumene will be transformed into a mosaic of contiguous metropolitan orbits. This is not a reversal of the trend to the metropolis. It is something much more significant, the end of the age-old distinction between urban and rural forms of human settlements.[37]

We may have new urban forms for old traditional values. As Herbert Gans two decades ago described the new arrivals to Levittown:

---

* Abram is commanded to leave the industrial area of Ur. According to tradition, his father had an idol factory. According to Blumenfeld, Ur even had a suburb.[36]

Perhaps the most significant fact about the origin of a new community is that it is not new at all, but only a new physical site on which people develop conventional institutions and traditional programs. . . .

Indeed the basic source of change comes from goals of homeownership, a free-standing house, outdoor living, and being with people of similar age and class, which has long been the aspiration of American working and middle class culture. . . .[38]

The motto of Chicago, *urbs en horto,* a city in a garden, summarizes the old aspiration and the new direction in which we are heading. As Daniel Elazar has stated:

The urban majority in America generally conceptualizes the United States as a network of cities with open spaces . . . in between. Perhaps the country should be reconceptualized in the reverse so that Americans will perceive the great wilderness areas as the country's heartland, with areas of progressively greater development radiating from them. The wild regions could then be connected with one another through preserved openings along rivers, roads and trails that cut through the developed areas to link with more developed parts and green edges surrounding and penetrating each urban area. These American cities would become cities in a garden in the fullest sense.[39]

Chapter 5

FROM THE FARM TO THE FUTURE

The migration to the suburbs was preceded by and followed by other migrations. During the past century the spur to much of the movement has been the revolution in the methods of production down on the farm. The spur in more recent years has been the revolutionary shift of jobs from the production of goods to the providing of services. Any attempt to see where Americans are likely to move in future years must take into account the subtle shift that has occurred in the relationship between the manufacturing and service sectors of the economy, and the fact that America, like the city, has lost its position as king of the hill and now is only one of the nobles in a global economy.

TECHNOLOGY COMES TO THE FARM

Malthus, gazing (or gasping) at America's rate of growth around the turn of the nineteenth century—by a third every ten years*— found additional evidence for his prediction that the population would inevitably outrun the food supply. Well, nobody's perfect. He would have been astonished had his gaze been clear enough to

* Each census between 1790 and 1860 found the population of the country one-third larger. Had this pace continued, the present U.S. population would be over a billion.

see the supply of food outrunning demand at the tail end of the twentieth century, and the workers of the earth—the farmers, foresters, and miners—shrinking to less than 3 percent of the labor force.[1]

In 1790, only 5 percent of the population lived in communities larger than 2,500. (When the Brooklyn Dodgers migrated to the West Coast in 1958, their home, Ebbets Field, was replaced by an apartment complex that housed about that number of people.) Although the trend toward urbanization began in 1840, it was not until 1920 that more than 50 percent of the population lived in communities that exceeded 2,500 in number. By 1980, 75 percent of the population were urban residents (though not, as the preceding chapter made clear, city dwellers, strictly speaking.) And rather than being clustered under the blue sky, they lived near the "blue water"—about 85 percent of the population lived within fifty miles of the Atlantic or Pacific oceans, the Gulf of Mexico, or the Great Lakes.

The farm population in 1920 stood at 32 million people (59 percent of the rural population). As a result of the mechanization of the fields, by 1970 there were fewer than 10 million people still living on farms. The postwar productivity gains in farming outstripped every other segment of the economy. Between 1947 and 1970, output per man-hour in agriculture was increasing twice as fast as other segments, at a rate of 5.9 percent, while the manufacturing rate stood at less than 3 percent, and the rest of the nonagricultural economy was at 2.4 percent per year.[2]

These improvements can be seen in the following table:

Table 6. Increases in Efficiency of Producing Three Basic Crops During Various Time Periods[3]

	Corn	Wheat	Cotton
	(100 bushels)		*(bale)*
Man-hours per Unit			
1800	344	373	601
1935–1939	108	67	209
1965–1969	7	11	30
Average Annual Percentage Increase in Productivity			
1800–1937	0.8	1.3	0.8
1937–1967	9.1	6.0	6.4

With machines moving through the fields, the farmers and field
hands were forced to move on. The effect of turning farming from
a family enterprise into an agrobusiness can be seen in the migration figures.

Table 7. Net Migration From Farms (1925–1969)[4]

Period	Net Migration (in thousands)	Period	Net Migration (in thousands)
1925–29	2,965	1950–54	5,576
1930–34	288	1955–59	4,552
1935–39	3,542	1960–64	3,968
1940–44	8,018	1965–69	2,972
1945–49	3,385		

THE BLACK MIGRATION

The black population has been on the move since they were allowed to move (and even before that). Between 1870 and 1970
there was a constant flow of rural blacks to the cities. The initial
moves were modest. For in spite of repressive conditions of the
post-Reconstruction South and the rapid industrialization of the
North, the close ties to familiar faces and places and the limited
job prospects (except as strikebreakers) as a result of the great
East European immigration at the end of the nineteenth century
greatly diminished the attractiveness of the North to blacks. Many
of the blacks who left the plantations moved into southern cities.[5]

The massive moves of blacks to the northern metropolitan centers on the Great Lakes and the eastern seaboard coincided with
the decline of European immigration as a result of World War I,
the enactment of discriminatory immigration quotas, and the arrival of the boll weevil in the South.

Blacks were actively recruited by northern employers, like the
packinghouses, which sent agents to the South to recruit black
laborers. The efforts of northern employers were aided and abetted
by the large Negro newspapers. The *Defender* acted as a cheer-
leader for "The Flight out of Egypt" to the promised land of Chi-

cago, which offered better jobs and somewhat greater rights. The cold weather of the North held risks, but as the paper informed its readers, "To die from the bite of frost is far more glorious than to die at the hands of the mob."[6]

The Great Migration north from 1910 to 1970 made the European migrations pale by comparison. The approximately 6.5 million blacks who left the South outnumbered the Irish, Italian, or Jews who moved from the Old Country to the New World. The peak Jewish flow between 1900 and World War I was at a rate of a million a decade, while the Italian migration was 2 million between 1901 and 1910 (some of the traffic, however, was two-way).[7] It is of note that approximately three-fourths of the population growth in New York, Pennsylvania, Ohio, Illinois, Michigan, and the District of Columbia between 1910 and 1940 was attributable to the arrival of black migrants.[8]

The peak of the flow coincided with the great exodus of white families to the suburbs in the forties, fifties, and sixties. The arrival of 1.7 million families in the forties, 1.5 million in the fifties, and 1.4 million in the sixties changed the flavor of the city. Washington, D.C., for example, went from 65 percent white to 72 percent black between 1959 and 1975.

The blacks did not push the whites out. Rather, the outmigration of the whites made room for the blacks. Sixty-two percent of Washington's racial change was attributable to white outmigration. The remainder was one part black migration (17 percent) and one part the natural increase of the black population (21 percent). Of the white residents who moved to Levittown, New Jersey, outside of Philadelphia, 20 percent listed racial change as a reason, among many others, for moving from the city. However, only 4 percent indicated that it was the most important reason for the flight from the city.[9]

The 1970s saw a reversal of the century-old pattern as northern cities were losing jobs, the rise in expectations was faster than the delivery of concrete accomplishments, kids were rioting in the streets, and the political, racial, and economic climate of the New South was improving. From 1970 to 1975, the flow between North and South was in balance. Between the second half of the decade and the first half of the eighties, over a quarter of a million have journeyed south, which remains the home of 53 percent of all blacks. The trip has been to the urban growth centers rather than the growing places—only one percent of the nation's blacks reside on farms.

THE INTERNAL MIGRATION

The tale of America's internal migrations can be capsulized by looking at the growth of California, which in 1970 was the most metropolitan state, where 93 percent of the population live in metropolitan areas. By the mid-1980s, a California-based magazine could boast "New York City may have the means to be the 51st state . . . but California has the clout to be a country! Welcome to The California Nation." [10]

California's post-Columbian history started in 1542 with the visit of Juan Cabrillo to the present San Diego. [11] For the next three centuries it was primarily a fringe colony, with a scattering of Spaniards, and later Mexicans, who held the land by virtue of the benevolence of the Indians. Gold wasn't discovered in California until 1848. When that played out, there were the gold of orange groves, the black gold of oil, the gold dust of Hollywood, the golden wings of the aerospace industry, the gold of the sun and ultimately even of silicon, all luring the wild, restless, and those seeking a better life.

When gold was discovered at Sutter's Mill, the best guess was that there were approximately 14,000 non-Indians in the state. By 1850, the year California became a state, the population had jumped to 170,000. The Gold Rush had brought a group of adventurers whose backgrounds were English, Irish, or Western European. The rush to build the railroads brought thousands of Chinese coolies. By 1869, California was linked to the rest of the nation, setting off a multinational influx. Between 1850 and 1900, about 900,000 people heeded Horace Greeley's dictum and added to the state's population.

The English, German, Irish, and French also came (these four nationalities and the Mexicans made up half of the foreign-born population of California in 1900). Italians also came to establish vineyards and orchards. They were followed by shepherds of German and Swiss descent who were attracted to the pasture regions beyond the valley.

The migration continued in good times as well as bad times. During the first three decades of the twentieth century, migration contributed an additional 3.2 million. During the 1930s growth slowed from the 66 percent pace of the twenties to a modestly impressive 22 percent. Much of the increase represented the Dust Bowl refugees—the first group to travel by car. In the first half of the decade the small farmers and sharecroppers from the Central and South Central states found refuge in the great valley of California centering around Stockton, Fresno, and Bakersfield. And as the hard times moved north during the second half of the decade, farmers from the northern midsection of the country arrived, and Los Angeles became known as "Iowa by the sea."

Naval war in the Pacific resulted in a sharp rise in the population. By 1950, the state's population had increased by more than 50 percent—80 percent of the growth was channeled into the metropolitan areas. The huge shipyards that sprang up in the Bay Area caused San Francisco to grow at a faster pace than Los Angeles for the only time since the 1860s. In the south of the state, San Diego, which became the major naval base on the West Coast, grew by over 90 percent.

The dominant source of the migrants in the previous decades—the Midwest—furnished only 28 percent of the new arrivals. The northeastern and the western regions provided the fodder for California's growth. This was the decade in which the Dodgers moved from Brooklyn to a ravine in Anaheim and the Giants moved from the Polo Grounds in Manhattan to San Francisco.

The postwar growth of California occurred primarily in metropolitan areas. In spite of its being the leading state in annual cash receipts from agriculture (with marijuana being at the top of the list of cash crops) and having a U.S. monopoly on kiwi fruit, almonds, dates, figs, dried prunes, pomegranates, olives, walnuts, and pistachios, the farm population of California comprises less than 2 percent of the state's population. California leads all other states in the proportion of its population living in urban areas. Ninety-five percent of its population live in urban areas, and Los Angeles has twice as many people as all of California in 1920.

As the country became "Californized," and as California became citified, its lure for Americans has been reduced. Between 1975 and 1980, there was a net in-migration from other areas of the United States of less than 100,000 (1.78 million people moved out, and 1.88 million people moved in). If the westward flow has slowed to a trickle, the northern and eastward flow continues. In 1982, 230,000 refugees, primarily Asians, settled in California. In addition, an average of over 500,000 illegal border-crossers a year are sent back to Mexico by the border patrol for another try.

California is not only metropolitan but also increasingly cosmopolitan. It is the leading place of residence for both the oldest and newest residents—American Indians (1.4 million), Chinese (81,000), Filipinos (77,000), Japanese (70,000), Samoans (42,000), Koreans (35,000), Vietnamese (26,000), and Guamians (30,000). Add 2 million blacks, 4.5 million Hispanics, and 14 million pinkish-colored people, and you have, if not a melting bowl, at the least a very colorful palette.

TO THE SUNNY CLIMES

At the national level, the census divides the country into four regions and nine divisions—the Northeast (New England and the Middle Atlantic states), the South (South Atlantic and East and West South Central states), the Midwest (East and West North Central states) and the West (Mountain and Pacific states). The South, which is bounded by the Atlantic on the east, New Mexico on the west, Mexico and the Gulf of Mexico on the south, and the Mason-Dixon Line on the north, is the largest region in the nation.

The South has been traditionally viewed as the poor, slow-moving, mint-julep-drinking, people-exporting region of the country. But it has been transformed. As in the rest of the country, the farmers have left the fields. In 1920 two-thirds of the South's labor force was employed in agriculture and mining. Today these sectors account for only 1 in 20 workers.[12]

The postwar rise of the South has been due to many factors. The sunny skies and the possibility of cool, air-conditioned retreats made the area a Mecca for people worshipping the sun or for those merely wishing to spend their sunset years in a fair climate, as well as a Disney World for vacationers. The benign attitude toward employers' rights and economic growth made it a safe haven for industries dependent on low wage rates and entrepreneurs. An unsafe world and a slew of congressmen in safe seats made the South a natural site for major military installations, which were followed by industrial complexes. With Latin America being an unsafe place for both dictators and democrats and with American tastes demanding something more exciting than nicotine, the American South became a haven for Spanish-speaking businessmen and Miami became the "capital" of South America. Add to this the overlay of interstate highways, the maturing of the air age, and the beginning of the space age, and we have a region that has had a lot going for it in the last few decades.

In the 1970s, the South gained 12.6 million people and in the eighties grew by 11.3 percent to reach a total of 83.8 million people in 1987—approximately one-third of the nation's population. It has also surpassed the West as an employment magnet. Between 1960 and 1985 it gained over 17 million jobs compared to 11 million in the West and 13 million in the rest of the country. Not surprisingly, in 1986 it overtook the Midwest for a brief period as far as average income in the region. The industrial recovery of the mid-eighties and the troubles of the oil industries have, however, enabled the Midwest to nose out the South for third place.

The West (whose Pacific division, which, thanks to the admission of Alaska and Hawaii, contains the most northerly and southerly states), has had the most impressive growth rate—increasing by 24 percent in the 1970s and between 1980 and 1987 by an additional 15 percent—reaching a total of close to 50 million and putting it on a par with the Northeast in terms of population. Although the Rocky Mountain states, helped by the energy boom, increased by three and a half times the national rate in the seventies, the big numbers are on the Coast (the eight mountain states contain less than half the population of California). Alaska has had the fastest growth rate in the 1980s and California, with a big boost from military spending in 1987, reached a population of 27.6 million (nearly 10 million more than the Empire State of New York).

The Midwest (which now contains about 60 million people) and the Northeast continued to grow slowly in the 1980s. They managed to account for only 2 million of the nation's 17 million increase in population. Since these regions have suffered a net migration loss over the last decades their increases were earned in an old-fashioned way—by the number of births exceeding the number of deaths.

Dropping to the metropolitan level, all of the fastest-growing areas in the 1980s were in the South and the West—Phoenix (22.4 percent), Dallas–Fort Worth (19.8 percent), Houston (17.8 percent), Tampa–St. Petersburg (15.8 percent), and Atlanta (15.6 percent). It was not a coincidence that when the owners of the St. Louis Cardinals football team looked for greener pastures, they found them in Phoenix. In contrast the biggest losers were Buffalo (−4.4%), Detroit (−3.6%), Pittsburgh (−3.5%), Cleveland (−2%), and Milwaukee (−1.3%).

The migratory habits of the American people have been generally seen as a move from the "Frostbelt" to the "Sunbelt"—at least until the oil bust put a dent in the economies of Texas and Louisiana (the latter in 1986 losing population for the first time in its history). While there was a germ of truth in the observation, it doesn't quite explain the growth of the cold and often nasty-weathered West, or the fact that New Hampshire grew three times as fast as Alabama, or the success of New England in not only weathering the 1980–1982 recession but also moving toward the nineties in a robust fashion.

The notion of Sunbelt growth relied heavily on the experience of Florida and Texas. The image of the flight from frost and cold stems from the trends of the aged from New York City and other aging northern cities. A substantial number of New Yorkers were moving to New York's southern suburb Miami. Of the 1.7 million New York emigrants between 1975 and 1980, more than 20 percent found their way to Florida. Bryant Robey, with the help of a friend, puts the losses and gains in a nonmeteorological framework:

> Demographer Peter Morrison . . . has joked, "Migration South and West is a long overdue correction for the mistake made by European immigrants when they failed to proceed directly to Houston." Had the United States 300 years ago been colonized from the West Coast, by Asians instead of Europeans, the Northeast might today be the nation's "Sunbelt" and the West the country's aging industrial heartland.
>
> As history has it, the Northeast and the North-Central regions have been below the nation's growth rate for the past 50 years. It has now taken half a century of above-average growth for the South and West to obtain a majority of the population.[13]

MANUFACTURING AND SERVICE— FROM PARASITIC TO SYMBIOTIC

Although moves in population were triggered in the past by movements in manufacturing, that era has ended. The American economy since World War II has been transformed into one in which the product is likely to be a service. For every two workers employed in producing goods, three are now in the service sector, and the gap is widening.

Manufacturing has ceased to be the engine of job generation. The manufacturing sector is producing the same share (approximately a quarter) of a larger gross product than it did thirty years ago, with but a negligible increase in employment. Industry will be with us for a long time; it is only the labor force that is being deindustrialized. The new jobs are coming from the service sector.

This change in the economy is a result of "how we produce" and "what we produce." As Peter Drucker has noted on the first point:

> In the 1920s one out of every three Americans in the labor force was a blue-collar worker in manufacturing. In the 1950s the figure was

one in four. It now is down to one in every six—and is dropping. While the trend has been running for a very long time, it has lately accelerated to the point where . . . no increase in manufacturing production is likely to reverse the the long term decline in the number of blue-collar jobs in manufacturing or in their proportion on the labor force.

. . . Today the United States employs around 18 million in blue-collar jobs in manufacturing industries. By 2010, the number is likely to be no more than 12 million. In some major industries the drop will even be sharper. It is quite unrealistic, for instance, to expect that the U.S. automobile industry will employ more than one-third of its present blue-collar work force 25 years hence, even though production might be 50 percent higher.[14]

The second factor represents a twofold change—a change of the product mix in the economy to items that are knowledge-intensive rather than labor-intensive, and the shift of the relationship between the service and manufacturing sectors from a parasitic to a symbiotic one—in which services have become an integral part of the production process. The manufacturing costs of a microchip are 12 percent labor and 70 percent knowledge—research, development, and testing. In the manufacture of drugs the labor costs represent 15 percent, while knowledge represents 50 percent. In contrast, even in a fully robotized car plant, labor would account for 20 to 25 percent of the costs.[15]

If the first change is in fields in which entirely new products are being produced, in the second we are dealing with a redesign of a standard product. Since the end of the war, the U.S. market has increased by 80 million, and disposable income has tripled. This growth in size and sophistication has forced industry to move from the homogeneous product to the product tailored to a specific market. There are large profits to be made in even small segments of this vastly larger pie. The faceless consumer, like the sneaker, is gone. We are in a post-sneaker age:

Reebok's rise has been meteoric. Eight years ago its entire line consisted of three different running shoes. . . . Today there are 250 . . . models to choose from in 12 different categories: running, aerobics, sports conditioning, walking, volleyball, cycling, golf, children's athletics, infant Weeboks, Metaphors casual and dress shoes, and, of course tennis . . .[16]

The result has been a proliferation of auxiliary services that have moved to the center stage of business—not to help produce but to decide what the product should be and how to package and promote the new product or the old product with a new image. In the more recent past we had lawyers, accountants, marketers, and advertisers. Today we have geodemographers and food technologists.

> From the office of Claritas, Robin Page can see the Potomac River clearly. From the computer printout on his desk, he gets . . . [a] vivid picture of Thomaston, Georgia.
>
> The printout shows that Thomaston is what Claritas calls Norma-Rae-ville. That label suggests that people there read the National Enquirer, watch roller-derby, buy plenty of curling irons, hair-setting lotions and deviled hams, love Hardee's—and are just like the people of Childersburg, Alabama. . . . Claritas . . . specializes in geodemography. . . . [I]t has reduced the vast, diverse, confusing U.S. market to its most basic common denominator, the neighborhood. . . . From such information as income, education, and occupations, it has pigeonholed the country's 240,000 neighborhoods and can often, with amazing accuracy, picture life in each, from the type of aspirin . . . to the magazine on the coffee table. . . .
>
> [U]ntil lately, its methods were considered experimental. . . . In recent years . . . Claritas is considered mainstream . . . and the information age has spurred dozens of competitors, who collect, analyze, package, and distribute minutiae about consumers.[17]

The food technologist creates new foods such as cheese analogues (fake mozzarella), restructured muscle products (fake steak), processed pollock (kosher lobster, crab, and shrimp).

The service sector has burgeoned in other areas as well. The nonprofit and government (primarily in the areas of education and health) segments now account for more than a quarter of the jobs in the country. There have also been significant increases in the numbers of people involved in the distribution and retail segments of the economy. Most of the latter growth has occurred in the Sunbelt. Since services cannot be shipped or stockpiled, new jobs are created to accommodate the shifts in population. Services in which there is a strong need for accessibility to the greatest number of people will usually be drawn to metropolitan centers (in contrast to manufacturing, which will locate to take advantage of material, labor, energy, and transportation costs).

Ironically, the one service sector that has declined has been the consumer services. America has beauty parlors, caterers, travel agents, hotel workers, and car renters galore but "what ain't we got, we ain't got maids." This has put, and will put, limits on what money can buy and affect the top and the bottom of society. As wealthy Washington hostesses complained:

. . . [T]here is the problem of catered food. "Most people don't have anyone in the house who can do it anymore. People had cooks in those days. And if it was catered you recognized it, you'd feel superior." [18]

Herman Kahn, talking about the future, noted:

I would guess that Americans 50 to 100 years from now will have . . . a median family income of $100,000 a year. What do you do with a $100,000 a year? You can have two or three houses, four cars, two helicopters and three submarines, but you will have to diaper the baby yourself. There are no maids. You wash your own dishes. [19]

AMERICAN JOBS AND ABODES IN A WORLD OF PLENTY

Where are the jobs and homes going to be as we move to this new level of deprivation? Professors Thierry Noyelle and Thomas Stanbach [20] have analyzed the economic structure of 140 metropolitan areas and come up with four major categories—production centers, consumer centers, specialized service centers, and diversified service areas.

In a world suffering from overcapacity in basic products such as steel and plastics, and in finished products from automobiles to microchips,[21] production centers have bleak futures as employment centers. Steel towns, such as Youngstown, Ohio, saddled with aging mills and the competition of cheaper foreign steel made in technologically advanced facilities, will have to create walls around their areas if they are to keep their residents from migrating.

Areas that have picked up industries, such as the textile center of Greenville, South Carolina, with the promise of cheap labor to keep the looms warping and woofing, are discovering that the area that lives by the cheap hand will die by the cheap hand. There are cheaper hands in such once faraway places as Sri Lanka and Thailand. The store fronts in the garment district in New York, in which every sign has the word "import," bear witness to this change. In the 1980s, U.S. imports of apparel rose from $10 billion to $25 billion, in spite of import quotas, faster distribution of garments, and promotional efforts such as Bob Hope hawking "made in the U.S.A." clothing. It is hard to compete when the hourly wages in Sri Lanka are 36 cents and in America $6.50. Major American manufacturers are throwing in the towel and see their future as provider of services to the retailer. In many cases they will stop making clothing and become middlemen between Third World producers and U.S. retailers. They will move into the knowledge business—translating American desires into Asian products.[22] And so will South Carolina. It is now "selling" its universities in order to attract employers. An advertisement by its State Development Board in the *Wall Street Journal* (April 24, 1987) read: "From the textile capital of America, designer genes . . . [a] state . . . reweaving the very fabric of American business."

If there is an excess of products, there is a glut of commodities. In areas that are dependent on agriculture (the farm belt), iron (Duluth), copper (Butte), oil (Louisiana and Texas), the busts will come far more often than the booms. There is a continuing migra-

tion from the farm. Every state in the farm belt experienced losses
to migration between 1981 and 1986, with Iowa losing population
in each year.[23] We are living in an age in which India is on the verge
of being a net exporter of food, cars are being made out of plastic,
and telephone wires are being replaced by laser beams.

The economic base of the second category, consumer centers,
is consumer-oriented. These areas are either bedroom communities of major diversified centers, such as Nassau and Suffolk Counties on Long Island; Anaheim, California; or resort and retirement
centers such as Orlando, West Palm Beach, Santa Barbara, Phoenix, Honolulu, and Las Vegas. These areas are safe bets for con-
tinual growth in population. Nevada and Arizona grew by 25
percent between 1980 and 1987 and Florida passed Illinois and
Pennsylvania to become the fourth most populous state.

The category of specialized service centers is divisible into three
different types of areas. The first group consists of areas in which
there is a strong concentration of production facilities as well as
corporate headquarters—Detroit in autos, Akron in tires, San Jose
in electronics, Rochester in scientific and office equipment. Their
success is geared to their ability to ward off foreign competition.
In contrast, the second group of cities, government and educational centers—like Washington, D.C., Austin, Texas, and Madison, Wisconsin, are nearly totally insulated from worries. Like
lawyers, they are busy in good times and in bad times. Even more
important, the educational centers are the economic base for the
future of the area. Harvard and M.I.T. were instrumental in trans-
forming the mill towns of Massachusetts into thriving centers. And
it is not a coincidence that in 1986, a shaky year for the economy
of Texas, the endowment of the University of Texas surpassed
that of Harvard. The third group of cities is based on education
and manufacturing—areas such as New Haven, which until the
departure of Winchester Arms was a gun-and-gown town. The
open question is whether with the gun gone the gown can fill the
gap.

The fourth and best-positioned metropolitan areas for economic
vitality in the future are the diversified service centers, which com-
bine the functions of distributing goods to their hinterlands and
supplying a high level of services.

At the bottom of the pyramid are subregional centers such as Omaha, Memphis, and Charlotte, which are key links in the wholesaling, trucking, and air-expressing of goods across the nation. Moving up the pyramid are such regional centers as Boston, Philadelphia, Atlanta, Houston, and Minneapolis. These areas have strong distribution networks with well-developed warehousing, storage, and shipping facilities and well-connected airports. In addition, they offer a high level of professional services and serve as the corporate headquarters of large food, retail, transportation, and utility firms.

At the top of the pyramid are the four largest cities—New York, Los Angeles, Chicago, and San Francisco. They provide firms with a large pool of accounting, legal, advertising, and commercial and investment banking resources, and the special expertise to engage in international commerce and plug into the global network of financial transactions. They serve as home for one-third of the nation's 1,150 largest firms, and about one-half of these firms have regional headquarters in each of these cities.

New York, in spite of losing 400,000 manufacturing jobs in the 1970s, is by far the first among the foremost. As of the late seventies, two-thirds of its labor force were employed in servicing the top layer of corporate America, Europe, and Asia, in nonprofit institutions or in the public sector. New York was where the gilt and the glitz was and (in spite of the drop in value of the gilt on Wall Street) still is. It has 30 percent of the nation's commercial bank deposits, almost all of the very large Japanese and American investment banks, and on Broadway and Madison Avenue the Great White Way and the great ad way.

This "nation in a nutshell" look at the economic strength and weaknesses of various areas of the country has value as an indicator of future settlement patterns in America and as an explanation of why cities that were once havens for the unskilled and the illiterate cannot serve that function anymore. The major cities are overcoming the problems associated with their loss of their industrial base. Unfortunately, these new cities have very few places for many of the black migrants whose timing was exquisitely poor. Their train came in as the boxcars of manufacturing were leaving. On it were the jobs that put a premium on sweat—the jobs on the docks of New York, the steel mills of Chicago. The first rungs of the ladder for many of the migrants were removed for those who came without a strong drive to succeed or entrepreneurial skills.

This move North turned out to be a move from dependency to dependency. As Nicolas Lemann put it:

> The one group of black migrants who in 1970, at the end of the great migration, had an above-average rate of welfare dependency consisted of those who had been in the North for less than five years and who were in female headed households. . . .
>
> The similarity between sharecropping and welfare are eerie; the dependency on "the man"; more money for having more children; no homeownership; an informal attitude towards marriage and child-bearing. . . . [E]verybody I met at the Robert Taylor Homes who was a migrant from the South had been in a sharecropper family right up to the move to Chicago.[24]

Chapter 6

RACE AND HOUSING

In 1979, in a HUD Report entitled *How Well Are We Housed . . . Blacks,* HUD replied to its own title:

> The answer to the question is—very badly.
> The housing of blacks is more than twice as often physically flawed as is the housing of the total population. . . .
> More heavily urbanized than the rest of the total population, blacks are often clustered in the central cities, where the housing stock is aging. Almost everywhere their neighborhood and housing choice remain more restricted than whites. . . .
> The picture is grim indeed.[1]

The traditional measurements of physical adequacy concerned themselves with the availability of plumbing facilities and the absence of crowding. The HUD report went beyond these standards. Housing was considered inadequate if it had one or more of the following flaws:

1. Plumbing—Unit lacks or shares complete plumbing.

2. Kitchen—Unit lacks or shares a complete kitchen (installed sink with piped water, a range, and a mechanical refrigerator).

3. Sewage—The absence of a public sewer, septic tank, cesspool, or chemical toilet.

4. Heating—No means of heating, or heated by unvented room heaters burning gas or kerosene or heated by fireplace, stove, or portable room heater.

5. Maintenance—It suffers any two of these defects: leaking roof; open cracks on interior walls; holes in the interior floors or broken plaster (over one square foot).

6. Public hall—It suffers from two of these defects: lacks light fixtures; loose, broken, or missing steps; loose or missing stair railing.

7. Privacy—Access of sole toilet through bedroom.

8. Electrical—Exposed wiring, fuse blew three times in the last 90 days or unit lacks a working outlet in every room.

The improvements made since World War II have been so great as to make the traditional criteria obsolete in measuring quality differences between the housing of blacks and whites. In 1980, blacks were housed quite well by the traditional standards. Nationwide, 95 percent were living in units that had a full complement of private plumbing facilities. In metropolitan areas, these numbers rose to 97 percent for renters and 98 percent for owners. And black residents in 52 percent of all homes and 47 percent of all apartments in metropolitan areas have at least two rooms per person, while only 6 percent of all owner-occupiers and less than 10 percent of all apartment dwellers have to make do with less than one room per person.[2] So by Western European standards, American blacks are quite well housed. Eight percent of the housing units in France lack indoor plumbing and 17 percent are overcrowded.[3]

Most black housing fares quite well even under intense scrutiny. Sixty percent of the deficient units of black housing have only one flaw, and close to four out of five black families live in flawless units. Yet, approximately 10 percent of America's housing is deficient and some of it is awful, and blacks are twice as likely as whites to live in housing at the bottom end of the scale.

The disparity between the quality of black housing and the housing of the total population is significant and the reason is simple—

blacks as a group have less housing and less good housing because they have less income. The median income of white families is 80 percent greater than the median income of black families. The proportion of blacks able to afford adequate, uncrowded housing is 10 to 15 percentage points below the general population. The percentage of black families living below the poverty line is three times greater than the percentage of white families. The percentage of black families headed by women is more than three times greater than the percentage of white families headed by women, and of these mothers, blacks are twice as likely to be in poverty.

A HISTORY OF DISCRIMINATION

What makes the situation of blacks special is the long history of racial segregation and the great deal of difficulty the country has had in overcoming it. It was not until well into the second half of the twentieth century that the country made a serious effort. Before then, governments at all levels often aided and abetted segregation, compounding large measures of racial discrimination with a combination of economics, cultural affinity, bad timing, and economic and demographic accidents (the arrival of large numbers of blacks to northern cities as the whites and industry were moving out).

The southern cities felt the first surge of the black migration off the farm and responded with a show of the "police powers" of the state. The attempt of a black professional couple—a lawyer and a teacher—to move into a white neighborhood in Baltimore in 1910 was deemed such a threat to the general health, safety, and welfare that the city fathers enacted a zoning ordinance that divided the city racially block by block. This legal defense of homogeneity was adopted in cities ranging from Norfolk, Virginia, to Oklahoma City. But in 1917, the Supreme Court, at the urging of the National Association for the Advancement of Colored People (NAACP), struck down these measures in *Buchanan* v. *Worley*.[4]

The North chose the private route: racially and often religiously restrictive covenants between property owners that barred the selling or renting of homes to "inferior races" or to "races that

had higher mortality rates than the Caucasian Race.'' These covenants had a much longer run. Ninety percent of the subdivision
plans filed in Milwaukee after 1910 contained restrictive covenants
against blacks. Such covenants blanketed the nation—reaching,
Chief Justice Rehnquist discovered, to the remote northern
reaches of Vermont—as the courts did not rush to interfere with
private property rights. It was not until 1948 that the Supreme
Court, in *Shelley* v. *Kramer,* held these covenants unenforceable.

The law was buttressed by business practice and the prudence
of financial institutions. Brokers who were gentlemen did not sell
to blacks except in certain areas. And since all bankers are gentlemen, even if a broker had poor manners the black family could not
get the money.

In 1943, a publication of the National Association of Real Estate
Brokers, entitled *Fundamentals of Real Estate Practice,* summarized the sense of outrage at a colored person who didn't know his
place:

> The prospective buyer might be a bootlegger who could cause con-
> siderable annoyance to his neighbors, a madam who had a number
> of call girls on her string, a gangster who wants a screen for his
> activities by living in a better neighborhood, a colored man of means
> who was giving his children a college education and thought they
> were entitled to live among whites. . . . No matter what the motive
> or character of the would-be purchaser, if the deal would instigate a
> form of blight, then certainly the well-meaning broker must work
> against its consummation.

If gentlemen couldn't work the matter out, the mob was always
lurking in the wings. Blacks could not shake the shadow of vio-
lence when they moved from the country to the city. The early
decades were characterized by rioting whenever the moving van
made a wrong turn and brought a black family to a white neighborhood. With the creation of the black ghetto, there also came the
pogrom. Then, as now, terrorism was a common occurrence. The
situation in Chicago is described by historian Allen Hirsch:

> Between . . . 1917 and . . . 1921, 58 homes were bombed—an av-
> erage of one bombing every 20 days for 4 years—by those trying to

restrict black areas of residence. Invariably, homes owned by blacks in fringe or "white" areas were targeted, as were the homes and offices of the real estate agents (white and black) who handled such properties. And under the cover of the riot itself, white gangs roamed the edges of the black belt committing, according to the State commission that investigated the riot, "premeditated depredations" against black individuals and property found outside of the popularly conceived boundaries of the ghetto. In but a single case, nine black families in the 5,000 block of Shields Avenue had their homes vandalized and torched by such mobs; blacks were driven out of the area, and it was 28 years before anyone sold or rented a home on that block to blacks again.[5]

In the period after 1940, the black ghettoes vastly expanded into the gray areas of the cities that the whites were leaving. In the mid-forties, when the housing shortage was at its peak, the expansion was met with violent resistance (Chicago had 357 racial incidents over housing between 1945 and 1950). But, the fact that the whites soon had elsewhere to move made the adjustment more tolerable and peaceful for all concerned. The new black areas now dwarf their earlier counterparts. In 1930, the largest black enclaves were in New York and Chicago, each containing 328,000 and 234,000 blacks respectively. By 1980, New York City had 1.8 million blacks (approximately twice the number of Mississippi, the state with the highest percentage of blacks) and Chicago 1.2 million blacks. Los Angeles, Washington, Houston, and Baltimore now have more blacks than New York had in 1930. New Orleans, Memphis, Atlanta, Dallas, and Cleveland now have more blacks than Chicago had at the start of the thirties.

Where has the federal government been while all this was occurring? Certainly not on the side of the angels. In the 1930s, when both the Federal Housing Administration and the public housing programs were toddlers struggling to get on their feet, they needed all the community support they could muster. They were not going to pioneer in the thicket of race relations. They were going to follow sound business principles in order to protect the solvency of their programs. The FHA wanted its housing to be in harmonious and stable neighborhoods. The insurance manuals suggested the use of zoning ordinances and physical barriers to protect racial stability, and racially restrictive covenants were a precondition of mortgage insurance. The FHA *Insurance Manual* used in the thirties and forties "read like a chapter of the Nuremberg Laws," according to Charles Abrams.[6]

The FHA was so wedded to its sound real estate concepts that it did its best to ignore the Supreme Court ruling that restrictive covenants were unenforceable. It took nearly two years and considerable prodding from the White House for the agency to announce that, beginning in February of 1950, it would not insure properties covered by restrictive developments. This should not be viewed as a ban on segregated developments. It merely shifted the decision from documents neatly filed away in the office of the recorder of deeds to the hurly-burly of the marketplace. The not surprising result was that only 2 percent of the new FHA-insured houses were open to blacks between 1946 and 1959.[7]

Public housing, to say the least, was also not an agent of integration. Although the program provided comparable housing for white and black families, in many areas it also reinforced segregated housing patterns. An article examining the workings of the program in Cleveland concluded:

> Yet, while housing projects rejuvenated certain slum sections, their distribution encouraged residential segregation. Before the advent of the New Deal, more than 90 percent of Cleveland's 72,469 Negroes were concentrated in twenty-nine contiguous census tracts, comprising a compact ghetto on the city's east side. . . . By constructing three projects . . . in the very heart of the ghetto, designating them as "Negro projects," and then failing to ensure Negroes free access to "white projects". . . . the federal government used its considerable influence toward preserving the local pattern of segregated housing.
>
> Moreover, several of the "white projects" actually had the effect of intensifying residential segregation. [O]ne was erected just inside the northwest border of the ghetto, [the other] was constructed on the southeast boundary of the Negro district. . . . In both locations Negroes had constituted 50 percent of the residents. However, when these projects were rented only nine Negroes were admitted [in one project] and none were accepted in the [other].[8]

The public housing program in the late forties was caught up in one of those classic congressional battles in which it is impossible to distinguish the good guys from the bad guys. In 1949, an amendment to the Housing Act of 1949 was proposed following the language of the Democratic and Republican platforms in the 1948 presidential elections that would have mandated that public housing be operated on a nondiscriminatory basis. It was defeated in the Senate by a vote of 48 to 32.

The decisive votes against the proposal came from liberal Senators whose careers are associated with the fight for civil rights— Paul Douglas, Hubert Humphrey, Wayne Morse. Paradoxically, they voted that way because they saw public housing in the North as a vehicle for racial integration.

The amendment was proposed by Republican senators John Bricker and Harry Cain in order to break the bloc of northern and southern supporters of public housing. The southern senators were more than willing to accept public housing on a truly equal basis for poor colored and white folks as long as it was segregated. As Senator Russell Long of Louisiana stated:

[A] large number of excellent housing facilities have been constructed exclusively for Negroes . . . many of the Negroes are very well pleased . . . and . . . the Negroes do not have to mix with the white people.

If the northern congressmen insisted on integrated housing, the amendment would pass but the bill would fail. They would face the same dilemma that HUD would later confront. They would have to choose between segregated housing or no housing at all.

Little (or too much) guidance about the matter was provided by the civil rights groups. The NAACP backed the amendment, along with the two representatives from Harlem and East Harlem—Vito Marcantonio and Adam Clayton Powell (who proposed the amendment in the House of Representatives). Against the amendment stood the National Council of Negro Women and the Chicago *Defender*. The position of the liberals was summed up by Charles

Abrams in an article in the *New York Post:* "If the device [the Bricker-Cain amendment] succeeds it will become the forerunner of a whole series of efforts to use the civil-rights issue as an instrument for killing off civil reform. . . . The maneuver is made not to advance equality but to destroy public housing."

Senator Glen Taylor directly addressed the black leaders who supported the amendment:

> I have been approached by Negroes who said, "We would rather go down fighting here and now and not have any housing, than to compromise in this fashion." However, . . . I believe these Negroes who spoke to me have houses, probably adequate houses, to live in. . . . We cannot be too self righteous and be ready to let other people go without housing in order that we may stand on our principles.

In truth, the issue was not perceived so starkly by Senator Douglas and his colleagues. A vote against the amendment did not force all public housing into a segregated mold. The choice between segregated housing and no housing was a southern choice. In the North, public housing could offer both good and integrated housing. As Senator Douglas stated:

> If it related only to the city of Chicago, I should vote for the Bricker amendment, to be applied to local housing projects in the city of Chicago. . . . the increase in public housing in the North will decrease the total amount of segregation which now exists. . . . The trend in the North is away from segregation, and while we have all varieties of practices in the housing authorities, we are moving away from it there. . . .

Senator Douglas held out the prospect that increased racial contact would further racial harmony. Various studies by social scientists in the 1940s lent support to that hypothesis. Striking differences in white attitudes toward blacks were found between residents of integrated and segregated public housing projects. Randomly selected women in integrated projects held their neighbors in greater esteem and viewed interracial housing with considerably more favor than did their randomly selected "sisters" in segregated housing. Alas, the social science the senator relied on was over-simplified. Thomas Pettigrew, a social scientist who has been a leader in the struggle for school and housing integration, has written:

> Many well meaning Americans have expressed the opinion that if only blacks and whites could experience more contact with each other, the nation's racial difficulties would solve themselves. Unfortunately the case is not so simple. . . . More interracial contact can lead either to greater prejudice and rejection or greater respect, depending on the situation in which it occurs. . . . Prejudice is lessened when two groups 1) possess equal status, 2) seek common goals, 3) are cooperatively dependent on each other, and 4) interact with the positive support of authorities, laws, or custom.[9]

The positive aspects of the Pettigrew doctrine and the great progress that has been made over the approximately twenty years that have passed since the enactment of fair housing legislation (as part of the Civil Rights Act of 1968) can be seen in a 1979 HUD report, "Measuring Racial Discrimination in American Housing Markets." It reported on a nationwide study of discrimination against blacks in the sale or rental of housing. The information was collected in forty metropolitan areas across the country by three hundred whites and three hundred blacks, in matched pairs, who shopped for housing advertised in metropolitan newspapers. The dour conclusion was that "The study provides definitive evidence that blacks are discriminated against in the sale and rental of housing."

As everyone knows bad news sells reports. But the message is in the measures. Racial discrimination was deduced from responses to questions in four categories: housing availability, courtesy, service, and household information requested. Although whites fared better than blacks and the differences were statistically significant, in an overwhelming majority of the questions the answers indicated that there was no difference in treatment.

Table 8. No Difference in Treatment Between Blacks and Whites (%) [10]

1. Housing Availability	% of Cases
Housing Availability	68
Multiple listing directory offered	67
Other listings offered	76
Houses volunteered	22
Invitations to inspect houses	23
Houses inspected	36

2. Courtesy	
Shorter wait before interview	70
Offer of drinks, cigarettes, etc.	73
Asked to be seated	69
Informal chatting during wait	64
Agent introduced self	73
Agent asked name	86
Shook hands	65
Addressed by title	56

3. Service	
Longer interview	6
Offer of literature	72
Offer of business card	70
House style desired	62
Special house features desired	64
Special neighborhood features desired	83
Request for phone number	72
Agent recorded information	61
Offer of assistance in obtaining financing	62
Invitation to call again	86

4. Household Information Requested	
Income	66
Spouse's income	66
Debts or other obligations	84
Occupation	57
Employer's name	76
Length of employment	86
Information about spouse's employment	60
References	96

THE BLACK MIDDLE CLASS—
PREFERENCES AND INTEGRATION

The increase in recent years of the number of blacks who have money to put on the table has resulted in a change in behavior of most of the real estate industry. Whether this represents a true feeling of equality is essentially irrelevant. As Paul Freund, former Professor of Constitutional Law at Harvard Law School, noted, "Two of the great civilizing human traits, it seems to me, are hypocrisy and greed. Hypocrisy is a bridge thrown up between attitude and behavior. Greed is a response to the equalizing power of money."

Money talks. Of blacks with incomes over $25,000, 76 percent are homeowners. Although the black homeownership is substantially lower than the national rate—44 percent versus 66 percent or two-thirds the national rate—it has risen substantially since 1940, when it was slightly over half the U.S. rate, 24 percent versus 44 percent. The present relationship between the black and the national rates (66.7 percent) is approximately the same as the relationship between the income of the average black owner and that of all owners ($13,900 to $19,800).

Yet, the statistics are misleading. If, instead of looking at the ratio of black to national income, we look at the national homeownership rate at and about the black homeowner median income level ($13,900), we discover that the U.S. homeowner rate is substantially higher—57 percent for families with incomes between $10,000 and $15,000. If income were the only factor, there should be very many more black homeowners. Still, the conclusion that there is widespread discrimination does not necessarily follow.

Current income is not an accurate yardstick for measuring current discrimination. Many of the lower-income white homeowners are elderly and reflect the widespread discrimination of the past. Income is only one of the hurdles that must be cleared before homeownership is attained. The requirement for a down payment and the need to pay settlement costs requires access to wealth. The young family often goes back to the source. Unfortunately, black in-laws have on average only one-twelfth the wealth of white in-laws. Although statistics are not collected based on the marital state of children, the median assets (not including housing equity) are $8,082 for white households and $678 for black households. Other factors explain portions of the disparity: blacks are younger than whites (median age of 26.6 versus 32.4), and black families are larger (higher costs) and are more likely to be headed by females (lower income).[11]

The lag in homeownership explains the lag in black movement to the suburbs. But things are steadily improving. After a decline in the percent of the black population in the suburbs between 1950 and 1960, from 21.9 percent to 21.5 percent as whites in some new suburbs displaced old established black rural communities, the percentage of the black population jumped from 21.6 percent in 1970 to 28.7 percent in 1980.

It might be remembered that in the fifties and sixties, developers who sought to introduce blacks into white suburbs had to go to extraordinary means to achieve their goal. The integration of Levittown, New Jersey, required money as a lubricant. Levittown, Pennsylvania was all-white at the time and the community had experienced a racial "disturbance" when a black family bought a house from a white Levittowner.

As a result of an impending decision by the New Jersey State Division Against Discrimination that it was violating the state law, the Levitt organization "freely chose" to sell to blacks. Levitt faced the problem that, although a good many potential residents were willing to live in an integrated neighborhood, most were hesitant about having a Negro next door. To overcome this problem, the Levitt organization developed an ingenious system of choosing lots, giving first choice in each neighborhood and its subsection to Negroes. Like other purchasers, they naturally preferred a private lot, one backing up on woods, creeks, or open spaces rather than other houses. Consequently, Negroes automatically located themselves at the edge of neighborhoods, where they were getting the best value for their dollar, adjacent to fewer white purchasers and less visible to hostile whites. It also forced whites who chose lots after them to decide whether they wanted a more private lot next to a Negro family, or a less desirable one in all-white company. If a white purchaser chose a lot adjacent to one selected by a black family, he was told so and given the option of changing to another lot. Most white buyers preferred privacy with Negro neighbors to interior lots. The policy of the company to scatter Negroes around the community (if possible, only one per block, and two Negro families were never allowed to reside in adjoining houses) resulted in only a 20 percent rejection rate by white families, even after the "private" lots were gone and Negroes were placed in the middle of the community.[12]

Today, there is a debate among scholars whether black suburbanization is merely the spillover of blacks from the city or movements into largely white areas. As summarized by William Clark, a Professor of Geography at UCLA:

During the 1970s at least two studies showed that black movers to the suburbs are younger, more affluent and better educated . . . [R]ecent black movers to the suburbs are relocating in white areas . . . [O]ver 40 percent of the city-suburban black movers in the mid-1970s went to tracts that were less than 10 percent black in 1970 and another 27 percent went to tracts that were between 10 and 40 percent black. . . .

The argument in favor of spillover seems to apply to the black suburbanization process up until the early 1970's, but the recent evidence is that although spillover still occurs, there is movement to all-white residential areas. . . . A recent paper . . . (1985) [concluding very much like Pettigrew] holds that black gains in social status will improve black-white relations, and will be shown in an increased suburban destination selectivity amongst black movers of all ages in the life cycle.[13]

There are real limits as to the level of integration that can be achieved if we take into consideration individual preferences and mathematics. As Thomas Schelling has pointed out:

Arithmetic plays a role. If blacks are a tenth of the population we cannot have the whole country integrated except in a nine-to-one ratio; if that ratio makes blacks uncomfortable and they withdraw in

the interests of less extreme "integration" the mechanism of withdrawal . . . may not be compatible with mixed living. . . . If blacks
are willing to be a minority but no smaller than one quarter, and
whites willing to mix equally but not in minority status, the limits
are 3:1 and 1:1 and in a population 90 percent white, two thirds of
the whites have to stay away or they swamp the whole arrangement.[14]

It would seem that the black pioneers to Levittown, willing to live
one to a block, were the exceptions rather than the rule. Survey
evidence of black and white preferences indicate that whites prefer
neighborhoods ranging from 0 to 30 percent black, while blacks
prefer neighborhoods that are half black and half white.[15] This real
difference in preference can play a critical role in residential patterns. (See Appendix A for a demonstration by Schelling that even
mild racial preferences over time can produce strong degrees of
segregation.) An article about race relations in the Washington
metropolitan area contained a section entitled "Why Are Neighbors Almost Always the Same Color." The following short excerpt
illustrates the importance of preferences in human terms:

For minorities who can afford to buy homes anywhere, personal
preferences sometimes leads to self-segregation. Many blacks who
could buy homes in Cleveland Park choose instead to live in well-
defined black neighborhoods such as DC's "Gold Coast." It could
be fear of being snubbed by white neighbors, but many blacks say
it's nothing of the kind.

"I enjoy living in a black community," says Prince George's civic
leader Bonnie John. . . . "I think blacks have reached a point in
their cultural sophistication that they enjoy, respect, and find their
own culture interesting. One does not have to prove anything by
moving into a community of all whites. What's to prove?[16]

As Professor Clark has concluded:

[A]s long as there is a fair amount of mobility in the city, and as long
as some blacks and whites value racial homogeneity in their neighborhoods, integrated neighborhoods are likely to be exceptional,

and not the rule. . . . We live . . . in a world in which private preferences account for a substantial fraction of the observed racial
separation. The effect of government action is limited." [17]

THE BLACK UNDERCLASS—
THE LIMITS OF GOOD INTENTIONS

There are not only limits as to what the government can do, there
are also at times excruciating dilemmas as to what the government
should do. A case in point is very poor blacks, who have no meaningful way of exercising choice and find themselves either in
government-subsidized housing or on the waiting lists for it. There
is no question that many of these housing projects are uniracial
(nowhere more so than in the Chicago represented by Senator
Douglas).[18] Although racism plays a role in creating and perpetu-
ating this situation within a development and management framework that includes 3,000 independent local housing authorities and
countless private developers, it is important to understand some of
the other complex factors that have obstructed meaningful progress, in spite of the federal government's good intentions.

A good point to start is the Housing Act of 1949 and the high
hopes of northern congressmen that the public housing program
could avoid segregation even without a formal provision of the act.
What they didn't realize was that other changes were made in the
legislation that would make a mockery of their hopes.

The crucial issue in extending the public housing program in
1949 was making it consistent with the main thrust of the legislation toward reliance on private enterprise. Congress responded
by targeting the program to the very poor, by lowering income
limits, barring discrimination against welfare families, and giving
a priority to families displaced by urban renewal and highway
construction.

Another factor that dimmed the prospects for integration was
tying tenants' rents to a percentage of income rather than the quality of the unit. In the early fifties, the ratio was set at 20 percent—
this rate was both too high and too low. For the new class of public

housing tenants, many of whom were in the lowest-income group,
20 percent of their income could not even cover operating expenses—leading to poor maintenance of the structures. The same
20 percent proved too high for the newly prosperous older tenants,
who could not understand why their rents should increase while
their buildings and neighbors deteriorated. For these upwardly mobile, primarily white families, the minimum ratio acted like a vac-
uum cleaner to suck them out of public housing. This process was
further accelerated by these families' need for more space than
public housing apartments could offer and by the availability of
cheap private alternatives.

By the mid-fifties, public housing authorities (PHAs) were peti-
tioning the federal government to drop the requirement that rent
be tied exclusively to income. Their wish was finally granted in
1959, but by then it was too late to forestall the flight of higher-
income, predominantly white families from public housing. Indeed, public housing had little to offer its higher-income tenants.
To families who had been paying steadily increasing rent and receiving steadily decreasing value, PHAs could offer neither rent
reductions—which would have threatened the projects with financial insolvency—nor newer housing. The influx of very poor minorities into public housing had begun to generate successful
organizing efforts by many neighborhoods to block the construction of new public housing projects which had come to be seen as
unwelcome intruders, unless they were specifically designed for
the elderly.[19]

The depth of the general public's aversion to projects is illustrated in the following account of an encounter between a salesman
and a buyer interested in a long-term real estate investment:

When we mentioned that perhaps there were similar cemeteries that
we should look into, the Parklawn man looked horrified. "Well you
wouldn't want to go to National Memorial Park," he said, "because
that's too far away. And as for Fort Lincoln, well, it is tragic what
happened there. The neighborhood has deteriorated so badly. And
now they are building a low-cost housing project just over the fence.
They will never be able to keep them out, even with a high wall. I

am so sick about it. I'm thinking about pulling my first wife out of there and transferring her to Parklawn.''[20]

The racism of the salesman was a bit extreme and otherworldly. Commenting on the hostility toward public housing, the National Commission on Urban Problems headed by Senator Paul Douglas found that white racism per se was too simplistic an explanation:

> A substantial part of the opposition to public housing is economic. It is based on the fear that if lower income folk, especially lower income Negroes, come into the neighborhood, crime rates go up and a slatternly pattern of house care develops, which, among other factors, tends to lower the price of real estate and endanger painfully acquired savings. . . . The objectors, whether vocal or silent, are not bad men or women and should not be treated as such. They are, instead, very human. They worry about their savings, their homes, their neighborhoods, and their children, and are often disturbed to find old, subconscious, and hidden prejudices coming to the surface.[21]

The passage of the landmark civil rights legislation of the 1960s brought a new attitude. HUD was not going to stand by—it was going to do something about segregated subsidized housing. These efforts were roundly criticized in a Pulitzer Prize winning series of articles in the Dallas *Morning News* in 1985. In an article entitled "Still Separate and Unequal,"[22] Craig Flournoy, the head of the team of Dallas journalists, presented a substantial amount of evidence that the public housing program was segregated and that black families were getting the short end of the stick. He saw the matter as a straightforward and simple question of weak-kneed administrators:

> . . . HUD secretaries during the past 19 years have not invoked the laws' strongest measures. For example: No HUD Secretary has ever used the authority provided under Title VI to cut off Federal funds to an . . . authority . . . or landlord who operated a Federal rent subsidy development. . . .

Top HUD officials seldom have revoked Community Development funds. . . .

To quote a quip attributed to former HUD Secretary Robert Weaver there are people who have "hearts of gold and heads of lead." What would be accomplished by cutting off the funds of a housing authority found guilty of discriminatory practices? Who would be hurt? The administrators who perpetrated the segregation may have been replaced by a new reform administration. But even if the same "bad old guys" are in charge, the rooms that would go unheated and the buildings whose roofs will leak would be inhabited not by the administrators but by poor tenants. Extending the circle of guilt for the failure of an independent local authority makes little sense. The loss of community development funds is likely to strike hard at the low-income person likely a resident of subsidized housing—currently benefiting from a job-training or Head Start program.

HOUSING ADVANCEMENT VERSUS HOUSING INTEGRATION

The uniqueness of subsidized housing causes difficult dilemmas when it comes to the issue of integration. Public education is a universal subsidy program, available to all. If a school is found to be segregated, the child is not deprived of schooling—some other arrangement is made for his schooling. Subsidized housing is available to only a relatively small proportion of the poor. The resident of even a segregated project is in a favored position. If he is deprived of the housing in order to aid integration, he has lost something of value.

The other unique aspect is that the minority residents are not only separate but unequal. *Nonwhites are more than equal.* They have more than their share of the available units. Of the 1.1 million occupied public housing units in 1978, blacks and Hispanics occupied 59 percent of the apartments, while whites occupied 34 percent (Indians, Orientals, and other government-designated minorities accounted for the remaining occupants.)[23]

These figures understate the disparity, since they include the elderly who occupy 46 percent of the apartments. Sixty percent of the elderly who moved into public housing in 1979 were white. In contrast, only 26 percent of the nonelderly moving into public housing during the same period were white. Fifty-three percent were black and 18 percent were Hispanic. In the private subsidized-housing program (that serves the same low-income group as public housing) the statistics are approximately the same for move-ins— 25 percent white, 62 percent black, and 8 percent Hispanic.

In the usual civil rights case the minority is not getting its fair share—whether it be police, firefighters, or medical school students. Even in the case of fair housing, the focus is the residential area in which the minority group is occupying fewer units than would be expected if the sole criterion were economic factors. If income were the sole criterion, the color distribution in subsidized housing would be quite different. Although the poverty rate of whites in 1983 was 12 percent, compared with 36 percent for blacks and 28 percent for those of Hispanic origin, there were 24 million poor whites as compared with 10 million poor blacks and 4 million poor Hispanics.

If integration is to be achieved, the traditional plowshares of minority improvement must be transformed into weapons against minorities. Goals and quotas have to be used to *limit* the number of blacks in public housing. The target of affirmative marketing must be the white community. In these cases, integration, if it is to be achieved, must be achieved at the "expense" of the blacks rather than whites. Yet, whose ox is then being gored? What is fair housing in such a different context?

The classic contest in this strange new world occurred in Starrett City, located in the outermost reaches of Broooklyn. Roger Starr (no relation) sets the scene:

After many years in which the goal of minority group advocates was the development of racially integrated housing, the local branch of the NAACP went to court . . . to oppose the efforts of Starrett City management to ensure exactly that. The Starrett City policy was endorsed by a firm majority of the residents both black and white. The cornerstone of the policy was . . . that pure color-blind policy would not be sufficient to ensure racial integration. Given that there was no shortage of well-qualified applicants . . . it would seem clear that only a token number of whites would live in the development unless they felt the percentage of blacks was to be less than overwhelming.

The Starrett management . . . deliberately limited the number of minority residents to approximately 30 percent of the total units. Since minority families tended to be larger than white families, the actual number of . . . whites . . . is little more than 50 percent. . . . That . . . would seem totally consistent with the racial distribution of the general population of New York City and thus the goal, long dreamed of, of racially integrated housing.

That numerical congruity . . . causes discomfort to many advocates of integrated housing. That is, the program is not itself colorblind. A number of black families were refused . . . admission . . . simply because of their race. . . . Many people . . . find that the policy of refusing admission . . . on the basis of race is troubling and distateful. But the NAACP supports the exclusion of some job applicants and the inclusion of others on the basis of race to meet quotas and guidelines.[24]

What has occurred is that the NAACP has gone back to basics in the advancement of colored people. At one time, advancement was through integration. Advancement and integration are not, however, synonymous. The NAACP would not complain that the work force on a construction job was not integrated if all the plumbers were black. No lawsuit has ever been brought against the National Basketball Association for the lack of white ballplayers. The purpose of the NAACP is not to make whites feel better at the expense of providing good-quality housing for blacks in subsidized housing. What is confusing is that in most other areas, including nonsubsidized housing, advancement is coming by means of integration.

When the self-interests of the parties are clear, settlements can be reached. The NAACP wanted more state-funded units for blacks (Starrett was state-funded and federally subsidized), and the owner wanted a racially stable project. A settlement was reached that allowed Starrett to continue its practices and imposed on the New York State Division of Housing and Community Renewal the obligation to use its best efforts to raise to 20 percent the black occupancy of other projects supervised by the agency. Everybody won.

The case did not end there. The Justice Department, after forcefully opposing affirmative-action preferences in employment for blacks in five Supreme Court cases and losing each one, decided to change its litigation priorities. It now started opposing affirmative-action preferences for another minority—whites—in the subsidized housing areas. Given the overwhelmingly large proportions of blacks on waiting lists, any project that was integrated was suspect. Affirmative-action programs initiated by HUD for the purpose of integration were now being attacked by the Justice Department for fostering discrimination against blacks.

Starrett City was an obvious choice. In addition, the federal government went after the Charlottesville Housing Authority, which against overwhelming odds succeeded in integrating its projects, and the nonprofit church-sponsored Atrium Village in Chicago, an integrated subsidized project only a block from one of the most dangerous public housing projects in the country—the all-minority Cabrini-Green.

The position of Assistant Attorney General William Bradford Reynolds was rigorously consistent. "Stripped of its rhetoric such conduct, no matter how well intended, constitutes discrimination plain and simple. Once again in the name of integration blacks are being discriminatorily denied housing on the basis of race."

There are historical echoes to the Attorney General's position. It sounds very much like the position of the supporters of the Bricker Amendment in 1949, who attempted to kill public housing by proposing an antidiscrimination provision. An analogy closer in time and closer in place (at least to Atrium Village) was recounted by Charles Abrams about a well-intentioned developer named Morris Milgram, who sought to build a development in an all-white section of Deerfield, Illinois, in the late 1950s:

> . . . He proposed to sell 10 to 12 of 51 houses to Negroes. After considerable harassment by white neighbors and by local officials,

Milgram brought suit to enjoin a condemnation of his property. The court held among other things that Milgram's "controlled occupancy" pattern was illegal and a violation of the Fifth and Fourteenth amendments. . . . "If there is to be controlled or forced integration," said the court, "it is most certainly a matter for action by the people through the government and not by a private corporation, which when all is said has as its object the motive of profit.[25]

It is hard to divine the motives of the Justice Department in its litigation choices. One can look to Emerson's epigram, "A foolish consistency is the hobgoblin of little minds, adored by statesmen, philosophers and divines." Or one can look to Paul Freund, a wise teacher of the law: "The issues are rarely right against wrong in the law, but right against right." We will have to wait for the memoirs of the Assistant Attorney General.

Chapter 7

POOR TENANTS— POOR LANDLORDS

Charles Abrams used to tell his students that if you wanted to propose a new housing program in New York City you first had to find a kid who had been bitten by a rat and print a picture of both in the *New York Post*. In our more sophisticated times, we can rely on the General Accounting Office[1] to announce the housing crisis:

Since 1970 renters' rent-to-income ratio has steadily increased . . . [I]n 1977 about 49 percent (11.9 million) of all renters paid 25 percent or more of their income for rent. About 30 percent (7.4 million) . . . paid 35 percent or more . . . with 4.2 million of these renters paying more than 50 percent. . . .

The national vacancy rate has been declining since 1974. During 1979 the vacancy rate ranged from between 4.8 and 5.2 percent. . . .

Our Nation's rental housing market has reached a crisis. The primary factors responsible for this crisis are low levels of moderate priced new private construction . . . and losses of existing units through abandonment and conversions to condominiums. Other factors, such as rapidly escalating operating costs and the increasing age of the existing rental stock, are also having a detrimental effect.

Historically, the private sector . . . dominat[ed] the market. However, the proportion of federally subsidized multifamily rental construction starts has increased steadily from 22 percent in 1972 to about 44 percent in 1978. HUD estimated that federally subsidized or insured units would account for about 75 percent . . . in 1979.[2]

There was a flurry of hearings and headlines and proposals, and bills were being drafted in both Congress and at HUD to solve this problem.

WAS THERE A HOUSING CRISIS IN THE SEVENTIES?

Although the policymakers and housers were ready to charge forth with new programs to address these "worst of times," researchers and scholars were uncovering evidence that indicated that the 1970s were the "best of times." Ira Lowry of the Rand Institute supplemented the GAO findings with the findings of the Pollyanna Institute about rental housing in the 1970s:

Between 1960 and 1980, the Bureau of Labor Statistics consumer price index (CPI) increased by 179 percent. The index of residential rents rose only 108 percent. For any renter whose income kept pace with the CPI, the real cost of a given level of housing consumption dropped by 25 percent. Most of this decrease . . . (18 percent) occurred after 1970.

Given its bargain price, rental housing consumption per capita increased. The average number of . . . rooms per person . . . rose from 1.32 in 1960 to 1.73 in 1978. The percentage of rental dwellings with more than one person per room fell from 16.1 to 5.9. . . .

. . . Between 1960 and 1978, the number of rental dwellings occupied by single persons living alone rose from 4.2 million to 9.6 million, an increase of 129 percent. . . .

Between 1960 and 1978, the nation's rental stock increased by about 6.4 million . . . despite the removal of about 375,000 obsolete or inappropriate dwellings a year. The additions . . . have been concentrated in metropolitan suburbs broadening the locational options of urban renters. By 1978 . . . 42 percent of [rental dwellings] in metropolitan areas were in . . . suburbs.[3]

To these observations, Larry Ozanne of the Urban Institute pointed out that in many ways it was "business as usual." Rental starts in the second half of the seventies were basically at the same pace as in the 1960s, and if units were being converted to condominiums, many of these same units were being rerented or were owned by their previous occupants. Finally, if the vacancy rate was at a twenty-five-year low, by all measures the quality of rental housing had improved between 1970 and 1977.[4]

These conflicting perceptions about the state of the rental market raise questions about the state of mind of landlords. With operating costs rising and vacancy rates dropping, why weren't they behaving like "economic men" and maximizing their return from their investment? How could they make a living by ignoring the economist's models of the market?

There are numerous explanations for this paradoxical behavior. First a fact. Landlords were making money. Operating costs are only a portion of the owner's costs. The debt-service portion of landlord's costs were fixed and were relatively low, since the mortgages carried relatively low interest rates. As Anthony Downs put it:

> [M]ost owners who did not refinance or buy recently gained because their fixed debt-service costs allowed them to increase profits even though rents went up more slowly than operating costs. Furthermore, some owners who refinanced took large sums of money out of their property. . . .[5]

The tax-shelter aspects of rental property, as previously noted, meant that rents were often not where the primary benefits were. The primary reason for investing was not cash flow arising from tenants, but cash flow arising from not having to pay taxes from other sources of income.

A third reason could be the fear of the imposition of rent control. Although rent control saw a revival in the 1970s, it seemed in such places as Santa Monica, Berkeley, and Cambridge to be more the dying last gasp of the radicalism of the sixties than a reason for landlord restraint in raising rents.

The primary reason is that the landlord in most cases is at worst only a sheep in wolf's clothing. There is very little reliable national data on the subject. Nevertheless, as expert Anthony Downs has noted:

[M]y impression is that ownership is scattered among many small-scale landlords. My impression is based on the high percentage of rental housing containing fewer than five units [60 percent] . . . and in my experience in talking to realtors and investors across the nation. . . . [S]mall scale investors who manage their own property rarely take full account of the cost of their time. So they have lower management costs—both apparent and real—than large scale operators who employ professional management and maintenance personnel.[6]

This subjective impression is supported by a survey of owners in New York City, the one area in the country where large-scale ownership of property would be expected. Arthur D. Little, Inc., found that 60 percent of the owners own only one building. Of the owners who bought a building in the late seventies and early eighties, 68 percent own only one building. In over 60 percent of the cases, the owners are making less than a quarter of their income from their rental investment—and not as a result of their great wealth. The majority of the owners had incomes between $10,000 and $40,000.[7]

Small-time operators with only a few units must play a much more conservative game than large-scale operators or the theoretical economic man. An owner with a few units has a stronger incentive than the larger landlord to avoid raising rents so fast that vacancy increases. The turnover of an apartment usually involves the extra cost of repainting and/or redecorating and the cost of finding a new tenant. More important, a vacancy to a small-time landlord involves loss of a substantial portion or all of the income of the building. As a result, to quote Anthony Downs, "This situation, plus the high rate of normal turnover among renters [in 1980, 37 percent were living in their unit for less than a year] makes most small-scale landlords *turnover minimizers* rather than *rent maximizers.*[8]

There is another factor that helps to explain what was happening to rental housing. Low rent levels are consistent with low vacancy levels when future tenants are likely to be poorer than their predecessors. As Frank de Leeuw has noted, "[V]acancies may be low when waiting has a low return. Waiting would have a low return when new renters coming into the market are increasingly low-income households . . . the longer the landlord waits, the lower the probable income of tenants interested in his vacant unit."[9]

In the seventies, the mix of tenants that the rental market had to accommodate was changing. The seventies witnessed the flowering of the "me generation" and the growth of singleness. The baby-boomers were coming of age and leaving the nest, the number of marriages postponed and disrupted rose sharply, wives continued to endure the trials of life better than their husbands, and everyone realized that homeownership was a blue-chip investment.

Going into the 1970s, married couples had dominated the rental market; 54 percent (12.8 million) of the rental households contained a husband and a wife. By 1980, this traditional family unit had dropped to less than 36 percent (9.8 million) of all the occupants of rental households. The missing households were alive and well, living in a home they owned. The homeownership sector captured 76 percent of the addition to the total households during the decade—12.6 of 16.6 million.[10]

The rental market was now dominated by women—the elderly, single, and divorced mothers, and single men. Female-headed households rose from 30 percent (7.1 million) of all rental households to 41 percent (11.2 million). The male-headed household, although only 23.7 of renter households in 1980, registered the sharpest rise, increasing by 76 percent in the decade—from 3.7 to 6.5 million.[11]

In 1980, one-third of all apartments were occupied by one person and two-thirds by two or fewer people. The expansion of rental units was not matched by the expansion of occupants. Five million rental units were added in the seventies (from 23.6 to 28.6 million). Nevertheless, the population of renters increased by less than a million persons (from 64.3 to 65.1 million).

The departure of higher-income renters to horizontal and vertical homes left vacant apartments for tenants who were either before or after their prime earning period or who had lost either through death or divorce the former prime earner of the household. The shift of higher-income households away from rental housing can be seen in the widening of the income gap between renters and homeowners in the 1970s. In 1970, the average income of a renter was 65 percent of the income of a homeowner ($6,300 as compared to $9,700). In 1980, it was only 53 percent ($10,500 as compared to $19,800).

The market matched lower-income tenants with good-quality housing that had "filtered down." Although the rents didn't rise as fast as other goods, neither did they fall sufficiently to make the acquisition of the better housing "cost-free." Tenants in the seventies enjoyed a relatively high level of housing services and paid a high fraction of their income. The average rent to income ratio rose from 20 percent in 1970 to 27 percent in 1980.

The typical renter had changed. The higher share of income going for housing was due to the changing composition of the renter population—the loss of middle- and upper-income households who had relatively low ratios and their replacement by younger households and single individuals who typically spend a higher share of their income on housing. To some renters it just meant better housing. To others it meant better housing and a heavier rent burden. Between 1970 and 1979 the median income of every household type (husband-wife, other male, female-headed, one-person) in the lowest-income group (the lowest quintile of the income scale) rose faster than rents. However, if we look only at the period between 1973 and 1979, the rent burden increased for two-or-more person households headed by women and unmarried men, as the rise in rents outpaced their income increases.[12]

The situation at the end of the decade was summarized by Michael Lea in a report to HUD:

[T]here is no current nationwide shortage in rental housing. While there may be some local shortages, in many areas there may be an actual surplus. . . .

One fact that is particularly relevant for the future course is that the rental population is becoming increasingly concentrated in the lower income segment of the society. Therefore, future rent increases are increasingly going to those households who can least afford such increases. . . .[13]

A HOUSING CRISIS AMID AN ADEQUATE HOUSING SUPPLY

The eighties seem to be far more turbulent times for rental housing. In the early part of the decade, interest rates soared into the stratosphere and almost put a stop to housing production. In the last part of the decade, after much huffing and puffing, Congress blew the tax shelters of the piggies down. And there are homeless in the streets (no connection between the two latter events).

The initial breezes in the beginning of the decade lifted rental housing higher than a kite. Faced with a faltering economy, Congress passed the Economic Recovery Tax Act of 1981, with the hope of spurring capital investment by business. The measure used more rapid depreciation schedules and therefore lower taxes as the carrot. It was expected that increased capital investment would result in higher national productivity and a lower inflation rate. What it meant for rental housing was an accelerated cost recovery system that allowed for the depreciation of a new building in fifteen years. This reduction substantially increased the paper losses of projects and as a result the attractiveness of rental housing as a tax shelter.

Although the high interest rates slowed the immediate impact of the legislation, by 1983 developers were lining up to obtain building permits for 570,000 units (the highest level since the early 1970s, when record numbers of federally subsidized housing units were authorized). In the four-year period between 1983 and the end of 1986, building plans containing 2.4 million units were approved by local building departments. By 1987, there was a glut of rental housing, and in many cities landlords were offering concessions to fill up empty apartments.

If developers of rental housing needed a reason to slow up, it was provided by the Tax Reform Act of 1986. Congress left the piggies out in the cold. The tax reform had four major features:

1. The depreciable life of rental housing was extended to about thirty years, and use of accelerated depreciation was eliminated.

2. The tax shelter was left in shambles as the ability to use tax losses to offset non–real estate income was severely reduced. The "passive" limited partners would only be able to use their losses to offset their gains from other passive activities. They would not be able to offset earned income or income from dividends or interest.

3. The maximum federal income tax was lowered to 28 percent. As a result the value of the deduction afforded by the losses was substantially reduced.

4. The special treatment of capital gains was eliminated. Therefore, the effective tax rate would increase from 20 percent to 28 percent.

The effect of these changes is to put a hold on development plans for rental housing until some supple mind learns to bend the tax code to provide shelter for some group of investors or develops a product that provides real profits. Nevertheless, the supply of rental housing should be adequate now that we are witnessing the aging of the baby-boom generation, which is now putting fiber into its cereal and replacing its running shoes with walking shoes. Two million, nine hundred thousand rental units were vacant in the third quarter of 1987. The vacancy rate of 8.1 percent (8.9 percent in central cities) was the highest level in over two decades.[14]

There are sharp contrasts between the 1970s and 1980s. The number of households maintained by young adults (under twenty-five), the front-end of housing demand, has declined by 17 percent in the 1980s. In the 1970–1975 period, this group increased by 34 percent. Households in the 35–44 age bracket increased by 25 percent in the 1980–1985 period, compared to no growth in the 1970–1975 period. And, although the total number of households increased by 7 percent it is half the rate of household formation in the 1975–1980 period. This slowdown has not been accompanied by an increase in "crowding," since population has been rising at an even slower rate, and the average size of household has steadily declined to 2.69 persons.[15]

Other factors indicate that the supply of rental housing will be adequate in the near future. The decline in household size is accounted for by a drop in the number of kids under eighteen. The growth of the nonfamily household has tapered off from its 36 percent increase in the 1975–1980 period to a 13 percent rate in the first half decade of the 1980s.[16] Finally, as the baby-boomers reach the great divide of the thirties, many a lingering relationship is finding itself on a fast track toward marriage and the union of two households into one.

An adequate housing supply can coexist with a housing crisis for families and individuals who cannot afford to pay the rent for the available housing. Housing does filter down, but if the rent roll does not equal the operating expenses the housing will filter right out of the market. There is no more graphic illustration of this phenomenon than New York City. The city owns (as a result of foreclosures for unpaid property taxes) 74,000 apartments that are either vacant or so far gone as to have lost their status as housing. And generally, for every city-owned unit that has been boarded up or demolished, two privately owned units meet a similar fate. At the same time, the city is the "home" of Rachel and her children. Although the problems of the homeless in many cases transcend a "housing solution" (although there is no evidence that society is saner, the number of residents of public psychiatric institutions dropped from 559,000 in 1955 to 122,000 in 1981), the total homeless population in New York City is substantially less than 50,000 people.

The average income for renters doubled in the 1970–1983 period, from $6,300 to $12,400. The gross rent (rent plus utilities), however, tripled for nonsubsidized renters, rising from $108 to $332 a month. These statistics reflect the skimming off of top-income layers of renters by condominiums, the inflationary rise in prices, and the removal of units at the bottom end of the rental scale. The gross rent of apartments removed from the inventory in 1983 was $98. The median rent burden rose from 20 percent of income to 30 percent of income.[17]

When matters get tough in the rental market generally, they get particularly rough for the poor:

> The changes in the rent burden distribution for the poorest households were particularly dramatic . . . By 1983 the median rent burden for households in this income class had risen to 46 percent of income, and over one-quarter of the households . . . had rent burden above three quarters of income. . . .
>
> These results must be interpreted with great care. . . . These rent burdens are based on household's cash income and therefore exclude income in kind, such as food stamps and Medicaid. Between 1974 and 1980, the in-kind benefits . . . increased significantly. As a result, the figures . . . overstate the increase in rent burden as a percent of total income. . . . [O]ne study estimates that including all such benefits reduces the median rent burden for the lowest one-fifth of the income distribution from 62 percent to 39 percent.[18]

From the perspective of poor tenants and academic scholars (often toiling in graduate school poverty jobs) the problem is affordability. From the perspective of the uneducated landlord (half of New York City's landlords never graduated from high school[19]) the

Table 9. Low Rents, Heavy Burdens

Sub-borough area	Median gross rent[21]	Median renter income[21]	Rent burden
South Bronx	$263	$ 6,874	47%
Northwest Bronx	$333	$13,984	29%
Northeast Bronx	$310	$12,421	30%
North Brooklyn	$274	$ 8,968	37%
Central Brooklyn	$340	$11,854	34%
South Brooklyn	$333	$13,938	29%
Northwest Manhattan	$309	$11,235	33%
Northeast Manhattan	$222	$ 7,071	38%
Upper Midtown	$463	$23,006	24%
Lower Midtown	$476	$26,801	21%
Lower Manhattan	$291	$12,784	27%
Northwest Queens	$347	$15,468	27%
Southern Queens	$354	$15,630	27%
Northeast Queens	$403	$19,648	25%
Richmond	$373	$15,761	29%

problem is pricing. The tenants with the highest rent burden are living in the lowest-priced units (the poor pay less but it hurts them more). This can be vividly seen in an area in which the median rent approximates the national average—New York City (in 1984 the average rent was $330[20]).

New York City is burdened with an arcane and byzantine maze of rent control, rent stabilization, and regulations designed to alleviate the plight of the poor and lower-middle-income renter. In practice, the system has turned rental housing into a public utility for the rich and famous. As William Tucker writes:

> 135 Central Park West [is] a magnificent ocean-liner of a building with stunning museum-sized apartments that could easily command five to ten thousands on the open market.
>
> [The] tenants are all rent regulated. Consequently [the] rent roll looks like this. Carly Simon pays $2208.75 for ten rooms overlooking Central Park; Mia Farrow pays $1870.31 for ten rooms overlooking Central Park; Whitney Ellsworth, publisher of the *New York Review of Books,* $1587.22 for ten rooms overlooking Central Park; . . . Jean Stein, heir to the MCA fortune, pays $1241.39 for ten rooms overlooking [the park]; James Levine, music director of the Metropolitan Opera, pays $1156.50 for six rooms overlooking the park. . . .
>
> Manocherian [the owner] says he loses $100,000 a year on the building. He keeps it for sentimental reasons (he lives there himself), plus the ever-faint hope that one day one of his tenant's great-grandchildren may die without an heir and the rights to the apartment will revert to one of his own great-grandchildren, who may be able to rerent the apartment at something like its market value.[22]

For the poor it is free enterprise. The rent regulations are almost irrelevant. Given the low income of such a large sector—one quarter of all renters were paying at least 50 percent of their income in 1984—it is almost impossible to squeeze out higher rents. As Michael Stegman (*the* expert on New York City housing) wrote in polite terms, in a report to the administrators of the New York City system, "[T]he more serious challenge to maintaining a healthy rental market might result from limited incomes of households who must depend on the rental market to meet their housing needs than from any unresponsiveness of rent regulations to the cost of providing decent housing."[23]

The most ominous occurrence in the New York City rental market is the rise in the operating and maintenance expenses as a percentage of rent. In an earlier report,[24] Stegman pointed out that the latter ratio has risen from 55 percent in 1971 to 70 percent in 1981. The rise meant that the percentage of the rent dollar available to cover vacancy losses, pay debt service, and return a profit has declined from 45 percent to just 30 percent.

An example using 1981 numbers illustrates the devastating effect on property values of this decline.

Rent (New York City median)			$265
Operating and Maintenance Expense (70%)			
Taxes, fees, and permits	$49		
Labor	30		
Fuel and utilities	66		
Contractor services	19		
Administrative	11		
Other	11		
		186	
Vacancy losses		26	
		212	
Income available for debt service and profit			$53

If we assume no profit, $53 would support a $5,000 mortgage, assuming an 11 percent interest rate and amortization period of fifteen years. If the potential buyer wanted a reasonable 10 percent of the rent as a profit, the resulting $27 for debt service would support a mortgage of about $2,500 a unit. Thus, while cooperative apartments along Central Park may be worth up to fifty times the annual rent, a few miles uptown a seller who obtains *one* time the rent is doing well.

THE POOR LANDLORD AS HERO

The battered but unsung heroes of housing for the poor are the buyers who have kept many of the buildings open despite the con-

ditions of the market. These are not absentee landlords astride
their steeds on their suburban estates. Sixty percent of New York
building owners own only one building, and 61 percent of owners
of buildings with less than ten apartments live in the building.[25]

They are not a particularly wealthy group. More than half of the
owners were not born in the United States, and of owners who
have bought within the last five years over 35 percent are either
black, Hispanic, or Asian. Thirty percent of owners report household income of under $20,000, and 9 percent have incomes of less
than $10,000. They did not buy for the tax-shelter opportunities.
The majority of the owners had incomes of less than $40,000.[26]
Although there are no statistics as to the relation between income
of the landlord and the income of the tenants, people generally
have landlords of their own social class.

What keeps these buildings going is quite often the "sweat equity" of the landlords. Thirty-nine percent collect the trash themselves (a further 5 percent use unpaid relatives); 36 percent clean
the public areas; 31.4 percent do minor plumbing repairs; 32 percent do minor electrical repairs; 23 percent repair leaky roofs; 87
percent collect the rent themselves; and 82 percent keep the books
themselves. Almost half the owners spend two to four days a week
on the operations of their building and only 16 percent receive any
salary.[27]

In spite of these economies, only one-third were making money
on a consistent basis and the remainder either broke even or were
losing money. Thirteen percent of the owners had to subsidize the
operating expenses every month and a further 16 percent have to
inject cash during the heating season. Since the statistics cover all
landlords it is likely that they understate the precarious situation
of landlords serving the poorest tenants. The owners are also
spending money on capital improvements. However, only 20 percent filed for rent increases—in no small part because of the
amount of red tape necessary to obtain a rent increase.[28]

The increase of improvements in the bottom end of the market
is substantiated by Stegman's analysis: "Of all the units that have
been counted as dilapidated at least once since 1978, only 2 percent
were dilapidated at the time of all three Housing and Vacancy

Surveys . . . [T]his suggests the chances a housing unit in serious disrepair will ever be improved are very good."[29]

The bottom line is that it is possible to make a modest profit on low-income rent buildings *if* the debt service, taxes, and vacancies are low, and the owner is handy and has time on his hands. Nevertheless, the operation is marginal. All it takes is one major repair —a boiler that needs repair, a roof in which there is no room for new patches—to bring the whole financial structure down.

The only major program aimed at the existing private market is the Section 8 leasing program. At present the fair market rent is $400 for a one-bedroom and $470 for a two-bedroom—substantially above the city's median rent. The money is thus quite unlikely to find its way into the lowest-income rental sector where it is most needed.

The present government policy seems paradoxical and narrowly defined. A government committed to the private market is standing by almost helplessly watching the major part of housing assistance being channeled into publicly owned housing. Its major effort is building levees around public housing projects which represent little more than 5 percent of the market while the river of red ink is inundating the surrounding areas.

In the coming years, federal policy will do little to preserve the private rental housing market that serves the poor in New York and the rest of the country. For Fiscal Year 1989 (which started October 1, 1988), the administration is proposing 100,000 additional subsidy vouchers for the entire nation when New York City alone can use more than 500,000. It is time to take a harder look at the structure of the country's housing policy.

Chapter 8

PERVERSE PROGRAMS BY PRUDENT PEOPLE

Subsidized rental housing in the United States has come a long way. Starting as a solution to a problem, it became a problem—some will claim it is a chronic condition. Five decades ago, Representative Henry Ellenbogen could state, "The money spent under the United States Housing Act will build monuments which 50 years hence will give concrete evidence that the Congress of 1936 was an enlightened and forward-looking body."[1] The House of Representatives in the fall of 1986 passed a bill stating, "The Congress . . . finds that the condition of public housing projects . . . is, in some cases, substandard, forcing many dwelling units to remain vacant, forcing many lower income families to live in substandard or dangerous living conditions."[2]

A RADICAL STEPCHILD OF THE NEW DEAL

Although born during the New Deal, public housing was both the last and least loved of the major housing initiatives. The prime concern of the New Deal was in firming up the institutional structure of private housing rather than in replacing it. Ernest Bohm, one of the early leaders in the public housing movement is said to have remarked, "If we wanted to have a convention of all those working for public-housing in 1934, we could have held it in a telephone booth."[3]

The immediate predecessors of public housing were in the area of public works and slum clearance. The initial public housing bill introduced in 1935 by Senator Robert Wagner mentioned the elimination of slums and the relief of congested areas before it mentioned housing. It marched under the banner of national recovery—the bill's purpose included "to further industrial recovery through the employment of labor and materials." The bill lingered and died—failing to be reported out of either the Senate or House committee to which it was referred.

Senator Wagner tried again in 1936. He did manage to get the bill out of the Senate committee, and it passed the Senate—apparently in such a rush that it caused Senator Arthur Vandenburg to raise doubts whether there were more than two senators "who could stand even a kindergarten examination of the bill."[4] However, public housing had something less than the lukewarm support of the Roosevelt administration. In listing the priority measures for Senate consideration in May of 1936, the President failed to mention public housing. Neither did the Democratic party platform's housing plank in 1936 make any mention of public or low-rent housing:

> We maintain that our people are entitled to decent, adequate housing at a price they can afford. In the last three years the Federal Government, having saved more than two million homes from foreclosure, has taken the first steps in our country to provide decent housing for people of meager incomes. We believe every encouragement should be given to the building of new homes by private enterprise; and that the Government should steadily extend its housing program toward the goal of adequate housing for those forced through economic necessities to live in unhealthy and slum conditions.[5]

Not heeding the advice of W. C. Fields ("If at first you don't succeed, don't make a damn fool of yourself"), Senator Wagner tried again in 1937. In spite of President Roosevelt's Inaugural

Address, in which he spoke of one-third of the nation as ill-housed, the bill did not have the initial support of the administration. Again the Senate passed the bill, although this time with greater deliberation than in 1936. The outcome in the House, however, was different than in prior years.

Roosevelt had overwhelmed Landon, and the lineup of Democrats to Republicans was 77–19 in the Senate and 328–107 in the House. Nevertheless, the legislative program had turned into a fiasco when the President attempted to pack the Supreme Court. As the session moved to a close, it became apparent to the White House that if the public housing bill did not pass, the legislative scorecard for 1937 would only have zeroes. Chairman Henry Steagall got a message from his chief and the House bill started moving. It steamrolled through the House making a shambles of the deliberative process. The House Committee on Banking and Currency had its first hearing on the bill on August, 3, 1937. By August 18, 1937, the bill passed the House of Representatives, after three hours of debate. The statements of the participants verify the haste of the process. The opening address by Representative Steagall (whose name the bill carries) seems to have been penned by the White Rabbit:

I must hurry on. We are necessarily limited in this discussion. I am not responsible for it. I am doing the best I can. . . . We have gone about it very hastily.[6]

Representative Hancock echoed the prior year's complaint of Senator Vandenburg:

There is not a member in the committee who would stand here in the Well and tell you he understands this bill in its present form.[7]

The Senate and House bills were reconciled in a conference committee. On September 2, 1937, President Roosevelt signed the "United States Housing Act of 1937."

The law was a brilliant technical feat. Public housing was blessed with an ingenious formula that permitted the almost painless birth (at least financially) of new housing. Amortization of the total development cost was covered by federal subsidies in the form of annual contributions. The maximum contribution was sufficient to pay the total amount of principal and interest on the local bonds issued to finance the development. Since the federal payment was on the installment plan—initially for sixty years—the resulting impact on the federal budget was very small. The subsidy was also carefully calibrated. If revenue from the project exceeded operating expenses and reserves, an equivalent reduction in the federal subsidy was required. There was another subsidy involved—the loss to the Treasury of income tax revenue—since part of the financing was done by tax-exempt bonds. But this subsidy was so well hidden it took decades for anyone to notice it.

The program was decentralized, in response to the 1935 court decision[8] that the federal government lacked the power under the Constitution to clear land and build public housing. The process was also painless on the local side. The United States Housing Authority stood ready to lend 90 percent of the total development cost (the balance to be obtained by issuing tax-exempt bonds to private investors). The borrowing was done by an independent local authority that was not subject to municipal debt limitations. A local contribution of 20 percent of the federal contribution was required, but it usually took the form of forgiveness of local property taxes. Localities could thus participate without contributing any cash.

The law was also, perhaps, the most radical piece of legislation passed in American history. It was not due to the adventuresomeness of Congress. Rather it was due to the unique nature of housing. In the case of clothing, welfare, or health care, the poor can be provided for in a way that leaves the donor in better shape (in material as well as spiritual terms) after the deed than the receiver. In the case of housing, however, the results run far beyond egalitarianism. The new program of production for the poor raises the prospect of leaving the recipient better off than donor.

A housing unit is built to provide decades of service. If it is to be functional as long as it is physically usable, when built it must be provided with facilities that were once (and may still be) considered luxuries. As a result, the unit is superior to the housing occupied by a large portion of the nonpoor. "A penthouse for the poor" housing program is analogous to a program providing new Buicks to families who are inadequately served by public transportation.

In a world in which a radical is one who proposes free transportation, a supporter of new housing for the poor should be deemed a madman. Nevertheless, this has been the mainstream of housing policy. When the basic format of public housing policy was created there was only a hazy understanding of this problem. It has remained to haunt housing policy for a half century.

The question of whom the program was to serve was raised but not resolved by Congress in 1937. The large percentage of poor and substandard housing made the issue difficult. The formula used for setting the eligibility limit made it a dilemma. A "family of low income" was defined as one that did not earn more than a given multiple of rent—for example, if income cannot exceed six times the rent and the rent is $1,000 a year, the maximum annual income for admission would be $6,000. The lower the multiple, the lower the income of the families the program would serve. If the multiple were three times rent, the program would only serve families with incomes under $3,000. However, lowering the multiple meant that low-income households would have to pay a more than "ordinary" share of their income for housing. And note that for all families below the income limit, the share would be extraordinary.

One solution is to lower the cost of construction. As a result, limitations were placed on the development cost of the apartment ($4,000) and of each room ($1,000)—$5,000 and $1,500 in cities with populations in excess of half a million. There were also prohibitions against elaborate design or expensive materials and a requirement that construction costs be below private costs. However, given the regional variation in costs and the expected life of the buildings, many in Congress were left disgruntled.

At various times between the bill's introduction and passage, the multiple of earnings was 4, 5, and 6. It ultimately settled at 5 (6 in the case of large families). Even so the measure only set a ceiling. The actual stratum of the population to be served was left to "the common sense and good faith with which it is administered by those who have charge of it."[9]

The management bible of the program, the *Housing Authority Management Manual,* informed local managers that the "first principle of . . . operations is to safeguard the public interests through business-like procedures." [10] This meant realistic rent levels, substantial reserves for repairs and replacements, *and* a limit to the number of very low-income and relief families served. The families to be selected had to be reasonable rent risks. One standard was that the family's income should not be so low that it would have to sacrifice budgetary essentials in order to afford the rent.

The emphasis on sound business procedures and the large pool of deserving poor (and war workers) left most local authorities in excellent financial shape in the late 1940s. If anything, their condition was too good. Congress complained about "excessive reserves," and the maximum amount of reserves was cut to one-half of the annual operating expenses. [11]

Supporters of public housing were quite proud of its record. Charles Abrams could ask rhetorically:

Can Government's administrative mechanisms attain the efficiency of private enterprise at its best while the people retain enough control . . . to assure democratic fulfillment of functions? The Housing record is short, mistakes have been made, policy may have to be modified, but the local authority experience has pointed the way. [12]

THE HOUSING ACT OF 1949:
FROM HOUSING THE POOR TO POORHOUSES

Unfortunately, the successful program found itself bucking the political tide. The war-induced postwar prosperity of the forties revived confidence in private enterprise and dramatically changed the country's political climate. In the elections of 1946, the Republicans captured control of Congress. Although this control was lost in the Truman upset of 1948, the combination of Republicans and Southern Democrats combined in a controlling conservative coalition. But, in spite of this, Congress authorized 810,000 additional public housing units over a six-year period in the Housing Act of 1949. What explains the survival and apparent strengthening of the program?

Many viewed the impressive performance of private enterprise with guarded pessimism. Even the gains in ownership were seen as more a matter of necessity than of choice. As the Housing and Home Finance Agency stated in 1949, "Whether the gains in homeownership will be held is yet to be seen, since many home purchasers bought only out of necessity of finding living quarters." [13] The private housing industry was regarded as needing assistance not only for its own sake but for the sake of the general welfare. The fluctuating building industry (from 937,000 units in 1925 to 93,000 units in 1933 and back to 930,000 units in 1948) was seen as a major factor in economic instability. A substantial public housing program could be a small price to pay for strengthening the economy.

There was also the matter of the serious existing shortage. A later estimate would place the need level at 21 million housing units at the beginning of 1950. [14] The trickle down of existing units was not a practical alternative. The only housing the poor could afford was substandard.

And the government was planning to make the situation worse. Title I of the Housing Act of 1949 provided authorization and federal funding of the urban renewal program. So housing would be needed for the dwellers of slum housing who would be displaced. As the House Banking and Currency Committee Report put the matter:

[T]he bill recognizes that the clearance of slums and the provision of decent housing for families who live in them are inseparable. Any slum clearance which fails to assure adequate housing for the families who presently live in slums would be merely forcing them into worse conditions. This applies particularly to minority races for whom the problems of relocation are particularly difficult. [15]

The public housing provision breezed through the Senate by a vote of 57–13. But it had to withstand a hurricane of criticism in the

House of Representatives. An amendment to strike the provision initially prevailed in the House. The decision was reversed by a razor-thin margin—209 to 204 (with Representatives Richard Nixon and Gerald Ford voting against).

The senators heard the likes of "Mr. Republican" Senator Robert Taft and southern senators describe public housing as part of the Anglo-Saxon heritage, as a bulwark against fascism and communism. The House heard different voices speaking about "free bread and circuses," and a "plundering of the producing group" and a trading of a contractual and civilized state for a police and barbarian state.[16]

Beyond the rhetoric, if public housing was to be continued by a conservative Congress, a new role had to be found. In 1948, Senator Joseph McCarthy was one of the first to understand how it would not compete with private housing. Public housing would be kept remote from the private market. It would be the province of the poor.[17]

Unfortunately, the proponents of a "separation of society into people served by the market and those outside the market"[18] are often the very same people who worry about the high cost and fairness of government programs. The latter point of view can be seen in the statement of Representative Joseph Martin, even if his math wasn't sound:

> It would cost between sixteen and nineteen billions of dollars in the period of its lifetime. That is a heavy obligation to assume. . . . Less than 6 percent of our people would be in a class available to benefit by the legislation, and less than 7 percent of those available could be selected. In other words, out of every 1,000 people . . . only 4 could qualify. The limitation placed in the bill provides for those 4. The other 993 persons get nothing but increased tax bills.[19]

If Mr. Martin had problems with what the economists refer to as the program's "horizontal equity," others would have problems with the program's "political equity"—its fairness to the non-beneficiary taxpayers. Mr. Allen made this point:

[A]t the present time, there are 12,000,000 citizens who are paying monthly installments . . . into cheap homes worth probably three or four thousand dollars. Many of these homes did not have modern conveniences; yet that individual in the good old American way works nights and Sundays to improve his bathroom and other parts of his home. If, however, this bill is enacted into law his neighbor will march in and take over a home with all the modern conveniences, while the first man . . . will have to help pay for the new home of his neighbor.[20]

Supporters defended the bill by stressing the annual cost and distinguishing the legal maximum cost from the actual costs. But cost arguments place supporters on treacherous grounds. In the heat of debate, an opponent on the basis of cost can transform into an opponent on the basis of equity. With the Devil's instinct for the jugular and a Catholic's concern for the poor large family, Senator Joseph McCarthy came back to remind supporters that the only way to reduce cost was to discriminate against the very poor. He offered the supporters an amendment that would increase the per unit subsidy to allow it to cover operating costs as well as debt service.[21]

The amendment placed proponents in a predicament. They had to choose between helping the very poor and fiscal prudence. If they accepted the McCarthy amendment and asked for more money to serve the same number of people, they underscored the argument that the program was too costly. If they accepted the amendment and didn't ask for more money, fewer families would be served. If they rejected the amendment, the subsidy would be insufficient to serve the very poor. By other provisions of the legislation, the administrator's hands were so tied that they would have to serve those who needed it most. Rejecting the McCarthy amendment saved the program in the short run, though it left some difficult problems for a future day.

The Housing Act of 1949 is conventionally viewed as a high point in the history of public housing. The Act authorized federal contributions and loans for 810,000 units. Also, by permitting the Federal Annual Contribution Contract as security for bonds, it made possible the permanent financing of all the capital costs of the projects by the sale of tax-exempt bonds to private investors. In order to make the bonds more attractive, the period of financing was dropped from sixty to forty years.

The new law, however, extended the coverage of the program in ways that made the federal contributions necessary but not sufficient. These changes included: 1. Prohibiting discrimination against welfare families. 2. Granting a priority to families displaced by public construction and urban renewal. 3. Imposing maximum limits for continuing occupancy and mandating the removal of overincome households. 4. Establishing a 20 percent gap between the top rent of public housing and the bottom rent of unaided private housing in the community (since public housing income limits were tied to rents, the lower rent resulted in lower income limits). 5. Directing the program to larger families by shifting the cost basis from a per unit to a per room basis and by mandating an exemption of $100 for each minor child in calculating income.

Public housing was not to be built at the pace of 135,000 units a year. The high production hopes ran up against the hostilities in Korea and the hostility of a significant sector of Congress. By 1953, the authorization rate was down to 20,000 units a year. During the entire decade, fewer than 250,000 units were built—2 percent of the nation's housing production.

Rising costs, however, began to materialize. The annual contribution, which between 1941 and 1953 totaled $116 million, represented only 44 percent of the maximum total contribution. By the end of 1955, the percentage had risen to close to 70 percent, and by the end of the decade to 87 precent.

The money wasn't buying much in the way of social improvement. By 1957, there was a feeling abroad in the land that the public housing that replaced slum housing was physically standard but socially substandard. As Catherine Bauer wrote, "Life in the usual public housing is just not the way most American families want to live."[22] Ironically, the housing that private enterprise had felt would offer unfair competition was being viewed as uncompetitive. Chester Rapkin raised this disquieting question to public housing officials:

An analysis of recent admissions shows that roughly 60 percent of the new tenants pay the same or lower rents in public housing than in their previous slum quarters. . . . this figure would seem to indicate that public housing must not only present a unit of superior quality but it also must be of lower rent. . . . Does the potential . . . tenant find the massive developments are too institutionalized and that they tend to segregate economic, social and racial groups? Do potential . . . tenants or their adolescent children prefer the anonymity of the slum to the public badge of charity. . . .[23]

The relationship between urban renewal and public housing was one-sided. Public housing took the displaced families. However, it did not receive the sites. Until 1959, localities had to contribute one-third of the write-down value of land used for public housing as well as lose future tax revenues (when compared to alternative redevelopment). Even more important, public housing would adversely affect other redevelopment.

High land cost plus the framework of the program necessitated the construction of the high-rise projects that became the trademark of the 1950 brand of public housing—austere exteriors and bare interiors. As the ubiquitous Charles Abrams noted:

Legislative architecture, financial tyrannies and political taboos design our houses. . . . Can Frank Lloyd Wright build a public housing project on land costing $5 a square foot at $2,500 per room cost that will not look like a housing project? With the economics of the elevator dictating nothing else than a 6 or 13-story project and the . . . limitation on room cost (which means using only a certain-size brick and . . . room) will Wright's project look different than Neutra's and Neutra's different from Sert's?"[24]

Another view of the design faults of public housing comes from the acerbic Tom Wolfe, who claims that the architectural problems resulted from the fact that public housing was in the forefront of architectural design:

[T]he reigning architectural style in this the very Babylon of capitalism became worker housing [characterized by flat roofs, sheer walls, the absence of decoration or color, 7 foot ceilings and 36 inch hall-ways]. Worker housing as developed by a handful of architects [in] . . . Europe in the early 1920's was now pitched high and wide, in the form of Ivy League art-gallery annexes, museums for art patrons, apartments for the rich, corporate headquarters, city halls, country estates. It was made to serve every purpose, in fact, except housing for workers.

It was not that worker housing was never built for workers. In the 1950's and early 1960's the federal government helped finance . . . public housing projects. But somehow the workers, intellectually undeveloped as they were, managed to avoid public housing. . . . The workers—if by workers we mean people who have jobs— headed out instead to suburbs. . . . They bought houses with pitched roofs and shingles and clapboard siding . . . and they put barbecue pits and fishponds with concrete cherubs on the lawn out back, and they parked the Buick Electras out front. . . .[25]

Pruitt-Igoe, which now is a symbol of everything wrong with public housing was opened in St. Louis in 1955. The design won an award from the American Institute of Architects. It was in the classic Corbusier style, following the design of a prewar building in Marseilles, and fulfilling the vision of a Radiant City of "highrise hives of steel, glass, and concrete separated by open spaces of green lawn."[26] It was demolished in 1972.

Things became so bad that the code of government silence was broken in the fall of 1959. The Housing and Home Finance Agency prepared a background statement for a symposium of letters (the government was short on travel money) about the program. The text,[27] like the biblical Book of Lamentations is a veritable catalogue of woes. The defects of public housing included: (1) poorly located sites, (2) economic and social segregation, (3) poor design, and (4) high development costs. Some criticized public housing for having income limits that were too low, others for having income limits that were too high. While some called for ending the program, others criticized it as being inadequate. (It was like the old joke in which the patron complains to the waiter, "'The food is lousy and the portions are too small.") The old critics had not died, but the old friends were fading quickly.

THE SIXTIES: THE PRIVATE
SECTOR DOESN'T DO MUCH BETTER

In the sixties, public housing was dethroned from its position as sole ruler of the subsidized kingdom (more a fiefdom). Given the success of private enterprise in meeting the needs of middle-income Americans, it seemed obvious (or at least plausible) that what was needed was subsidy plus private know-how. The National Association of Home Builders, a traditional foe of subsidized housing, realizing it had nothing to fear from public housing, were willing to try their hands at producing for the poor.[28] The 1960s saw not only a succession of programs (a jumble of numbers) in which public subsidies to private enterprise became the vehicle of housing production for the poor but also the increasing "privatization" of public housing through a variety of "turnkey" programs that sought roles for the private sector ranging from site assembly and development to management and ownership.[29]

The 1960s also witnessed attempts to increase the volume of the programs by providing housing subsidies to families with incomes that could be classified as "moderate," as opposed to "low." The rent supplement proposal in 1965 sought to serve an "in-between" group—too poor for standard housing and too rich for public housing. The smaller subsidy per unit would result in a bigger bang for the buck.

In spite of an overwhelming Democratic majority on the tails of the Johnson landslide in 1964, the proposal ran into a great deal of legislative flak. From the left came the argument (primarily from an old friend of public housing—Senator Paul Douglas) that the program was unjustified when there were still vast unmet needs to lower-income families. So the income limits were pushed down to public housing limits. And again the problem, "A policy of taxing Peter to provide housing for Paul, who would otherwise have to live in squalor, may rest on sweet virtue. A policy of taxing Peter to provide better housing than his own for Paul is a bitter pill."[30]

The solution was to remove whatever sugar coating the project might have and to limit the location of the project. As Elie Wiesel has noted, "Generally my fellow townspeople, though they would help the poor, were not particularly fond of them." In America there was also a racial overtone. As one of the congressmen noted, "I think it is time to call a spade a spade" and then went on to discuss the possibility the program would force the integration of better-class neighborhoods.[31] Congress tinkered with the program (with the effect of limiting monthly rent for a new two-bedroom apartment to $120). The result was that there were but a few areas in the country in which units could be built. The introduction of new players from the private side did not change the rules of the game.

After the experience of the rent-supplement program, the Johnson administration was ready to give up. The major item on HUD's housing agenda in 1967 was rat eradication. Senator Charles Percy made a new and surprisingly popular proposal: the housing program of the poor could be solved through a homeownership program.

The administration at first scoffed, seeing it as a Madison Avenue solution. But a response was needed, since the proposal "A New Dawn for our Cities—A Homeownership Achievement Plan" received a glowing media reception, and at the time, the President was still planning to run for another term. What was being promised was the replacement of high-rise ghettoes, housing sullen and morose generations of welfare recipients, by pleasant and stable communities of tax-paying freeholders who, at the very least, would not burn what they owned.

THE PRODUCTION BOOM: WHEN LEGISLATIVE ACCIDENTS PRODUCE MANAGEMENT DISASTERS

The Administration reluctantly hopped on the homeownership bandwagon and as a matter of legislative symmetry added a rental program—Section 235 and Section 236. A strange thing happened: without a shift in legislative attitudes, both programs were to achieve high levels of production. It was an accident by a Congress that was in a state of innocence with regard to the mechanics of mortgage financing.

As in 1965, the Administration set out in 1968 to obtain a high-volume program. High volume requires targeting the program to higher-income families, since they require smaller subsidies. The income limits were pegged near the local median. The new feature in the proposals was an interest-differential payment to the lender (in order to permit the owner to pay only a one percent interest rate).

Congress was not enamored of the new proposal. The liberals deplored such high income-limits; the conservatives deplored the subsidies. The liberal-dominated Senate cut the income-limit to 70 percent of the median. Republican senators were critical, with Senators Wallace Bennett, John Tower, and Bourke Hickenlooper stating: "To allow that 46 percent, or almost half, of our nation's families must be supported by their government, is certainly not acceptable. . . . [B]enefits [should] be generally restricted to families with incomes ranging from $3,000 to $5,000."[32]

To assure that the households affected were genuinely interested in housing and not merely taking advantage of a good thing, the minimum rent-to-income ratio (the percentage of income that had to go for rent) was raised by the House from 20 to 25 percent. The figure was plucked from the air. (In fact, Congress in the following year used 25 percent as a *maximum* rent-to-income ratio in public housing.) The U.S. Census for 1960 showed that 80 percent of the families in the $4,000 to $4,999 income level were paying less than 25 percent. The rationale for the ratio was given in the following colloquy involving then Representative William Brock, the author of the House amendment (who had unsuccessfully attempted to impose a 25 percent ratio in the homeownership program):

> Mr. Eckhardt: If the . . . first amendment had been passed, would he offer this amendment at 30 percent . . . ?
>
> Mr. Brock: I think that I probably would and maybe 40 percent. . . . I honestly hope we could reduce this program. . . .

The more conservative House was also not satisfied by the rollback of the income limits to 70 percent of median income, and cut back (they thought) the maximum permissible income even farther

—to a figure representing 130 percent of the income that would make one eligible for public housing admission. The conference committee finally settled on a 135 percent figure.

The most knowledgeable people in the House and Senate thought that these amendments caused grave damage. Representative William Barrett, Chairman of the House Subcommittee on Housing, thought that they "cripple[d] the program. Senator William Proxmire, on the Senate side thought that the program would be limited to "paupers plus 30 percent." The main result of this arcane game of income limits and rent/income ratios, contrary to *everyone's* expectations, was to prime the program for production and to price the poor right out of the program.

The synergetic effect of bringing the wonderful world of FHA mortgage financing into the Wonderland of the Internal Revenue Code was not taken into consideration. The one percent interest rate meant that each dollar of net income had a powerful leverage effect. It would support the debt service on $27 of mortgage. If a developer were to have sufficient mortgage money to build an attractive project, he would need the highest estimate of income and the lowest estimate of expenses. As it turned out the actual income limits in most areas of the country for public housing were quite high (not to be confused with the actual income of the residents)—close to 90 percent of the local median. In estimating the gross rents in the project the assumption was always made that the project would be inhabited only by people with the maximum permissible income. And the requirement that they must pay at least 25 percent turned out to be a boon rather than a disadvantage for projecting income.

The expenses turned on "guesstimates" of future operating expenses. The name of the game was production. Congress had proclaimed a goal of 6 million new subsidized units for the decade. The Republican victory in 1968 brought George Romney to HUD. He was deeply committed to helping the poor and demonstrating that the genius of American business could be brought to government housing programs. If congressmen are attuned to the voice of their constituents, government employees are attuned to the political winds. The estimates of future expenses were low.

Developers were in heaven. The key obstacle to the production of subsidized housing is frequently neighborhood opposition. "Subsidized housing" conjures up the specter of drab and dreary projects and homeowners immediately see a decline in their most precious possession—the equity in their house. The best possible defense for HUD and the developer is to prove to the neighbors that the units, although labeled "lower-income housing," are in fact nothing of the sort. They were now able to offer this proof.

Placing a heavily subsidized rental program in the "sale of tax losses for profit" world stacks the cards in favor of higher-cost units. The size of the depreciation deduction is determined by the amount spent in developing the building. The developer is penalized if he attempts to save money during construction. This occurs in a number of ways:

(1) The more the project costs, the greater the tax shelter. A reduction in the cost results in a reduction of the mortgage, which in turn reduces the available tax benefits and lowers the syndication price of the project's equity.

(2) The mortgagor's return is equal to 6 percent of 11.11 percent of the mortgage. The lower the mortgage amount, the lower the return.

(3) The size of the construction fee and other fees paid out during the construction process is based on a percentage of cost.

Of course, higher costs and higher rents reduce the potential market for the project's units. The effect of this factor is diluted by the subsidy, which results in rents approximately 35 percent below the unsubsidized rent. And just as the market constraints are diluted, the usual HUD constraints are diluted by the nature of the subsidy payment. A $1,000 increase in costs results in only a few-dollar increase in the monthly subsidy per tenant. The increase in cost need not even result in increased expenses to the government if the project draws higher-income and therefore higher-rent-paying tenants to the project.

The increased initial cost can also be justified on the basis of improving the economic soundness of the project. The mortgage that is insured is to be amortized over forty years. A well-built and well-appointed building is an investment with a future. To paraphrase Eugene Gulledge, the head of the program, who was a builder and former president of the National Association of Home Builders, "Cost is forgotten and only the quality remains."

The consequences of this exotic brew of legislative unawareness, legal sleight of hand (in defining income limits), haphazard patterns of public housing income limits, financial leveraging, liberal administration, and tax-shelter economics was a fountain of profits that attracted producers and investors like flies to honey. A lot of housing began to be built. By the end of 1972, FHA had written insurance for close to 400,000 homes and 335,000 apartment units.[33]

The high production totals brought with them a high budgetary cost. The problem was stated as follows in the *Third Annual Report on National Housing Goals* submitted by President Nixon to Congress in June of 1971:

> In calendar year 1968, the Federal Government subsidized about 10 percent of all new housing units produced; last year, the figure was up to almost 25 percent. . . . It is estimated that subsidized units started or projected for the three fiscal years 1970–72 have already obligated the Federal Government to subsidy payments of perhaps $30 to $40 billion over the next 30 to 40 years. And assuming completion of the six million subsidized units . . . called for in the 10-year housing goals by 1978, present estimates suggest that the Federal Government will by that year be paying out at least $7.5 billion annually in subsidies. Over the life of the mortgages this could amount to a staggering total of more than $200 billion.

The second problem was one of equity. Neither the homeownership nor the rental program was able to serve the poor. The poor could not afford even the reduced debt service on the new suburban units. The poor in the program went into existing units in inner-city areas. The program, in effect, offered homeownership opportunities to marginal mortgagors in marginal neighborhoods. There was no way (except by additional subsidy) to avoid exposing the homeowner to the danger of unexpected major catastrophes without pricing him out of the market. Returning to the automobile metaphor, the low-income buyer could not afford the new subcompact. The program offered lower-priced ten-year-old gas-guzzlers. As in the used-car business there is a trade-off between lower debt service and higher operating and maintenance costs.

In the case of the rental programs the production miracles turned into management disasters when the program was directed to the poor. The mortgage processing that produced the high mortgages assumed high income and low expenses. Neither turned out to be accurate. This meant that the poor had to pay extremely high percentages of their income for rent. At one point FHA mandated that a tenant was not eligible if he or she had to pay more than 35 percent of income for rent. HUD was caught between a rock and a hard place. Owners were pleading for higher rents to cover higher than "projected" operating expenses and tenants were bleeding over the exorbitant proportion of income they were already paying. The only way the program could survive would be to attract higher-income households. However, in the words of the National Tenants Organization, this would be a "perversion of subsidies from the neediest families."

The number and geographic spread of the subsidized units highlighted the "penthouses for the poor" problem. As the following letter from a concerned constituent to his congressman indicates:

As a member of the usually silent majority . . . I believe that I should bring to your attention some things that . . . should be corrected. . . . I am a young man of 25 employed as the personnel supervisor of a growing concern . . . where my wife is also employed. Between us we earn approximately eleven thousand dollars per year and live within our means in a modest three-room apartment in a 40-year-old building. A new [subsidized] housing area . . . is now open for tenants who earn less than six thousand per annum. *These apartments are as large or larger than ours and in beautiful condition, and the rent is actually less than I am paying. Is it possible that this situation can be justified?*

SECTION 8: HOW THE WISE OWLS MADE THINGS WORSE

In January of 1973, Secretary Romney suspended the programs and resigned. President Nixon sent in a troop of the "best and the brightest" he could find, under the leadership of James T. Lynn, to set housing policy aright. After much study, they rejected the old programs and managed to find a new way to screw up. Building on philosopher George Santayana's observation, Charles Wolf has suggested the Law of Historical Lessons—"Those who don't study the past repeat it; those who do study it, will find *other* ways to err."

The choice of the new approach, "the Section 8 Leasing Program," has a fairy-tale quality to it. Until 1965, the sole approach of housing assistance was through producing new units for poor people. The Housing and Urban Development Act of 1965 contained a program that followed a different path. Dubbed Section 23 (the twenty-third section of the United States Housing Act of 1937), the local housing authority (LHA) was granted the power to lease units in privately owned buildings. The LHA would then sublease the apartments to low-income tenants. The LHA would pay the landlord the market rent and the occupants would pay what they could afford and the federal government would make up the difference.

The then HUD administrators looked down their noses at the program. The program came from the wrong side of the aisle. Sponsored by Representative William Widnall, it was the Republican alternative to the rent supplement program that relied solely on new construction. The Democrats perceived the major problem as a shortage of decent housing. They could not, therefore, see much use for a program limited to older units. It was accepted as a sop to gain Republican support for the "important" construction-oriented rent supplement program.

In spite of its dubious pedigree, Section 23 gained a foothold— primarily because it could provide instantaneous assistance. It began to blossom when an astute lawyer read the term "existing" as the opposite of "nonexistent"—the LHA lease could not take effect until the building was completed. The interpretation meant that the program could be used to support new construction. By the end of 1972, there were, under management, 30,000 new and 19,000 "nearly new" (substantially rehabilitated) units. In addition, another 38,000 new leased units were in various stages of development.

As a program that produced new units, the best that could be said for Section 23 was that it was no worse than its predecessors. Thus, HUD's Assistant Secretary could enter into the following exchange at a congressional hearing:

> Mr. Boland: Most long term leases (10 to 20 years) are barely financially feasible. . . . If escalation clauses cannot be fully funded . . . LHA's will face disastrous financial consequences. . . .
>
> Mr. Gulledge: Yes, but no more disastrous than they will on all the other units they have in management.[34]

When all the other housing programs expired in September of 1973, the leased program managed to survive. The part of the program that relied on existing units had been evaluated favorably by the scholars. The mountainous and hurried HUD housing study produced only a molehill of evidence before the witching hour (when HUD promised Congress results of its study). As a result of the absence of any evidence, Section 23 was viewed kindly as a low-income housing construction program. And so in the fall of 1973, the leasing program was spruced up, given a new title—up fifteen notches from Section 23 to Section 8—and nominated as the sole heir to the low-income throne before Congress.

Alas, after clumsy reshaping by Congress and the Executive Branch, the latest version of a new construction program for the poor was to set a new record for cost. It had a shape only a developer could love.

Stung by the defaults and troubled projects that resulted from their prior efforts, the craftsmen came up with a seemingly foolproof solution to the inadequate rent-paying ability of the tenant. The subsidy would be equal to the first year's rent, and to the extent that a tenant could contribute *anything* toward the rent the amount would be placed in a reserve. With the average rent hovering around $500 a month this meant an annual subsidy of $6,000 and a 20-year commitment by the U.S. Treasury to lay out $120,000 for each unit constructed.

Ironically, even that amount would be insufficient. The legislators overlooked the Iron Law of Section 8—the larger the initial subsidy, the sooner the project would need more funds than were initially committed. This is a matter of simple arithmetic. Assume an initial rent of $500, a tenant who can afford $100 a month, and an inflation rate of 5 percent a year. Although there is a surplus in the initial year, by year 10 there is a deficit in the reserve fund.

Table 10. The Iron Law of Section 8

Monthly Rent	Tenant Contribution	Surplus (deficit)	Reserve Fund
1. $500	$100	$100	$100
2. 525	105	80	180
3. 551	110	59	239
4. 579	116	37	276
5. 608	122	14	290
6. 638	128	(10)	280
7. 670	134	(36)	244
8. 704	141	(63)	181
9. 739	148	(91)	90
10. 776	155	(121)	(11)

The Reagan administration thought that it could help matters by requiring tenants to pay a larger share of their income, and raised the minimum contribution to 30 percent of income. A case of institutional amnesia. It forgot (or never knew) that such a high rent-to-income ratio drives higher-income people out, to be replaced by lower-income people, and increases the total subsidy or, if the total is kept constant, decreases the number to be served.

With 800,000 units either completed or under construction and a budget commitment over twenty years that would run in the hundreds of billions, the new construction program fell through the safety net. After close to half a century, the federal government had all but given up in trying to help the poorly housed by building new apartments.

Chapter 9

HOUSING ASSISTANCE AND ASSISTANCE TO HOUSING

Trying to kill two birds with one stone is a simple and powerful idea that every child learns and few adults forget. It has been reinforced in the case of housing by the addition of two powerful elements—goodness and greed—that has resulted in a powerful lobby supporting the status quo. Unfortunately, it is a sure way of missing both targets. In the case of subsidized housing, the missile has at times gone astray and ruptured the fabric of communities and neighborhoods.

The basic goal of American housing policy was set forth in the Housing Act of 1949—"the realization as soon as feasible of . . . a decent home and a suitable environment for every American family." To accomplish this goal, two things must be done. First there must be enough housing units so that decent housing exists for every family (and, with the fission of the nuclear family, every individual). If there are not enough units, it will be necessary to produce more. Second, every household must be able to afford decent housing. If this is not the case, it will be necessary to provide financial assistance to some households.

The distinction was blurred in housing subsidy programs because of the substantial housing shortage at the initiation of the programs. And, over the years, the blurring became a cataract that clouded the vision of policymakers. The basic programs for over forty years attempted to solve the housing problem by providing

180

new housing for the poor. Because there is a shortage of standard units and many of the poor live in substandard units, the production of new units for the poor has the virtue of conceptual simplicity.

As an economic matter, one can imagine a system built entirely on an incomes approach (housing allowances, housing assistance, housing vouchers, rent certificates, housing stamps, rent relief), even in the face of a housing shortage. With housing allowances, poor families would be able to pay for standard units. In response to the increase in demand, would not suppliers produce more units?

There are at least five possible scenarios for an assistance program that (1) increases the number of poor households covered and (2) provides payments at a level sufficient to permit the poor to bid for higher-quality housing without being so generous as to enable them to afford new housing.

1. The poor outbid lower-middle-income households for standard units. The latter move into the units vacated by the poor.

2. The poor do not outbid lower-middle-income households for standard units and remain residents of their original units.

   Charles Abrams describes the second scenario as a case history:

   During the depression in the 1930s, New York City's emergency bureau spent $30,000,000 annually for rent—a sum which, if paid annually, would have been sufficient to subsidize modern, low rent housing for more than half the city's slum dwellers. Yet, not a single family got a decent home. . . . The dumb-bell flats that were 30 percent empty simply filled up with the undoubling of families encouraged by rent relief and slum values zoomed. *The plan would produce no new housing for slum dwellers and would extend the life of old ones.*[1]

3. Either (1) or (2) is the case and the landlords raise prices on the units originally occupied by the poor.

4. Either (1) or (2) is the case and landlords raise prices on the units originally occupied by the poor but also improve their quality.

5. The poor pay more and obtain the standard apartments of lower-middle-income households. The latter, in turn, pay more and obtain better housing. This ripple effect ends when developers add to the housing supply, in so far as the price of the new units is competitive with the rents of older units.

Even at best, the allowance is like a game of musical chairs, with the private sector calling the tune and the public sector paying the piper. An upward shift in demand, as a result of subsidizing rents, may induce an increase supply in the long run by short-run increases in prices, according to classical economic theory. But, in the meantime, the middle-income voter is doubly taxed, first in terms of subsidizing the allowance and again in higher housing costs.

In fact, the advocacy for housing allowances preceded the enactment of the Housing Act of 1937 and continued to be the basic position of representatives of the building, real estate, and financial industries through the 1940s. The National Association of Real Estate Boards, for example, in 1943, advocated that, "Public assistance should be given directly to families that cannot pay economic rents. This assistance should be administered through local welfare boards in the form of rent certificates adjusted to the needs and requirements of the family."[2]

No favorable action was taken on any of the proposals by any committee or by either the House or Senate.[3] Before enactment of the public housing legislation, the House Committee on Education and Labor was convinced "that in dealing with the housing of families of low income, systematic low-rent housing should be substituted for relief."[4]

PRODUCTION AND ASSISTANCE

The housing allowance was considered during the debate over the public housing provisions in 1949. However, by then the thought of assistance could not be separated from the thought of building for the poor. Even as intelligent a market-oriented senator as Robert Taft could not imagine it:

I hope we may gradually solve this problem, so that we will not have to go on with public housing; but in the meantime I know of no other method of meeting the problem of low-income families, except by starting at the bottom and replacing existing slums with permanent buildings; and subsidizing the rentals sufficiently so that these buildings will not deteriorate, but will be kept up, and will not themselves become slums.

The low-income groups, of course, could be taken care of with rent-relief certificates; but the difficulty is that nobody would build any new houses on the chance that, 5 years from now, somebody would continue to issue a great many rent-relief certificates. It would not be known if the city would continue that policy or not. There could be no assurance such as there is in the pending bill, that a subsidy would definitely continue for 40 years, so that the money would ultimately be returned.[5]

A commission set up by President Eisenhower again considered the matter in the early 1950s and provided a catalogue of reasons for rejecting rent certificates. These reasons are indicative of what a long time ago the fifties were, in terms of welfare and public housing, and at the same time how persistent some of the issues are.

One of our principal objections . . . is that it would create a "dole" for housing. Every responsible social service agency has opposed it. . . . We have always, to the greatest extent possible, avoided a "dole" as being degrading to the individual. Money invested in public housing, on the other hand, adds permanent wealth to the community and to the Nation which can be liquidated and the investment recaptured when the need disappears.

A "rent certificate" plan would cause a vast number of families to go on relief despite the fact that it is only decent housing that they cannot obtain for themselves.

"[R]ent certificates" will not add to the housing supply. Even if they could be used only for standard housing, as some of its advocates now urge, we cannot see any expansion of the supply of new housing. . . .

Furthermore, there is no way of limiting the applications . . . and its aggregate cost would be far greater than the public housing program. For its proper administration—inspection of dwellings, adju-

dication of disputes between landlords and tenants, certification of
reasonable rents, the continuous selection and constant checking
upon a vast number of tenants—there would be required such a
tremendous organization that the program would fall by its own
weight.[6]

Housing allowances did appear in the panoply of housing and
urban development in the fifties and sixties, in the apparel of relocation payments. Families and individuals who were displaced
from an urban-renewal area and who were unable to obtain public
housing could receive payments to supplement their rent-paying
capacity. The payments had to be used for standard housing. The
amount of the payment was calculated by subtracting from the rent
20 percent of the recipient's income. A maximum payment of $500
per year for a two-year period was available. As of June 30, 1968,
17,687 relocation payments had been made.

Nineteen sixty-eight was an important juncture, since it was the
year in which housing allowances were looked upon favorably by
no less a body than the President's Committee on Urban Housing
(the Kaiser Committee), and a liberal President at that. The premise of the committee was that there were no production panaceas
to the housing problem:

> [T]he primary problem is not some gross inefficiency in homebuild-
> ing or some exorbitant element in the production of housing. The
> root of the problem in housing America's poor is the gap between
> the price that private enterprise must receive and the price the poor
> can afford. In short, the basic source of the problem is not poor
> housing or a faulty production system. It is poverty, itself.
>   . . . The economic gap separating millions of deprived families
> from adequate housing can only be bridged by government subsi-
> dies. Such subsidies create an effective and real market demand to
> which private enterprise has proved it will respond. . . .[7]

Once in the market mode, it was but a short step to question the
sole reliance on project subsidies to a specific dwelling for deliv-
ering housing subsidies for the benefit of the poor. The Kaiser
Committee raised the possibility of an income maintenance pro-

gram that would provide unrestricted cash payments to families or housing allowances that were tied to the family rather than to the project. With regard to the latter, the commissioners were tempted to dive into the water, but they didn't want to get their feet too wet:

> A housing allowance system appears to have several potential advantages. It would permit the consumer to make his own choice in the marketplace, a freedom which tends to enhance personal dignity. By relying on market forces, it should bring about a better matching of consumer demands and housing supply. Low-income consumers would make their own decisions of location and housing style rather than have others make these decisions for them. . . . Lastly, it is possible that a housing allowance approach would eliminate adminstrative processing of projects and would involve lower administrative costs for government than the present project subsidy systems.
>
> Several factors militate against a full-scale housing allowance program and have led to the conclusion that such a system initially be attempted on an experimental basis only. There is a strong need to stimulate new construction as quickly as possible and the project subsidy approach best lends itself to this purpose. In addition, the immediate adoption of a massive housing allowance system would be likely to inflate the cost of existing housing, at least in the short run.[8]

INCOME VERSUS HOUSING TRANSFERS

The housing allowance had broken through its eggshell. There were fledgling programs being run by 1970 (in Kansas City and Wilmington, using Model City funds), the existing portion of the Section 23 program was alive and well, and Congress authorized an experiment in the Housing Act of 1970 to demonstrate the feasibility of a housing allowance. Most of this activity was, however, below the sight line of most policymakers. During the early part of the Nixon years, HUD was hell-bent on making the Great Society production programs work and the White House was concentrating its domestic attention on the Family Assistance Plan—a radical reform of the welfare system.

Even before structural problems with the production programs aimed at the poor brought the Great Society housing programs to their knees, the New Deal foundations of the program—the existence of a housing shortage—had all but rotted away. Frank Kristof, commenting on the 1970 census noted:

> The nation's housing problem has little relationship to physical shortages of housing. If anything, the evidence suggests housing surplus rather than housing shortage. For two decades the nation has produced an average of 1.5 new housing units for each new household added. . . . Any talk of housing shortages in America constitutes one of the great mythologies in America.[9]

The task force—heavily peopled by economists who came to HUD in 1973 to examine the cadavers of the old housing programs, hoping to breathe new life into the dream of providing a decent and affordable house to every American—almost unanimously agreed that the problem facing the nation's poor was not a housing problem but an "income" (or lack thereof) problem. In the heart of their hearts (assuming economic men have that organ), they wished that the poor could be allowed to express their preferences and not be limited to housing. They would have opted for an income-maintenance approach.

Unfortunately, the administration's welfare reform proposal had just gone down to defeat. The reason was the inability of the proponents to keep the three balls of welfare reform in the air at one time—a reasonably high level of benefits, a moderate phase-out of benefits to encourage work, and a low cost to the taxpayer. As Martin Anderson, one of the jugglers,[10] noted:

> The three basic elements . . . —the level of benefits, the marginal rate of taxation and the overall cost to the taxpayers—are *inextricably linked to one another*. . . .
>
> When any two of the three basic elements . . . are set at politically acceptable levels, the remaining element becomes unaccept-

able. For example, if both the minimum welfare benefit level and the tax rate are . . . acceptable . . . the cost balloons into tens of billions of dollars, adding millions of Americans to the welfare roles. . . . [I]f the welfare benefit level is set at a politically tolerable level and the overall cost is held down, the result is a tax rate that approaches confiscatory levels and destroys the financial incentive to work. And, finally if the cost is acceptable and the tax rate is low enough . . . the level of welfare benefits . . . must be reduced to such a low level that the plan would have no chance whatsoever of being enacted. *There is no way to achieve all the politically necessary conditions of radical welfare reform at the same time.*

There are also political advantages to restricting cash transfers to specified essentials. As James Tobin has written, "The social conscience is more offended by severe inequality in nutrition and basic shelter . . . than by inequality in automobiles, books, clothes, furniture. . . ."[11] Even from a purely economic perspective, restricted transfers may have an advantage when viewed within a broadened analytical framework. As Roger Scott has written:

I have taught my students that such taxes and subsidies were "economically inefficient." Now . . . I fear I may have been mistaken. . . .

If a starving moron freely spends his money on balloons instead of food, who am I to say he is irrational in his behavior? I am forced to presume his happiness is best served by his "revealed preferences." But if I am to ask to help pay for his care then should my preferences have no weight in deciding what he will consume?[12]*

If welfare reform was not an alternative, why didn't HUD's task force recommend housing allowances? The short answer was that

---

* The matter was put more realistically by a medieval moralist's comment on Chapter 22, verse 24, of Exodus: "If lending to the poor is an obligation . . . why does the Scripture employ the conditional 'im'[if]? It is to cover the following contingencies: If you are dealing with . . . one who drinks but leaves his children without food; or one who keeps a prostitute or a married woman. In such a case better to give him food and not lend him even if you put him to shame by providing him food as charity every week." "Sefer Hasidim," cited in Leibowitz, Nehama, *Studies in Shemot,* Part 2 (W.Z.O.: 1976), 406.

they had screwed up administratively. They had promised a report to Congress by September of 1973, and after having been geared up to propose an income-maintenance approach could not shift gears quickly enough when Congress rejected the administration's Family Assistance Plan. They couldn't get their housing-allowance act together. As a student of the study, Robert Bell, has written:

> The team charged with developing alternative policies needed either a structured adversary process designed to explore the arguments for and against all plausible courses of action or explicit guidance from policy level officials about which policies to study. . . . If HUD had begun this way, it might have made better use of its staff and produced a more policy relevant report. It might, for example, have developed better answers to the objections of housing allowances raised by Congress." [13]

Instead, housing allowances were shunted off to an experimental side-rail during the seventies to provide answers to the question that concerned Congress—what would be the inflationary effects of a large-scale housing allowance program?

The segment of the Section 8 program—enacted by the Housing and Community Development Act of 1974—that was based on existing housing served as a replacement for the Section 23 program and as a surrogate for the housing allowance. In the Section 8 Certificate program, the participating tenant is usually subsidized to the extent of the difference between the rent of his apartment and 25 percent of his income. Different "fair market rents" were set for new, recently completed, and existing units by apartment size and building type for each market area.

In spite of their similarity to housing allowances, there are at least two differences. A purpose of HUD's setting the fair market rent is to insure that the beneficiary of the program gets a decent unit (the rent is set approximately at the median rent for recent movers in the market area) and that the tenant is not being overcharged. The tenant's choice is limited to apartments whose rent does not exceed the government-set rent. Good intentions, however, can lead to strange results.

In a given metropolitan area, the fair market rental for a new two-bedroom unit in an elevator apartment building may be $600. The comparable "right" rent—as defined by HUD—for an older unit may be $350 in an elevator building and $275 in a nonelevator building. If the family decides it wishes to live in a flawless non-elevator building and pay $300 a month, it cannot receive the subsidy (unless the $25 is paid "under the table"), since the rent exceeds the "right" rent.

The rent a family pays is purely derivative of its income, and HUD pays exactly the difference between the apartment rent and 25 percent of the family income. Let us return to the prior example and assume the tenant can obtain the unit for $225—$50 below the government "right rent." He has no benefit—the subsidy is just reduced by $50. A tenant in such a program has no reason to object when the landlord seizes the opportunity to obtain an extra $50 in rent. When the money belongs to everyone (i.e., the government), it belongs to no one.

ASSISTANCE TO HOUSING

Many of the Section 8 certificates lacked the characteristic of being tied to the beneficiary rather than the project. In the early seventies, many of the subsidized projects had "loan-management" problems—a euphemism for going broke. Owners were faced with rising expenses, which raised the specter of mortgage defaults. HUD had it within its power to allow the owners to raise rents. However, this would mean that many of the tenants would not be able to afford the rent. Section 8 came to the rescue and HUD granted rent certificates to the tenants (in 1986, 20 percent of all certificates were so used) of these projects. There was a hitch, however: if the tenant moves out of the unit he cannot take the subsidy with him. In effect, HUD had moved from subsidized housing assistance to assistance to subsidized housing. The latter subject more or less characterizes the history of public housing in the last quarter century.

In the early 1960s, HUD came up with a way of untying the

Gordian knot (of race and low income) that held back production by tying up the site selection process in endless tangles. Public housing agencies (PHAs) began to focus their efforts on a new strategy—building for the elderly. Although it originated as a program for families, public housing began a major transformation when, in 1956, the definition of "family" was amended to include a single person over the age of sixty-two. Armed with a new definition and a little extra subsidy money, PHAs suddenly saw site problems disappear. As Abner Silverman put it in a paper entitled "Everybody Loves Momma":

> The elderly don't make waves. They don't have children to overuse project facilities. They generally get along with their neighbors, irrespective of religion, social status or color. They try to take care of their dwellings. They live by middle-class standards.[14]

In 1952, approximately 10 percent of the tenancy in public housing was elderly. In 1960, it was still less than 20 percent. During the mid-sixties, over 50 percent of the public housing starts were in units specifically designed for the elderly. In addition, a high percentage of previously constructed efficiencies and one-bedroom units were being occupied by the elderly. By the end of 1968, 38 percent of all public housing units were occupied by the elderly.

The federal push and the locality's rush to build for the elderly is akin to the less than sage businessman who loses a bit on each sale and attempts to compensate by increasing volume. In 1959, the average income of the elderly family moving into public housing was only 57 percent of the nonelderly family. The income of the elderly could not begin to meet the required rental of the new public housing projects that were being built. In 1968, expenses on a new elevator apartment equaled $76 a month. Assuming a 25 percent rent-to-income ratio, the required break-even (assuming the federal government made all the debt-service payments) income would be $3,600. The average income of the elderly tenant moving into public housing in 1969 was under $1,800. So the operation of these new shiny buildings had to be financed by "milking" older projects.

Tenants in family projects were forced to bear either higher rents that were not in the proportion to the improvement in services or a drop in the quality of services. Either event would speed the exodus of higher-income tenants. Attempts to skimp on maintenance in order to find the money to feed the new projects backfired. The older units were once economic bargains. By the late sixties, 180,000 tenants were paying more than 25 percent of their income for rent, and some PHAs, to meet operating expenses, were charging many families rents of 50 to 75 percent of their income.[15] Ironically, the competition from other HUD programs would often heighten the dissatisfaction and provide alternate housing opportunities. The growth of the Section 235 and 236 programs in many areas was at the expense of local public housing. By 1969, many authorities were on the verge of bankruptcy.

HUD in 1969, made aware of the fiscal plight of the housing authorities, attempted to solve it by stretching the debt-service subsidy a bit. Congress, more specifically Senator Edward Brooke, wanted something more. Many of the 1968 rioters were public housing residents. Having visited low-rent projects, Senator Brooke, as a member of the Kerner Commission, could understand the rioters' dissatisfaction with the high price they were paying for their often poor housing. Tenants in Pruitt-Igoe in St. Louis had completed their first successful rent strike to protest rising rents and deteriorating conditions. The limitation of the federal subsidy to debt service had outlived its usefulness.

With Senator Brooke in the vanguard, Congress decreed that rents in public housing were to be limited to 25 percent of income, and funds to cover operating expenses were to be authorized. Congress came face to face with the ultimate horror—an open-ended authorization that it could not sweep into the future.

The seventies and eighties have been marked by an intensified emphasis on sound management focused on two areas—reducing the need for subsidies by increasing the revenues of PHAs, and imposing some system and standard for two open-ended authorizations—operating subsidies and capital improvements. Management failure is a wonderful and ubiquitous villain. Saddled with a mess, Republican administrations could (at least before Irangate) blame the Democrats, who know how to tax and legislate and next to nothing about how to manage and operate. Democratic administrations can always place the blame on the uncaring attitude of Republicans and their lack of commitment to the welfare of the poor. Congress need not take the responsibility for faulty legislation if it can berate the Executive Branch. In an exercise of true federalism, the latter blames local housing authorities who easily toss the blame back at the federal level—giving full credit to all three branches. When all else fails, there are the victims—the tenants. All bemoan the passing of the good old days when public housing served the deserving poor—the working lower-middle class.

In 1974, Congress, "greatly disturbed" with the fiscal problem, tried to turn the clock back. The Housing and Community Development Act of 1974 instructed HUD to instruct the PHAs to establish tenant selection criteria designed to assure that each project would include families with a "broad-range-of-income." In 1979, the General Accounting Office reviewed the affect of the change. What they found was that the attempt to obtain higher-income families had little effect, since it imposed a dilemma on most authorities. "No simple solution exists to motivate housing agencies to house a broad range of low-income families instead of the poorest households. Housing poor families in preference to very poor involves hard choices. Formidable problems of a moral and administrative nature exist." [16]

In the 1980s, there has been a continuing attempt to balance fiscal concerns and the needs of the poor. The Omnibus Reconciliation Act of 1981 raised rents from a maximum of 25 percent of income to a flat 30 percent. At the same time, while retaining the broad range of income requirement, the legislation severely limited the number of "lower"-income (the notch above the "very low") households that could be admitted. The discovery that the 30-percent-of-income requirement was pushing out the most economically successful tenants and decreasing the total income for some PHAs brought the Housing and Community Development Act of

1987, which allowed PHAs to drop the 30 percent requirement for their highest-income tenants. This exercise in fine tuning can easily be mistaken for the sharpening of the horns of the dilemma.

THE PRICELESS WORLD OF PUBLIC HOUSING

The public housing subsidy has to pay the difference between what the tenants are required to pay and the cost of providing the services. The setting of the cost level is difficult since there is no way of knowing whether high costs are a result of controllable factors —such as a high level of services; poor management; or fraud, waste, and abuse—or uncontrollable factors such as inflation. Usually, there is countervailing pressure against high costs because they must be reflected in the tenant's rent. But, there are no market signals in public housing. Rent is entirely a function of income and family characteristics. Higher costs are passed on to the government rather than the tenant.

In the early 1970s, the federal budget reviews were haphazard, *ad hoc,* and unsatisfactory to both the government and the housing authorities. A comprehensive, equitable, and predictable cost regulation and funding system was needed that promoted good management and constrained costs. Starting in 1974, HUD had tried, and is continuing to try, to produce such a system.

In theory, HUD could have set absolute standards for the numerous cost components, ranging from response time to maintenance calls to utility consumption. They would consider the myriad differences in over 3,000 housing authorities ranging in size from 100 to 100,000 units, housing tiny tots and centenarians, in hamlets and metropolises bordering the Caribbean Sea and within the Arctic Circle. Even if HUD had the desire and capability, it had months rather than decades to come up with a system.

To cope with the immediate problem, HUD developed the Performance Funding System (PFS). As a standard for regulating cost, it chose the "well-managed authority." The criteria used to measure performance were primarily subjective—the satisfaction of HUD field staff, PHA personnel, and tenants with the local authority. It was assumed that well-managed authorities would be more efficient and have lower costs (adjusting for items beyond the control of the PHA—for example, the age and height of the buildings). The assumption was correct in 1974.

The expense level of an authority was based on its expenditures. It was accepted if its costs were within the range of costs of a comparable well-managed authority. Utility costs were not included in these cost calculations. HUD lacked any standard, and they were treated as a "pass-through." The expense levels of authorities that were above the range (over by more than $10.31 per month) were frozen until inflation and other adjustments brought their cost within range.

Unfortunately, the system could not fulfill its ambitious mission. The performance element crumbled first. The costs of the high-performing authorities were remeasured in 1978. They were not significantly different from those of the low performers. As for energy, PHAs were passing through heating and water costs that were based on consumption that was approximately twice the national average. By 1980 the system was in crisis. Subsidy amounts were increasing steadily to the billion-dollar level as costs outpaced income. There was a growing reluctance to pay the total bill estimated by the system.

In response to a request by Congress to examine alternative methods for distributing operating subsidies, HUD, in 1981, looked to the "fair market rent" used in the Section 8 leased existing housing program. The latter would have one great advantage—avoiding the incestuous nature of the PFS, in which the standard for "public housing" was "public housing." The payment standard would be based on the rents charged in private housing. As in the Section 8 program, the PHA would receive a subsidy equal to the difference between a percentage of the tenant's income and the fair market rental. The use of the Section 8 system would also provide management incentives in public housing (to take just one example, a PHA need not concern itself with energy conservation, since HUD is paying based on its prior energy usage) and reduce the administrative complexity of tailoring the subsidy to the particular circumstances of each authority.

The system would bring uniformity to HUD's major assistance programs. Alas, it would be a Procrustean uniformity. Some authorities would obtain windfalls, while others would drop by the wayside. There is a relationship between the full costs (debt service and operating costs) of public housing and private housing in a particular city. As the HUD report to Congress acknowledged:

> [T]he system is not based on an estimate of what it costs to run the current stock of public housing projects. . . . The market rents used as a proxy for legitimate costs do not necessarily reflect the inherent costs of, for example, running older multifamily structures, paying high wages required by Federal statute, or serving large proverty-level families.
>
> Thus, it is possible that some PHAs would be unable, even through a carefully managed transition and stringent economies to reduce their costs to the levels provided by an FMR-based funding system. . . . Some PHAs might go out of business.[17]

Uniformity between programs is not necessarily a virtue. In programs in which a tenant pays the same rent irrespective of the quality of the apartment it can produce internecine warfare. The Cincinnati Housing Authority explained the high vacancy level in its smaller units as follows: "The rate of turnover is . . . exacerbated by HUD's actions to fund . . . elderly housing to the extent that elderly residents can readily move from conventional public housing to . . . units with many more amenities while paying the same rent they were charged for a public housing unit."

Charles Abrams was once heard to say that one of the problems of public housing is that the structures are built of brick instead of cardboard. With an aging, much used, and often abused housing stock, the deferral of maintenance has hastened the need for capital improvements. With housing authorities running on empty as far as reserves for replacement, the problem of funding is thrown back to the federal government, which has the choice of walking away from what in many cases is a valuable resource or spending money. Federally funded modernization is now a big-ticket item. Between 1980 and 1987, not one of the high points of federal generosity, over $8 billion has come out of the federal Treasury.

The availability of money has not produced peace. The modernization is a bitterly fought contest between PHAs, which take the position that the federal government is obligated to fund modernization of every project in America, and HUD, only too aware how little money is available in a milieu in which there are many voices eager to solve the problem by disposing of the housing problem, using the wrecker's ball if necessary.

The crucial problem is again the lack of any pricing system in public housing. A private entrepreneur has limits and guides when it comes to capital investments—the cost must bear a reasonable relationship to the expected rents. Public housing modernization is an exercise in grantsmanship. The Monopoly money aspect of federal dollars and the desire of tenants for the best when they don't have to pay for it drive PHAs to do a really bang-up job and spend the largest amount possible. Priceless housing is a costly commodity.

HUD and the PHAs are racing forward like trotters wearing blinders. Public housing, however, isn't the only game in town. Most of the poor are living outside of the walls of public housing. In many cities, at the same time expensive modernization is being carried out, private landlords are unable to make a go of it and are boarding up units or allowing the city to take them rather than continue to pay taxes. Given limited federal dollars, the choice should be between supporting one public housing unit whose costs put it into the luxury class or to support two tenants so that they can pay enough rent to enable private units to stay in the inventory and continue to pay taxes. The end result of a "successful" modernization program is likely to be a longer waiting list for public housing.

Chapter 10

MONEY AND HOUSING

During the past two decades, the arrival of money into the mortgages that finance housing has gone through a radical transformation. After a long and difficult gestation during the seventies and early eighties, which nearly killed the mother of mortgage financing (the savings and loan associations), new players and new instruments were created and with them a whole new world of mortgage financing.

The statutory and regulatory framework for the housing finance system dates back to the New Deal response to the Depression (see Chapter II). The measures adopted during the 1930s to strengthen the system established a highly regulated group of institutions that specialized in home financing—savings and loan associations and mutual savings banks ("thrifts"). As a result of the availability of federal mortgage insurance, the centerpiece of the system was the widespread acceptance of the fully amortized, fixed-rate, long-term, level-payment mortgage.

During the postwar years the thrift institutions were fruitful and multiplied. Steady economic expansion brought a plentiful supply of savings and a constantly increasing demand for mortgages. There was a substantial spread between the rates paid on savings deposits and the rates charged for mortgages. In 1960, for example, the average rate paid by thrift institutions was 3.86 percent, while the yield on mortgages was 6.22 percent. The thrifts were growing at a phenomenal pace, doubling their total assets every five years and increasing their market share of savings deposits (from less than one-fifth to more than one-half), at the expense of commercial banks, which were paying their savings depositors only 2.56 percent in 1960.[1]

By the mid-1960s, the thrifts were rudely expelled from the Garden of Eden into a world in which they would have to earn their money by the sweat of their brow. Large commercial banks began to compete more vigorously for funds. In 1964, the rate differential between commercial banks and thrifts had dwindled to 0.5 percent. As inflation moved into high gear in response to a guns-and-butter economy, the Federal Reserve clamped down on the money supply, and a severe credit crunch ensued. During 1966, interest rates jumped, and the commercial banks were allowed to raise their rates to 5.15 percent. The thrifts discovered the real world.

Money, unlike water, flows upward—to the highest interest rates. When interest in other banking institutions rises more quickly than in the thrifts, savers, especially the large ones, leapfrog the thrifts and place their money elsewhere—*disintermediation*. This occurred first when the increase in deposits in savings and loan associations precipitously dropped from $8.5 billion in 1965 to $3.6 billion in 1966. Actually more money went out than came in—the increase was a result of interest being credited to the accounts of depositors.[2] As the flow of money dried up, the drought spread to the housing industry. New housing starts dropped from 1.5 million to 700,000 units.

The thrifts were saved by Congress. But they had to pay for their protection. In September of 1966 Congress passed the Interest Control Act of 1966, in which the thrifts traded in their right to raise their rates (as long as they were in a sound condition) for the umbrella of Regulation Q—a much tighter control over their rates but one that protected them from interest-rate competition by banks. The Regulation permitted thrifts to pay depositors one-half of a percent higher interest rate than commercial banks. The differential was to offer savers a prize for choosing a thrift with limited services as opposed to a full-service bank.

THE RISE OF THE SECONDARY MARKET

The umbrella, however, offered insufficient protection from the cold winds of inflation, as savers were drawn to a wide variety of nonbank investment outlets that reflected the real rather than the regulated price of money. And the thrifts were disintermediated in 1969–1970 and in 1974–1975. Luckily for housing in the late 1960s, a new emphasis began to make the secondary market institutions more efficient suppliers of mortgage funds.

The secondary market was already active as a result of the existence of the Federal National Mortgage Association (FNMA—Fannie Mae), but was limited to FHA and VA loans. This was fine for mortgage bankers, acting as brokers and middlemen, who, being dependent on secondary sources of funds, tailored their business to standardized, readily acceptable FHA and VA underwritten loans. Thrifts, on the other hand, held most loans they originated and needed a secondary market to replenish funds when available deposits were low relative to demand for loans. Until the middle sixties, this was a problem for lenders in rapidly growing areas in the West and South; it was solved by selling participations in loans to thrifts in capital-rich slower-growing areas of the country. However, a new source of funds was needed when the fat cats in the East also had to scrounge for funds.

In 1968, Fannie Mae was partitioned in an attempt to give stronger support to the secondary mortgage market. A new agency, the Government National Mortgage Association (GNMA —Ginnie Mae) was established to carry out special assistance functions, such as purchasing below-market-interest-rate loans used in subsidy programs at 100 percent of their face value and absorbing the loss when the loans were resold. Its mission was to "buy high and sell low." FNMA became a quasi-private corporation, stockholder-owned and federally regulated, designed to provide secondary market services for FHA and VA loans.

Although Fannie Mae was also authorized to deal in conventional loans, savings and loans did not feel comfortable dealing with an institution that had been attuned to the needs of mortgage

bankers. They wanted and got their own secondary market institution—the Federal Home Loan Mortgage Corporation (FHLMC
—Freddie Mac). It was a child of the Federal Home Loan Bank
Board (which was owned by its members) and thus had the same
bloodlines as Fannie Mae—quasi-private and federally sponsored.
It was hoped that the desire for both profit and public purpose
would increase the efficiency of mortgage trading.

The major innovation came from Ginnie Mae. In early 1970,
GNMA began allowing mortgage originators to create pools of
FHA or VA loans and prepare securities backed by the monthly
mortgage payments on these loans. For a fee, GNMA would add
its guarantee. The new instrument offered investors the high yield
of mortgages that were either government insured or guaranteed,
without the usual administrative hassle of mortgage financing. The
money would be paid on a monthly basis and GNMA guaranteed
that the money would be passed through and that proper and
timely payment would be made even if underlying mortgage payment was not made.

These "pass-through" certificates created a source of mortgage
funds among institutions and people who would never have
dreamed of being mortgage financiers. It cloaked the mortgage in
the garb of the capital market. Freddie Mac followed Ginnie Mae
in 1971 and by the 1980s large private banks, such as the Bank of
America, had begun issuing pass-throughs. In the latter case, the
underlying loans were insured by private mortgage insurers. Fannie Mae was also in the marketplace guaranteeing not only FHA
mortgages but also certificates on older (and therefore less risky
since there was a greater cushion between the amount of the loan
and the value of the property) conventional loans. From the first
issue in 1970, the security issue grew to cover over $275 billion in
1984 and there is an active market in the buying and selling of the
certificates making the securities, unlike the underlying mortgage,
quite liquid.

These measures helped the mortgage-financing system muddle
through the seventies, although it was clear to everyone that any
business that was "borrowing short" and "lending long" in an
inflationary era was involved in a giant shell game. As a practical

Table 11. Residential-Mortgage Pass-Through Certificates Outstanding[3]

Millions of Dollars

Year	Total	GNMA-guaranteed	FHLMC-guaranteed	FNMA-guaranteed	FmHA-guaranteed	Private	Total as percent of residential mortgage debt outstanding
1970	$ 2,592	$ 347	$ 0	$ 0	$ 2,245	$ 0	1%
1975	29,344	18,257	1,598	0	9,489	0	5
1980	134,099	93,874	16,854	0	19,295	4,076	12
1981	153,425	105,790	19,853	717	21,804	5,261	13
1982	208,045	118,940	42,964	14,450	24,349	7,342	17
1983	278,456	159,850	57,895	25,121	25,494	10,096	20

Cumulative issues of private pass-through securities not adjusted for amortization and prepayments.

SOURCES: Government National Mortgage Association (GNMA), Federal Home Loan Mortgage Corporation (FHLMC), Federal National Mortgage Association (FNMA), Farmers Home Administration (FmHA), U.S. Department of Housing and Urban Development (HUD), and Federal Reserve Board.

matter, the deposits in these banks could be withdrawn at the whim of the depositor, without any prior notice. Yet the money of the banks is tied up in long term-mortgages. The profitability of these banks depends on the difference between their cost of money (the interest rate they paid to depositors) and the price they charged for money (the interest rate they charged their borrowers).

The borrowers held all the high cards. The fixed rate protected against subsequent interest-rate increases. The borrower held a one-sided option; if interest rates decline, he could prepay the mortgage, usually without any penalty, and obtain another mortgage at a lower interest rate. These benefits ran with the property. If the borrower decided to sell the property, the buyer could assume the mortgage under the same terms. Although this right was initially limited to FHA/VA loans, the latter feature became so ingrained that many state courts and legislatures permitted new buyers, even of conventional loans that explicitly stated that they were "due on sale," to assume the old mortgage. When this was coupled with the fact that the cost of borrowing new money was substantially less than the interest return banks were receiving on these older loans it was obvious that trouble was brewing.

Through the sixties and seventies many a commission met and many a committee held lengthy hearings on deregulating the thrifts to make them more competitive, and many a measure was proposed—the "intense political conflict among rival financial institutions, real estate interests, and the construction trades precluded the passage of any of these measures." [4]

THE TURBULENT EIGHTIES

Going into the 1980s, the thrift institutions, composed of savings and loan associations and mutual savings banks, dominated the housing finance sector. They accounted for approximately one-half of all mortgages issued. In almost all cases, the interest on these mortgages was fixed for the lengthy life of the mortgage. As interest rates rose through the seventies, the gap between the yield on new and existing loans widened. As a result of the unanticipated increases in the rate of inflation and interest rates, the thrifts had created their own subsidized mortgage scheme for borrowers, as the rates on a substantial sector of their portfolios were below the market. In some ways the operation was even more perverse than some of the government programs, since most of the depositors had lower incomes than the borrowers.

Many of the thrifts were blissfully unaware of the situation. In the late seventies, the U.S. Savings and Loan League concerned itself with traditional concerns of inflation and shortages of capital:

> Inflation has a particularly damaging impact on the housing market, mounting a dual attack on home-buying activity. In an inflationary environment, not only are housing costs pushed upward, but also household savings flows, the primary source of mortgage credit are reduced . . . Inflation thereby produces a particularly distressing environment for first-time home buyers; there can be no doubt that this must be an overriding concern in the 1980s.[5]

God was cruel to the thrifts—their wishes were granted. Major legislation in 1980 and 1982 expanded the flexibility of the thrifts and allowed them to make commercial and consumer loans. Even more important, thrifts were able to get a major infusion of new funds by offering insured money market accounts (which can be quickly converted to cash and whose rate of return is based on that of high-grade short-term instruments such as Treasury bills and certificates of deposit) with relatively low minimum deposit requirements.

In the early 1980s, the Federal Reserve Board was strangling inflation with a tight money policy that pushed interest rates into the teens. In 1981, the interest rates on new Treasury bills were over 14 percent and the prime rate was close to 19 percent. The ability to pay higher rates to attract funds succeeded only in toppling the unbalanced financial structure the thrifts were building by borrowing short at high interest rates while they had large portfolios of long-term mortgages at lower interest rates.

In 1981, the paper profits went over the cliff accompanied by many of the thrift institutions themselves; 1981 and 1982 proved to be years of record losses for the thrift industry. Of the 4,002 federally insured savings and loans in operation at the end of 1980, 843 disappeared by the end of 1982 and the number of savings banks dropped from 463 to 424 in the same period.[6]

The thrifts were experiencing the truth of the Chinese curse, "You should only live in a time of transition." The skyrocketing interest rate and the great advantage borrowers had over lenders under fixed-rate mortgages brought in their wake new mortgage instruments in which the interest rate was not set for the life of the loan. In the adjustable rate mortgage (ARM) the interest varied over the life of the loan according to the cost of funds to thrift institutions. The monthly payments would go up or down following an index based on the market rate of borrowing.

The graduated-payment mortgage (GPM) is an adjustable-payment mortgage on which the monthly payment increases according to a fixed schedule. It is designed primarily for younger families whose incomes are low (in relation to the required monthly payment, based on current interest rates) but may be expected to rise faster than average as they enter the more productive years of their life. The initial rate of interest was below the market and the low early payment was often smaller than the interest on the outstanding balance—in which case the difference was added to the balance of the loan.

The thrifts, flush with funds and faced with a weak demand from consumers were willing to take on increasingly risky loans. Builders eager to sell homes in a weak market would "buy down" mortgages by paying for a portion of the interest rate during the initial years and bankers would deem the buyers qualified at the time of origination. In other cases, banks on their own would provide discounts in the initial years to induce customers to accept ARMs or approve borrowers who would have been turned away in earlier years because the mortgage payment represented too large a percentage of their income.

When the "Devil's Birthday" came around and the first upward adjustment was made, many borrowers were hit by the shock that they could no longer afford the payment. Many discovered that as a result of negative amortization (the higher interest rate that was not paid by the borrower was added to the principal), the outstanding balance was greater than when they had started.

Unfortunately for the banks, the granting of their second wish—the end to the inflation of housing prices—discouraged homeowners from continuing to make payments. In many cases, the loans were greater than the worth of the houses, and mortgagors walked away. Unlike the 1970s the sins of underwriters were not absolved by house price inflation—the banks took their lumps when they foreclosed.

If the thrifts were doing badly in their traditional field of lending for housing, they really went astray when they used their new authority to roam in strange fields. They plunged into ill-advised real estate development, construction loans, and other high-risk ventures, as well as all of the "sure" things (at least in the 1970s) from farmland to oil patches. The outcome was disastrous. As the *New York Times* reported in June of 1986:

> The number of savings and loan associations that are effectively bankrupt—but still open—has increased fivefold since 1981, to more than 400. . . .
>
> Moreover, another 400 thrift units whose assets barely exceed liabilities will also have a hard time surviving. In all perhaps one-third of the 3,150 federally insured . . . associations now open are likely to disappear by the end of the decade. . . .
>
> Depositors should not be hurt, because the . . . Government stands behind the Federal Savings and Loan Insurance Corporation, the agency that insures the deposits up to $100,000 each. The effect of the casualties will be most acutely felt by the F.S.L.I.C., whose pool of $4.7 billion in usable assets could easily be exhausted if a large thrift unit were liquidated.
>
> . . . Indeed the thrift units that are effectively bankrupt . . . have been allowed to stay open . . . to avert an abrupt shake-out that would deplete the insurance fund and might also, by disrupting public confidence, trigger runs on smaller institutions.[7]

Since 1985, although interest rates have substantially declined, there have been runs on banks insured under state programs in Ohio and Maryland, where a combination of bad loans and bad guys have bankrupted banks and the state insurance funds. And the federal government is still grappling with the issue of the close to 600 insolvent thrifts that they have "warehoused"—allowed to stay open.

The lifesaving operation by the FSLIC (by applying the latest advances in accounting procedures) has not been a cheap one for the insurance agency. Auditors from the General Accounting Office in the first week of March in 1987 informed Congress that the FSLIC's balance sheet was $3.8 billion in the red.

Fearing that the public might respond by making a run on the federally insured savings and loans, the FSLIC responded by running to its bank—the U.S. Treasury—seeking a line of credit for the sum of $750 million. This was truly a modest sum. It is estimated that the FSLIC will need approximately $25 billion during the next five years if it pulls the plugs from the hundreds of terminally ill savings and loan associations and allows them to die in peace.

The deregulation of the thrift industry had Darwinian effects—only the strongest in human terms (smartness and plasticity) survived. After the long winters of high interest rates the winners emerged. They have prospered by adopting a new strategy. They have wised up and tried to assure that their cost of money was less than the price they were charging for mortgages. They have also shown less interest in possessions and growth for their own sake.

In 1986, thrifts made record profits through a "make and sell" approach. With interest rates dropping sharply, thrifts originated or refinanced a record $255 billion in loans. Rather than retaining all these loans, they sold a record $172 billion—much of it for packaging and sale as mortgage-backed securities. The thrifts thus earned fees for making the loans and servicing the loans after the sale and made profits selling some of their older higher-interest loans. Just as important, they reduced their reliance on the whims of depositors, and by the sale of fixed-rate mortgages insulated themselves against future interest-rate fluctuations.

Some thrifts sought to reduce the latter risk by aggressive marketing of adjustable-rate mortgages. In an atmosphere of dropping interest rates and strong demand of borrowers for the certainty of fixed-rate mortgages, it was a hard sell. The use of adjustable-rate mortgages dropped from 61 percent in 1984 to 31 percent in 1986 of all originations. When interest rates rose in 1987, the adjustable-rate mortgage again moved up in the charts. The adjustable mortgage has become a fixture on the housing-finance landscape.

The success of the thrifts has been made possible by a revolution in financing. The ultimately parochial interest, the family homestead, has been tied into the network of global money markets. The money to finance housing is primarily coming from holders of securities rather than mortgage lenders. In 1986, two-thirds of the $410 billion of new originations were passed through into the general money market and sold as securities. And the thrifts have begun to bypass American sources to directly tap European investors. Although the first Eurobond issue was made in 1984, over $2 billion was raised in 1986. The floating rates on these bonds are more likely to be pegged to the "London interbank offered quotation for three-month U.S. dollar deposits" ("Libor") than to an American index.

The innovations that marked the beginning of the decade centered on the mortgage instrument itself. In the mid-eighties, "the innovations of the mortgage market centered on mortgage securities rather than on the underlying mortgage instrument."[8] In 1983, creative underwriters, eyeing the largely untapped billions in pension funds, developed the collateralized mortgage obligation (CMO) to overcome shortcomings that had limited the market earlier.

In the past, many investment managers shied away from mortgage-backed securities because the ability of home buyers to prepay their mortgages frustrated investors who wanted a predictable yield over a predictable period. The CMO provides protection against the "prepayment" hazard. Freddie Mac divided the issue into 5 year, 12½-year, and 30-year bonds. It reduced the risk of prepayment for holders of longer maturity bonds by earmarking all early mortgage retirement payments for holders of the shorter maturity bonds.

By 1986, $48 billion in CMOs were being issued in a single year as issuers created more and more exotic instruments to meet the requirements of specific investors. There are now "Multiple 'Z' bonds," "Y tranches" with sinking funds, floating-rate "A" tranches with and without inverse floating rate "O" tranches, stripped interest certificates, senior and subordinated classes. As long as investment bankers can keep their minds on honest endeavors, one can be fairly sure that there will be a steadier flow of funds for mortgages at comparatively (to Treasury and corporate bonds) low rates and from more diverse sources in the future.

Chapter 11

THE REALITY IS ALIVE AND WELL

The Age of Aquarius arrived in the sixties. It was soon followed by the Age of Malaise in the seventies. The "sky is falling" syndrome was abroad in the land. And nowhere was it more evident than in the field of housing:

> The chief economic pulsetaker of the nation's homebuilders says the industry is in the "worst state since the depression." . . . Dr. Michael Sumichrast . . . warned that even if money markets improve there won't be a turnaround in housing without government help. The industry faces possible collapse. . . .[1]

The media focused on the sexier issue of affordability of homeownership. Would homeownership be only a dream for the baby-boom generation? Although there were crises aplenty, ranging from the shortage of resources to the shortage of stable marital relationships, in some magical and mysterious way (at least to the media) the seventies in hindsight were viewed as a golden age for single-family housing.

In 1977, Bernard Frieden, who headed up the MIT-Harvard Joint Center for Urban Studies stated the problem of homeownership:

> From the late 1940s through the 1960s, a new suburban home was within the reach of most middle-income families. Since the late

210

1960s, sales prices . . . have gone up faster than incomes and operating costs have gone up faster still. As a result, the young family
trying to buy its first home faces high prices and few choices. . . .

. . . [I]n a country where homeownership is the middle class
norm, where consumers have high expectations for their living standards, and where increases in real income have been the typical
experience for a long time, the problem is serious.[2]

George Sternlieb put the matter more succinctly: "[T]he housing
delivery system of the United States is an endangered species.
New housing costs have soared well beyond the reach of many
middle class Americans."[3]

In the first half of the seventies, housing costs seemed to have
crossed the great divide. The purchaser of a new home in 1970
faced monthly costs of approximately $217 a month ($221 in the
case of existing housing). By 1975, these costs had jumped 83
percent to $396 for a new home (63 percent to $360 for an existing
home). In those five years, the cost of new housing rose almost
twice as quickly as income. The average price of new homes went
up 89 percent, from $23,400 to $44,200. Average income rose 47
percent—from $9,867 to $14,500.[4]

Middle-income families dominated the housing market in 1965–
1966. Families earning between $5,000 and $10,000 bought 53 percent of new homes. Ten years later, new housing was for the
well-to-do. The range of the middle-income group had jumped to
between $10,000 and $20,000. Housing jumped higher, and this
group represented only one-third of the buyers. Families with incomes below $10,000 represented a paltry 4 percent of the market.

The following breakdown of monthly housing cost increases
summarizes most of the bad news.

THE GUYS IN THE WHITE HATS

Can the rise in housing costs be explained? Is there an obvious
culprit? Are the statistics suspect? The answer is yes to all three
questions. The place to start is with the biggest-ticket item—the
mortgage debt—which still represented 63 percent of the total

Table 12. Changes in Components of Homeownership Costs Median Priced New Homes, 1970–1975[5]

	Total Costs	Mortgage Payment	Insurance	Property Taxes	Maintenance & Repairs	Heat & Utilities	Interest Rate
1970	$217	$141	$ 5.65	$31.76	$12.15	$26.74	8.45%
1971	230	143	10.09	37.89	13.20	26.27	7.74
1972	256	154	6.50	47.45	15.88	31.87	7.60
1973	305	187	7.84	50.63	20.82	38.54	7.95
1974	370	224	13.12	62.80	24.00	45.35	8.92
1975	396	248	10.68	64.98	26.45	45.21	9.01
				Change 1970–1975			
	$179	$107	$ 5.03	$33.22	$14.30	$33.77	—
	82.4%	75.9%	89.0%	104.6%	117.7%	72.8%	6.6%
				Percent of Cost			
1970	100%	65%	3%	15%	6%	12%	
1975	100%	63%	3%	16%	7%	12%	

cost, although its percentage of total cost dipped slightly. Since interest rates went up only a slight bit, the key element is the price of the new house. And the culprit is the "good guys" and the government.

To return to George Sternlieb:

The standard criticism leveled at American tract development frequently focused on the failure to provide appropriate infrastructure. While the housing unit was by world standards uniquely finished . . . the infrastructure surrounding the house was relatively primitive. Sewerage facilities, sidewalk construction, school and recreational development were often inadequate. . . . In recent years, steps were taken in many jurisdictions to insure a full panoply of support elements built into the original development. . . . Much of this has been applauded as an overdue acknowledgement of the real costs of housing and . . . as being much more rationally provided at the initiation of the housing unit life cycle. . . .

What has not been appreciated . . . is that the provision of the infrastructure on the installment plan, while an economist's nightmare, tended to . . . parallel the income growth cycle of the residents. . . .

The supposed crudeness of the system, as well as the impact of those whose income did not increase commensurate with the new . . . costs, as well as a new community consciousness fearful of increasing tax rates, produced a general response requiring all infrastructure to be supplied in advance. . . . The results are far more rational, provide a better living environment . . . but effectively *exclude* a substantial portion of the market.[6]

By the mid-seventies the typical developer was being nibbled to debt. A subdivision in suburban Maryland required thirteen permit fees and four bonds during the land development stage. A south New Jersey development had to submit to a total of fourteen reviews of various stages of water, sewer and site plans, seven agency fees, four permits, and the payment of a bond before housing construction could start. At each step, there was not only the direct cost but the indirect increased cost of financing. The list of government regulations[7] that could affect the cost of housing was staggering:

Federal	Localities
Clean Air Act	Bonding Requirements
Coastal Zone Management Act	Building Codes
Consumer Product Safety Act	Energy Codes
Noise Control Act	Engineering Inspection
Water Pollution Act	Environmental Impact Reviews
FHA and VA Programs	Mechanical Codes
Flood Insurance Programs	Plat Review
Occupational Health and Safety	Sewer Connection Approval and Fee
Real Estate Settlement Procedures	Shade Tree Permits
State	Site Plan Review
Building Codes	Soil Disturbance Testing
Coastal Zone Management	Utility Connection Fees
Critical Areas Restrictions	Water Connection Approval and Fee
Land Development Acts	Zoning
Sewer Moratoria	

The scope of the government regulation went beyond the land-development stage to cover the construction and the occupancy stage. A good portion of government regulations and controls went beyond minimum health, safety, and welfare considerations. Using a hypothetical example, the Center of Urban Policy Research at Rutgers University estimated these "excess costs":

(a)	length of rezoning request—9 rather than 4 months	$ 385
(b)	environmental impact statement—9 rather than 6 months	231
(c)	ban against burning as a way to clear land	1105
(d)	excessive frontage—100 rather than 90 feet	966
(e)	underground electric utilities	273
(f)	10 inch rather than 6 inch sanitary pipe	21
(g)	underground cast iron or copper rather than plastic pipe	223
(h)	excessive floor space	1040
(i)	excess settlement costs	500

The total could push the price of a $40,000 house to $50,000, and since operating costs (property taxes and insurance) are tied to the purchase price of the house, the total cost of ownership would rise from $400 to $500 a month.[8]

The statistics and the way affordability is measured are also open to challenge. As two professors at the University of Pennsylvania put the matter:

First of all . . . they badly understate the proportion of households potentially in the new construction market. They make no adjustment for family size, either in computing likely funds available for acquiring new housing or likely demand for dwellings other than those of median size. Given the decreasing average size of households this oversight is not trivial. . . . Accumulated savings available for larger than average down payments are ignored, as are intergenerational transfers. No distinction is made between the characteristics of households likely to be in the market and characteristics of all households. . . . Finally, no significance is attached to the fact that the proportion of households who can ''afford'' a new home at any point in time is . . . substantially less than the proportion potentially in the . . . market during their life.[9]

John Weicher supports this notion, by looking at the cry of crisis historically:

The notion that new homes are suddenly getting beyond the means of typical home buyers is a hardy perennial. . . . During 1947 and 1948, the Joint Committee on Housing heard complaints that houses used to be affordable right after the war, but weren't then. It concluded: ''The field hearings . . . in city after city fully corroborate the fact that the vast majority of families today cannot afford to buy housing at present prices.''
     The price of new homes was also seen as a problem ten years ago. In the mid-1960s, Bernard Frieden wrote that ''the cost of new housing today prices most American families out of the market. . . . Ownership of new homes is effectively limited to the top quarter of American families, who earn $8,000 year or more.'' Now, however, Frieden and his co-author believe that the 1960s were a good period but that the 1970s aren't. . . .[10]

As always, there was another way to look at the statistics. The early 1970s were an abnormal period in housing because a substantial portion of single-family houses that were produced were subsidized under the section 235 housing program. Average housing prices and incomes of homeowners were thus atypically low. When the programs came to a halt, and the statistics only represented the usual collection of home buyers, it was only natural that a sharp jump should be recorded.

The standard for judging affordability (25 percent of income) was not given on Mount Sinai. In 1965, the average first year's housing cost was 28.7 percent of household income. The figure dropped to 25 percent in three years and by 1975 was less than 20 percent. The price-income ratio—the median new home sales price divided by median family income—was the same in 1965 and 1975—2.9.[11]

The mid-1970 house was not the same house as the early 1970 house. It was bigger and better. It was built on a larger lot and was more spacious. It was more likely to have a garage, central air-conditioning, fireplaces, and built-in dishwashers. If quality were held constant, the increase in price would have been 48 percent, rather than 83 percent.

While the economists heaved missives in learned journals, single-family construction continued merrily along. More than a million single-family homes were built annually in the 1976 through 1979 period. The 1.43 million built in 1977 even exceeded the totals of the early 1970s that were bloated by subsidized construction.

Rather than shutting people out of the markets, housing inflation actually gave people an opportunity and a reason to buy homes. In California, where the housing boom started, 85 percent of the buyers of new homes in 1977 were prior homeowners. This was in part due to the drop in the average age of the first-time home buyer from thirty-eight in 1965 to thirty-three in 1975 [12]—having bought an existing house at a younger age, they rode the wave of inflation to a new house.

In the bad old days, bankers would look askance at the income of the spouse. The coming of Women's Liberation and the Pill changed all that. The wife was now an unchallengeable income source. Families with double earners, in 1976, represented 43 percent of all home buyers and 59 percent of all first-time home buyers. While many relied on what was previously referred to as the

Table 13. Estimates of Real After-Tax Mortgage Rates [13]

	Average Mortgage Rate	Marginal Tax Rate (1)	After-Tax Mortgage Rate (2)	Annual Rate of Change Consumer Price Index	Real Mortgage Rate (3)
1965	5.81%	17.0%	4.82%	1.70%	3.12%
1970	8.45	19.5	6.80	5.90	.90
1975	9.01	22.0	7.03	9.10	−2.07
1976	8.99	22.0	7.01	5.80	1.21
1977	9.01	22.0	7.03	6.50	.53
1978	9.54	25.0	7.16	7.70	−.54
1979	10.77	24.0	8.19	11.30	−3.11
1980	12.65	24.0	9.61	14.40	−4.79

1. Estimated marginal tax rate for median taxpayer with family of four.
2. Average mortgage rate times (1 minus the marginal tax rate).
3. After-tax mortgage rate minus annual rate of change in CPI.

"GI Program"—Good In-Laws, others were willing to scrimp and stretch their resources. Nevertheless, half of the first-time home buyers had acquired two cars before they acquired their first house.

THE HOME AS A HEDGE AND AN INVESTMENT

There was good reason to stretch resources. The home represented more than shelter. Between 1970 and 1979, the average value of a home tripled ($17,100 to $51,300). In a poll of home buyers in 1976, 45 percent gave as their reason for purchasing the fact that the house was an "investment to dwell in." The poll also found the stretching of resources was inversely related to income. The median relationship between the value of the house and income was 2.5. However, for families with incomes over $25,000 the relationship was over 2.7. The 1977 Home Buyer Survey by the United States League of Savings Associations was entitled *Homeownership: Realizing the American Dream* and later described as a "celebration."

The savings and loans did their part. They were flush with money and they were making home buyers offers they could hardly refuse—negative real interest rates. The high rates of the late 1970s (between 9 and 12 percent) were more than canceled by the rate of change in prices and the rising tax rates of the average home buyer. As the following table indicates, the highest real rate of interest (interest rate less the marginal tax rate and annual rate of change in the consumer price index) during the fifteen-year period between 1965 and 1980 was in 1965, when the rate of interest was 5.81 percent.

It is only right that this look at the housing affordability problem in the 1970s should end where it began, at the Harvard-MIT Joint Center for Urban Research. A study on housing affordability by H. James Brown, Karl Case, and Kermit Baker [14] in the 1980s came to two conclusions. First, the total cost of owning a home relative to income declined fairly steadily from 1965 to 1979. It was a period in which tax savings and equity buildup more than offset the cash costs of homeownership. Second, there would be a housing cost problem in the 1980s.

THE ROLLER-COASTER EIGHTIES

The titles told the story of the roller-coaster decline in the homeowner sector of the market in the early 1980s. The U.S. League of Savings and Loan Associations reports on home-buyer surveys were *Homeownership: Realizing the American Dream* in 1978, *Homeownership: Coping with Inflation* in 1980, *Homeownership: The American Dream Adrift* in 1982. The last report in fact opined that it was the beginning of the end:

> The U.S. League's 1981 Home Buyer Survey . . . documents and quantifies the fact that 1981 was an extremely bad year for housing. But these findings also indicate that the 1981 housing market may not be a temporary aberration, but the beginning of new trends for the future. [15]

In mid-1983, Arthur Young, who headed up the Census Bureau's Housing division envisioned an even darker future:

We are on the verge of breaking a fundamental social compact among economic classes that we've had for decades: Work hard, be part of the capitalistic system, and one day you and your children will become property owners.[16]

It wasn't that there was a housing shortage and prices of housing were rising. It was worse. There was a drop in household formation, and vacancy rates were rising. "Let the trend keep growing, and 'you're going to see too many housing units chasing too few households who can afford to pay for them' later in this decade— eventually triggering declines in property values, he [Dr. Young] warned."[17] Nobody asked the next question. And, if prices drop, is it not true that more people will be able to afford homeownership?

The beginning of the eighties also saw the return of Calvin Coolidge's portrait to the walls of the White House. John Kenneth Galbraith's comment on the former President sheds some perspective on the harbingers of gloom:

A whole generation of historians has assailed Coolidge for . . . superficial optimism. . . . This is grossly unfair. It requires neither courage nor prescience to predict disaster. . . . Historians rejoice in crucifying the false prophet of the millennium. They never dwell on the mistake of the man who wrongly predicts Armageddon.[18]

The rapid rise in homeownership costs and a weak economy in the early eighties pushed private housing construction starts through the floor. The 2 million yearly level in 1977 and 1978 fell to a little over a million units a year in 1981 and 1982. Households formed at a slower rate. The percent of the population that were homeowners dropped. The size of new houses dropped. House price appreciation ground to a virtual halt—from 16 percent in 1978 to 2 percent in 1982. The only indicators going up were unemployment, mortgage delinquency, and interest rates.

The latter hovered around 15 percent and as Table 14 indicates a 2 percent hike in the interest rate raises the payment on a $72,000 mortgage by $100 a month, pricing about 4 million families out of the market.

Table 14. What a Difference a Point Makes in Housing Affordability[19]

Based on a 30-year mortgage, 10% down payment and assuming expenses equal 28% of income

Interest Rate	Monthly Principal and Interest Payment	Property Taxes & Insurance	Total Monthly Expenses	Annual Income Needed to Afford	Number of Families with Income Needed	Percent of Family Income Needed
			$80,300 purchase price, $72,270 mortgage			
9%	$ 582	$95	$ 677	$29,003	23,697,698	38.6%
10	635	95	730	31,273	20,996,406	34.2
11	688	95	783	33,544	18,233,721	29.7
12	744	95	839	35,943	15,900,787	25.9
13	802	95	897	38,428	14,243,176	23.2
14	860	95	955	40,912	12,643,218	20.6
15	918	95	1013	43,397	11,016,312	17.9
16	976	95	1071	45,882	9,393,129	15.3
17	1033	95	1128	48,324	7,796,911	12.7
18	1091	95	1186	50,808	6,446,265	10.5

But even during the bad time, the predictors of a long-term trend and increasing difficulties for a new generation of home buyers were using common sense and reading the tea leaves incorrectly. As a report by the National Association of Home Builders pointed out:

> [T]he number of previous owners purchasing a dwelling unit fell from 3.0 million in 1978 to 2.0 million in 1981 . . . Over the same years . . . the number of first-time buyers dropped only 20 percent, from 2.0 million to 1.6 million.
>
> Common sense alone would suggest that first-time buyers would be more adversely affected during cyclical downturns than would repeat buyers, because they tend to be younger and have smaller incomes and savings. However, unlike trade-up buyers, they are not faced with the problem of selling an existing home at a time when high interest rates are likely to reduce the sales price of that home and increase the carrying costs of a new home. . . . [They] can defer a new purchase until financial conditions improve.[20]

Not surprisingly, when the trade-up buyers returned to the market, analysts at the Joint Center of Gloom and Doom found cause for concern that the first-time buyers now made up a smaller percentage of the market.[21] A long-range report done three years earlier put the matter in a better perspective:

> While the mix of first time and trade-up buyers can fluctuate cyclically, over the long term demand should shift to the trade-up market. As the baby-boomers age, the number of young, first time home buyers will trend downward and the number of middle-aged homeowners with children will trend upward. . . . The growth of the trade-up market can therefore be expected to provide important . . . pressures that favor the construction of larger single family detached homes at a high level during the rest of the century.[22]

THE PATIENT RECOVERS

All the dire predictions came to naught as the economic and housing cycle took an upward turn, and inflation and interest rates took a downward turn in the mid-eighties. The U.S. Savings and Loan League, commenting on its 1985 housing survey, reported that home buyers were spending less and buying more. Home-buyer income had risen 18 percent since 1983 (first-time home buyer by 22 percent), and average monthly housing costs were below the level in 1981. Fewer than one-third of the home buyers were paying more than a third of their income for housing (the lowest figure since the League began its study in 1977).

And 1986 was even a better year. Interest rates continued to decline, and by December they were at 9 percent—a nine-year low. One million eight hundred thousand housing units were started—over 100,000 units above the average production level in the 1975–1979 period. The number of Americans behind in their mortgage payments by more than thirty days was down sharply— declining in each of the last three quarters of 1986 (the first time in nearly a decade that the rate has gone down for three consecutive quarters).

The only "bad" news was that the increased demand for single-family houses pushed the prices to higher levels. Prices rose faster than at any previous time in the decade—10.4 percent higher in 1986 than in 1985. The news is tempered by the fact that the average house sold in 1986 was a higher-quality house. When adjusted for differences in amenity level the average price increase was only 4.3 percent, and the plunge in interest rates more than offset the upswing in purchase prices.[23]

By November of 1987, the housing-affordability index, published by the National Association of Realtors, hit a ten-year high of 115.7—meaning 25 percent of the income of a family earning the median income ($30,963) was 115.7 percent of the income needed to qualify for a mortgage covering 80 percent of the price of the existing median-priced house ($84,200). In spite of the fact that more than half (53.6 percent) of the home-buying households in 1987 had no more than two members, the housing expense burden continued to decline—only 30.5 percent of the buyers were paying more than a quarter of their income.

The homeownership sector weathered the storm of tax reform with most of its benefits intact. Mortgage interest payments and property taxes remained deductible. However, the value of the tax deduction was cut substantially for the higher-income homeowner as the tax rate was cut to 28 percent—so that each dollar of deduction reduces taxes only by 28 cents. These changes are unlikely to greatly affect most homeowners. In 1984, one-half of owner-occupants[24] had no mortgages on their homes. And only 23 percent took itemized deductions for mortgage-interest payments.[25]

The national homeownership rate has declined from the 65.6 peak it hit in 1980. In the third quarter of 1987, it was at 64.2 percent. However, as an example of the need to be wary of statistics, the national total was smaller than the sum of the parts. *The homeownership rate, both for married couples and singles, has increased since 1980.* The rate for the former has gone up from 74.7 to 78.8 percent and the rate for the latter has increased from 45.0 to 46.9 percent. The explanation is that the decline in the overall rate reflects the strong shift in the eighties toward more single-person households, with their lower propensity to own.[26]

Homeownership, as a way of life, is alive and well in America. Although there is much noise about the difficulties the young will have in achieving their dream, there is a difference, as Paul Freund has noted, "between the sound of popguns and the crack of doom."

Chapter 12

NEW WAVE PROGRAMS IN AN AGE OF AUSTERITY

This chapter, which consists of my solutions to America's major housing problems, takes as a premise the words of Irving Kristol:

> Indeed the trouble with the thing . . . is that it is just too simple, too easy to understand. Accustomed as we are to the increasing complexity of the natural sciences, and the occult jargon of the social sciences, we are inclined to be suspicious of . . . simplicity, which we are likely to equate with naivete or wishful thinking. The average person, listening to an exposition . . . will nod his head to every point but, after it is done, will remain incredulous: if it is that obvious, what is the fuss and controversy all about? The average [expert] on the other hand, is likely to be indignant, outraged and contemptuously dismissive: what is the point of this hard won expertise in sophisticated . . . theory if . . . policy can be reduced to such plain terms.[1]

The first part will describe a homeownership program for people who are presently overhoused. The second part will present a nationwide program for production of rental housing in a country that may have more than enough decent, safe, and sanitary housing units. The third part will describe a housing assistance program that breaks all the rules about how the housing needs of poor people should be met. Finally, I will take a shot at making the public housing program manageable and describe a method of bringing the program out of the projects and into the mainstream of American housing.

NEW HOMES FOR THE ELDERLY—
OLD HOMES FOR THE YOUNG

The elderly have the highest rate of homeownership in the nation. Eighty percent of households in the 55–65 age group are homeowners; 77 percent are homeowners in the 65–74 segment; and 72 percent of those over the age of 75 own their homes. In the overwhelming proportion of the cases they have also paid off the mortgage on their homes.

Although the elderly appear to be among the best-housed segments of the population, many find that they have more house than they need or can adequately maintain. Many of the elderly remain homeowners for economic reasons. As one observer noted, "Few better alternatives exist that would not result in a major increase in the proportion of income consumed by housing costs."[2] In a substantial number of cases—either because of indifference, cost, or the inability to do it themselves—the homes fall into disrepair. This depreciation of property serves no one well. In addition, the usual house is designed for larger, younger families. As a result, the elderly often underoccupy shelter that is ill-designed for their present use, and close off a significant portion of potential housing to a new generation of prospective homeowners beginning their family cycle.

This is not a uniquely American problem. Surveys of homeowners in England found that half of the elderly respondents felt that their present home was unsatisfactory as a place to retire. The reasons seem universal:

The greatest number of responses concerned the size of house [⅓] . . . particularly for those whose families had grown up and left.
Reference was frequently made to the difficulties of maintaining

. . . for example, decorating or cleaning windows; in addition the cost of services such as heating . . . which are related to size were a concern to many (20 percent).

Almost a sixth [mentioned stairs] . . . the toilet not being on the ground floor presented difficulties. Over a third . . . felt the garden was likely to be a problem in the future . . . [referring] to . . . mowing the lawn, cutting hedges, and generally keeping it tidy.[3]

This housing mismatch is also causing problems in suburbia. A recent article in the *Wall Street Journal* entitled "Suburban Population Ages, Causes Conflicts and Radical Changes" states:

The aging of suburbia is causing radical changes in the character and politics of countless bedroom communities. It is leading to school closings, property tax revolts and demands . . . for services for the elderly. Few suburbs are prepared to meet the needs of an older population. Subdivisions of single family homes sprang up like crab grass outside of major cities, and their town zoning laws and institutions catered to households with young children.

At the other end of the age spectrum, the cost of housing has priced many out of the homeownership market. To make matters worse, many landlords have decided that they do not wish to cater to kids. A 1980 study for the federal government revealed that one-quarter of the nation's rental units banned children entirely and an additional 50 percent limited them by number, age, or other factors.[4]

The condominium subsidy program described here would help solve both of these problems, while at the same time minimizing the cost to the government. It would be open to all elderly households who elected to move into condominiums and live there for at least nine months of the year. A condominium arrangement (whether high-rise, garden-type, or townhouse), is well suited for occupancy by the elderly because each household owns its unit and a proportionate share of the common space. The residents are free both physically and fiscally. They are free from mowing the lawn and raking the leaves, and free to make mortgage arrangements that suit their particular situation. The program in some areas would merely reallocate existing housing in a way that accommodates the desires of both old and young. In other areas it would increase housing production at a relatively low cost and thereby eliminate the need for building large high-cost units for younger households.

The average value of the elderly couple's home in 1983 was $52,300; for the elderly single, $49,200. The median value of a four-room owned unit (most likely a condominium) was $37,800.[5] In areas in which the costs of condominiums are high, it is likely the value of homes would also be high. In the typical case, however, the household could purchase the unit from the proceeds of the sale of its home and could be left with a few thousand dollars of pocket money. It might be noted that a recent rating by Rand–McNally of Retirement Places (based on cost of living, climate, personal safety, services, housing, and leisure living) listed the following places in the top ten: Murray–Kentucky Lake, Kentucky; Clayton–Clarkesville, Georgia; Hot Springs–Lake Ouachita, Arkansas; Grand Lake–Lake Tenkiller, Oklahoma; Fayetteville, Arkansas; St. George–Zion, Utah; Brownsville–Harlington, Texas; Bloomington–Brown County, Indiana; San Antonio, Texas; Port Angeles–Strait of Juan de Fuca, Washington. Miami was fifty-first.

The traditional way of aiding homeowners is through subsidies that lower either the down-payment requirements or the monthly debt-service payment. Concentrating on the mortgage is appropriate for young, asset-poor families with good future income prospects. It is inappropriate for asset-rich households with poor future income prospects.

The subsidy in the proposed scheme would be tied to the non-debt-service components (that is, real estate taxes, insurance, and operating expenses) of housing cost. It would be paid only when these expenses exceed 20 percent of household income and would be limited to the amounts in excess of 20 percent. Thus, the program would protect elderly owners from increases in housing costs that were not matched by increases in income. And, unlike reverse annuity mortgage schemes by which the owners draw down the equity of their homes in monthly installments, there is no danger that the owners will "outlive" their equity and be forced to repay the loan with interest out of what may be quite limited resources. This assures the elderly household that it will never have to invade the principal of its home to cover its housing costs.

The condominium has the added advantage that there can be independent verifications and checks on operating costs. The monthly fee provides a convenient measure of the expenses to be subsidized while the existence of other owners who will not necessarily be subsidized provides a check on costs. To further ensure that owners do not take a free ride on maintenance costs, the subsidy could be limited to, for example, 50 percent of the first $1,000 of non-debt-service costs, 25 percent of the second $1,000 and 10 percent of an amount over $2,000, up to an amount set by regulation. The maximum subsidy for a unit with expenses of $2,400 would then be $790 ($500 or 50 percent of the first $1,000, plus $250 or 25 percent of the second thousand, plus $40 or 10 percent of the next $4,000). In 1983, the monthly median operating expenses for new units without mortgages was $170 per month (within metropolitan areas, $202 per month). The median size of these new units was 5.2 room.[6]

Table 15 shows subsidy payments for households at various levels of income and expenses. We can see that the subsidy program meets the twin goals of hedging against high costs of the elderly while keeping the overall program inexpensive for taxpayers.

There are approximately 7 million households 65 and older with incomes between $5,000 and $12,500.[8] A program covering 100,000 units, assuming an average subsidy of $600, would cost $60 million a year. Unlike present programs, the subsidy would have accomplished its purpose once the moderate-income elderly family moved and there was a reallocation of old space or the production of new space. The subsidy, therefore, ceases when the initial household moves on or passes on. If we assume an average tenure of ten years, the total cost would be $600 million.

There is an extra benefit that will affect the well-being of the elderly. Gerontologists have studied the reaction of a group of elderly who voluntarily moved to smaller units. They found:

Table 15. Estimated Subsidy Payments for Operating Costs and Utilities[7]
(By Income Class)

Income	Operating Costs	Maximum Subsidy	Actual Subsidy[a]	Subsidy/Cost (Percent)
$12,000	$1,600	$ 625	$ 0	0
	2,000	750	0	0
	2,400	790	0	0
	2,800	830	400	14
10,000	1,600	625	0	0
	2,000	750	0	0
	2,400	790	400	17
	2,800	830	800	29
8,000	1,600	625	0	0
	2,000	750	400	20
	2,400	800	790	33
	2,800	1,200	830	30
6,000	1,600	625	400	25
	2,000	800	750	38
	2,400	1,200	790	33
	2,800	1,600	830	30

[a] The lesser of (costs − 20% of income) or (50% of the first $1,000 of costs, 25% of second $2,000, and 10% of amount in excess of $2,000).

The effect of the dwelling size was always such that the *smaller* size was associated with improved well-being. It is probable that the most favorable moves were from those large units in unfavorable settings to small ones in improved settings.

In addition, this finding suggests that there may have been something satisfying the competence of residents in reducing the size of the dwelling and concomitantly the demands of their energies.[9]

The present mission of the Office of Management and Budget is to search, using its standards of efficiency and equity, for demerits in any program that has any dollar figure connected with it. A cheap program is not necessarily an efficient one. If some of the elderly being subsidized would have moved to smaller units even without a subsidy, each dollar spent would produce less than a dollar in benefits. The number of such households in the latter category is an issue of program design and conjecture. Although the program is not aimed at the poor elderly,* an income limit would ensure that the critical factor in the move would be the "possibility" of a subsidy payment. An income limit of approximately $12,000 (or 120 percent of the median elderly income in the locality) would seem to be the level at which the subsidy would make a difference to stay or move. The word possibility is in quotation marks to indicate that the receipt of a certificate and the receipt of a payment is not necessarily the same. HUD program officials are well aware of the number of needy certificate recipients who are unable to find a unit that meets HUD's standards and who, therefore, never receive a subsidy.

The condominium program presents a different scenario. The homeowner sells his house and moves to a condominium because he has a lifetime limited guarantee as far as housing costs. It then turns out that because his income did not decrease as quickly as he expected or housing costs did not increase as quickly, the subsidy is never used or used only during the later years of the household's tenure. The government would then realize more than a dollar's worth of benefit for every dollar expended. In addition, there are benefits to the young families who are able to obtain homes and also savings to local governments (and the federal treasury) that need not float bonds to build up-county roads and schools at the same time down-county schools are being closed.

Is it fair? Can we justify a program that is not directed to the neediest? The question wrongly assumes that the program is meant to replace present programs that are directed to poor renters (although many public housing projects have their highest vacancy rates in elderly projects). A reallocation of housing will help young couples looking for homes and poor renters looking for apartments. The loosening of the market will transform certificates into leases. The "elderly" are not a homogeneous group. There is a world of difference between the fifty-eight-year-old empty-nester and the eighty-five-year-old nursing-home patient. All sorts of

---

* Note, however, almost all the families would qualify as *very low income* under HUD rules. To give some representative income limits for a one-person household: Yazoo, Mississippi—$7,500; Hickory, North Carolina—$9,750; Passaic, New Jersey—$13,950; Norwalk, Connecticut—$18,300.

housing options are needed, covering ownership as well as rental —ranging from maintenance assistance for poor elderly homeowners to high-rise boardinghouses for the very poor elderly who have been displaced from single-room occupancy hotels.[10]

Since this is not a universal subsidy program, how will the participants be chosen? The program is only tangentially based on need. The main objective is a better use of the nation's housing inventory; the benefit given to the elderly household is incidental to the program. If homeownership, a moderate level of income, and a geographic spread are the only criteria, can we do better than a first-come first-served basis?

Yes, at least in a financial sense, if the right to distribute the subsidy certificates were auctioned off. Who would pay to take over the government's job? Here's a list of candidates—real estate brokers, builders, children of eligible parents. The broker, ever eager to have a leg up on the competition, will be buying a better chance of closing a deal. He will have an answer to the question posed by the elderly prospect, "Where will I live if I sell my house, and will I be able to afford it?" The broker, because of the availability of the lifetime guarantee, can allay the latter fear. The bottom line is the possibility of two commissions—one for the sale of the house and one for the purchase of a condominium. It is especially attractive to nationwide real estate networks, since they can show not only local alternatives but also alternatives in other and perhaps warmer climates. The fact that the holder of the commitment is a person or a firm that has put up cold-cash guarantees that a strong effort will be made to publicize the program.

Builders or owners of buildings that are undergoing conversion (or even investors who may own a block of condominium units) will also be interested in a scheme that could provide their apartments with a unique feature. It makes far more sense to buy a commitment for $3,000 than to slash the price of an apartment by $10,000.

The purchase of the subsidy certificate by the middle-aged children of an elderly couple could buy peace of mind. For the price of a four-week vacation in Arizona, the "kids" could provide their parents with a lifetime of carefree housing that is only a telephone call away. And the more mercenary could assure that their inheritance will not be dissipated. The commitments would be negotiable. Even if the parents do not want the condominium, it could be transferred to someone who would use it. Since the commitments are meant to be more than speculative items, there would be a time limit (with renewal for a fee).

The federal government's role would be limited to consumer protection. A face-to-face meeting would be required between a HUD representative and the recipient before he sells his home. The building into which he moves would have to meet HUD local standards, be in a moderate-cost range, and have a management scheme that is fair and reasonable (for example, no recreational leases). The recipient will also be informed that operating costs are limited to traditional housing items and would not include such services as health-club fees.

The possibility that the government will run a surplus on a subsidy program (assuming the distribution rights are sold for $3,000 a unit and the subsidy is $600 a year) raises the possibility that OMB will instruct HUD to increase the volume of the program— running a Ponzi scheme (that the next administration will have to pay for) is better politics than selling oil-drilling rights in Yellowstone Park in order to reduce the budget deficit.

CARROTS, NOT CRUTCHES

The conclusion of prior chapters was that a stortage of rental housing was not where the problem was. Facts may not make good politics, or a production program may be the price that has to be paid for a large-scale housing assistance program. In this section, before setting out a number of production programs, I will discuss the criteria that should govern their selection.

1. **Effectiveness.** The program should work. This requires that the designers know the real world of sticks and bricks as well as the paper world of words and numbers. The history of housing legislation is littered with programs that failed to perform. The public housing program's authorization in 1949 of 800,000

units in six years took two decades to fulfill. The initial 500,000-unit rent-supplement proposal in 1965 fizzled to a total production of less than 100,000 in less than a decade. Section 243 of the Emergency Home Finance Act of 1970 (HOAP—Housing Opportunity Allowance Program) resulted in fewer than 10,000 units (out of 125,000 authorized) before it disappeared from sight.

There are three sources of failure—conceptual, structural, or administrative. The problems encountered by public housing in the fifties and sixties were in the first area. The program machinery was able to pump out the subsidy dollars. The site selection and other problems that plagued family projects and hampered production resulted from fundamental dilemmas of the production-for-the-poor strategy. The inability of the rent supplement and Section 235 programs to produce new housing in northern metropolitan areas, on the other hand, were structural. The statutory mortgage limits were simply too low. The unworkability of the Section 243 program, a shallow subsidy production program operated by the Federal Home Loan Bank Board, was caused in large part by the lack of administrative machinery and experience of the Bank Board.

2. **Efficiency.** The program should not merely replace an unsubsidized unit with a subsidized unit. The crucial measure is the cost of the incremental unit. One of the advantages of the production-for-the-poor programs was that the measurement of the incremental unit was fairly simple. Although the cost per unit was high, it was fairly certain that the housing unit would not have been built but for the subsidy.

Conversely, a small subsidy to a buyer of a new home may not be a particularly efficient production program, or in the end cheap if he would have bought the home anyway, and the subsidy only allows the purchase of a more expensive house. The need is for the golden mean—the subsidy must be targeted to a family whose income is high enough not to necessitate a large subsidy, yet low enough so that it would otherwise not be able to afford new housing.

3. **Effective Incentive.** Building the incremental unit is not enough. Although there may be a shortage of decent units in the

nation, there are many places, either because of population and industry shifts or overbuilding, where there is more than enough housing. The developer should only be rewarded for building the unit where it is needed. A profit should not be reaped if it involves the rape of the taxpayer. The subsidy should not bail out a poor lender, builder, or marketer.

One of the great weaknesses of the production-for-the-poor programs was that the developer was so insulated from competition that he could ignore market considerations. The fact that there is an oversupply in the private market does not deter the seller of a product who is able to undercut the market price by a substantial margin. Beneficiaries of a program cannot be relied upon to police it. They will be quite ready to take part in a program that offers a bargain of $50 a month, although the cost to the taxpayer may be $100 a month. Sophisticated consumers bought overappraised Section 235 homes as long as the monthly payment was below that of unsubsidized homes.

One of the great ironies is that the federal government is often hoist with its own petard. Many of HUD's production successes exacerbated its own management problems. It is difficult to dispose of low-priced foreclosed homes in the vicinity of new subsidized units that carry a lower monthly cost. It is difficult to keep an older subsidized project fully rented when a newer one opens next door with a lower rent schedule because of a larger subsidy or a lower minimum-rent requirement.

A tax-credit proposal passed in the spring of 1975, providing a household with a $2,000 tax credit if it purchased a previously unoccupied home completed prior to March of 1975, was a marvelously perverse incentive. In was basically a bailout of builders who had misjudged their markets and were stuck with an inventory of unsold homes. Rather than letting the builder and lender take their losses, with the ripple effect putting downward pressure on the market, the provision propped up the less competent. Even worse, new starts were delayed since they had to compete with the subsidized units.

4. **Administrative Simplicity.** The program should be simple to administer and streamlined to permit speedy action. Since time

is money, time is the most precious commodity available to the private entrepreneur—especially one as heavily leveraged as the developer. To the maximum extent possible the government should rely on existing institutions to take care of the day-to-day processing and administration. If it wishes to have a volume program the government must assume the role of a wholesaler rather than that of a retailer.

The term "maximum extent possible" is used since there is a conflict in criteria. The necessity to target a given population for the purpose of efficiency will require means testing and a selection process, and so some red tape will alway accompany a subsidized program. In addition, in a program that lacks effective incentives and in which the discipline of the marketplace is absent, strict adherence to this criterion can be an invitation to disaster. In turning over management of the Section 235 program (a program that required wise counsel and personal tailoring) to wholesale-oriented mortgage bankers, HUD managed to bury itself in the rubble of urban decay.

5. **Minimized Opportunity for Fraud.** Whenever a subsidy program provides someone with a large benefit and the process involves a great deal of discretion, temptation rears its ugly head. When a program is structured so that only a small percentage of either the developers or the consumers partake of the government's beneficence, we are asking for trouble.

A program that maximizes temptation also maximizes the need for government regulation and supervision. A large part of the red tape that ensnarls programs represents attempts to secure movable objects from the sticky-fingered among the general populace. In like manner, ineffective incentives tend to produce walls of paper. When it turned out in the late 1940s that developers could obtain large profits by "mortgaging out," leaving FHA holding tenantless buildings, the ensuing scandal brought requirements that are now criticized as bureaucratic red tape.

When a mortgage in the Section 236 program can only be justified by overestimating the income of tenants and underestimating expenses, there is an ultimate day of reckoning. When that day came, all of HUD's masons and all the heavy layers of administrative patchwork were insufficient to shore up a program whose surface was undermined with structural defects.

6. Minimize Unfairness.   There will always be traces of unfairness in any nonuniversal subsidy. The subsidy, however, may be necessary in order to achieve social justice. Much of the debate over social programs is a debate between justice and equity. Perfect equity can be synonymous with the unjust society. Since the decision in the debate must wait until Judgment Day, we are usually left with both sides banging the table while one stresses the unfairness of the program and the other the fact that a journey of 1,000 miles must start with a single step. The $64,000 political question is how to do justice while causing a minimum of unfairness.

There are three aspects to this problem. The program should minimize unfairness between the beneficiary and his economic peers (horizontal equity) and between the beneficiary and those above (political equity) and below him (vertical equity) on the economic totem pole. If the opportunity to benefit is available to all and the selection process is fair, the horizontal equity is satisfied. The pain of not receiving a subsidy is no worse than the pain of "losing" a lottery an economic equal has "won." If the subsidy enables the economic recipient to obtain better housing but at a greater effort (a higher rent-to-income ratio) than a household with higher income, the higher-income household may overlook the recipient's good luck. If the subsidy assists the higher-income household to obtain new housing, any sting of unfairness to those lower on the totem pole can be salved if there is also a benefit to them in the form of increased housing opportunity—if the subsidy to some middle-class households is the lubricant for a smoother housing-assistance program.

Begin at the beginning. There is housing *production* and there is housing *assistance*. The focus of housing production is the creation of new dwellings; its prime justification is the nation's need for additional dwellings. The focus of housing assistance is the need of some citizens for a subsidy if they are to be able to afford decent housing, and not necessarily new housing; its prime justification is the community's obligation to provide to all its citizens the basic necessities of life.

The key to a new form of rental subsidy program is the establishment of a new market and time frame. The fact that the program would be aimed only at increasing production and not at maintaining long-range financial assistance would enable the relationship between the government and the producer to be shorter and sweeter. The subsidy would be a carrot and not a crutch. It would be a reward for competence, and the drop in the subsidy amount would be matched by an increase in profit margins, if the producer competently manufactured, marketed, and managed his merchandise.

Under the program, the subsidy would be available only for occupancy of new buildings, and only to the initial tenant. The beneficiary would be required to pay at least 25 percent of his income for rent. The subsidy would be the lesser of (1) the difference between the rent and 25 percent of the tenant's income, and (2) 25 percent of rent (so that if the rent were $500 a month the maximum subsidy would equal $125). The unit's rent would have to be equal or less than the rent of a well-designed and well-managed middle-income unit in the locality.

The program would operate in this way. For each housing market, HUD, as it has been doing for the new construction segment of the Section 8 program, would set a market rental for new units taking into account the size and type of dwelling. The subsidy would be available to *all* developers of new units under the fixed rents. The developer, when the units were ready for occupancy, would certify that the rents were at or below the amount set and would receive a commitment for a full subsidy for 25 percent of his units. For a 100-unit project with $500-a-month rentals the total monthly subsidy would be $3125.

The developer would be free to distribute the allocation any way he chose. He could reduce the rent on 25 percent of his units by the full $125 a month, or on 100 of the units by $31.25 each, or in any other combination and permutation, as long as (1) no unit subsidy exceeded $125, (2) the subsidy was used for moderate-rent units, and (3) the beneficiary was spending more than 25 percent of his income. The developer would choose the tenants and present an income certification to HUD.

The landlord would not have to use the commitment. Under the plan, the developer would be free to rent without the benefit of the subsidy to anyone at any rent. In fact the rent on a unit would be fixed (although adjusted annually to take into account changes in operating expenses in the market) only as long as a subsidized tenant lived in it. If the tenant graduated out of the subsidy or moved out of the apartment, the subsidy would be forever lost.

Unlike current programs in which it is heads the developer wins and tails the government loses,* HUD does not take the loss if the developer builds into a housing glut or misses his market or manages the property poorly.

The advantage of such a program is that it involves a minimum of regulation (even the income-certification requirements can be done on an exception basis—after the initial year, tenant income is assumed to rise sufficiently to cut subsidy by 20 percent unless the tenant can prove that his income has not increased). The program is far cheaper than current programs. Given turnover, the average subsidy of $1,500 a year can be expected to run for five years, or $7,500, and if the subsidy commitment is used to get the developer off the fence and into a market that needs the units, almost nothing. There is little risk for the government, since the projects don't need insurance as a prerequisite for participation and there is a strong incentive for good management. The major disadvantage is that this is a new ballgame; more important, there is no way of knowing how high the caloric content of carrot has to be to entice the developer without allowing him to get fat on units he would have built without the subsidy.

* The phenomenon occurs both at the initial stages and at the end of the subsidy period. There is a ticking time-bomb situation in terms of assisted housing since the interest-based subsidy programs (which started in 1961) allow the owner to refinance and get out from under the regulations requiring that occupancy be limited to the poor (after twenty years). The successful projects will bail out of the program (requiring HUD to expand its housing-assistance program) and the unsuccessful ones will remain, many of the latter needing major repairs (requiring a major input of capital).[11]

A variation of the program may provide an answer. Instead of partially subsidizing all the owners, HUD would be willing to subsidize all the units at the rate of $1,500 a unit (or $150,000 for 100 unit project) a year for some of the owners in a given area. The owners would be selected by a "Dutch auction"—by low bids; $150,000 would be the most HUD would offer. The developer who would be willing to build the units at the lowest subsidy amount would be awarded the commitment.

At present, all the pressure is to receive the highest subsidy. The reverse auction reverses the pressure and provides HUD with a firm market basis. It also ensures honesty in the allocation process. This program could be refined by a willingness of the government to buy back the subsidy when the payments actually needed are less than the contract commitment (since the rules as to who can receive the subsidy would still apply). This would provide a strong incentive not to use the subsidy. And to reiterate, we would not be taking the money from needy tenants. Quite the contrary. The savings could be used to expand the production program or extend assistance programs.

Many of the features of these proposals will sound strange to the cognoscenti in the field. However, given the track record of those who know how the game is played, this may not be a disadvantage.

RESPECTING THE INTELLIGENCE OF THE POOR

Over the decade of the seventies HUD ran an Experimental Housing Allowance Program that involved tens of thousands of households at a cost of about $200 million. At the end there were more questions than answers. There was even the question of why the experiment had imposed housing standards. Katherine Bradbury and Anthony Downs, summarizing a conference sponsored by HUD in 1979 that brought together academic specialists and the contractors who ran the experiment for HUD, asked:

[S]hould society try to impose housing quality standards on *anyone*, in the absence of a clearly established relationship between such standards and the quality of human life? . . . Even expert, highly trained housing inspectors did not agree how to classify specific housing units. . . . Even more important, there is almost no evidence that moving to a high quality housing unit (as defined by traditional standards) improves the health, incomes, welfare or happiness of households formerly living in low quality or substandard units. So why should society try to force people to reside in the former housing. . . . Moreover, no matter what housing standards are used, there will be many cases in which specific houses will be disqualified for what appear to be trivial reasons, such as having windows that are several square inches too small.[12]

There was evidence that the federal housing standards were out of touch with the preferences of many poor families. In order to qualify for an allowance, a family had to live in a standard unit, in line with housing codes developed by building code or public health officials. A family who did not live in a standard unit had four options: (1) remain in their unit and get it repaired and obtain a subsidy; (2) move to a unit that met the standard and qualified for the subsidy; (3) remain in their unit and not get it brought up to standard and pass up the subsidy; or (4) move to another unit even though it did not meet the standard.

The repairs necessary to bring the units up to standards were usually quite small. After the families made their choice, the researchers returned to ask the households if they were "very satisfied" with their housing. The most satisfied (70 percent in the very satisfied category) were those who remained in a unit that was brought up to the standard necessary to qualify for a subsidy. Surprisingly, however, 45 percent of those who remained in a unit that failed to meet the standard were also "very satisfied," compared to the 30 percent who moved and qualified for the subsidy and the 19 percent who moved and failed to qualify. The poor were ready to take the money and not run. However, if the choice were to lose the money and stay put or take the money and move to a higher-quality unit, the poor preferred to stay put. To Bernard Frieden, the high satisfaction level of the families who did not move and did not receive an allowance made the experiment a success because it raised a new and troublesome issue of housing policy:

An important question for the next wave of housing programs is: Who should decide how much a family ought to consume and where it ought to live, the family or an administrator who sets the standards? . . . There may conceivably be public benefits involved that would justify overriding the preferences of the poor themselves and requiring them to pay for better housing than they would otherwise choose to do. If that is so, federal officials have a responsibility to present the case for setting aside the wishes of the poor.[13]

This section will attempt to answer Frieden's question and present a new wave program that can accommodate the desires of the poor and those of the federal government. Among the issues to be discussed are:

1. Can we trust the judgment of the poor in the case of housing?

2. Should different rules apply to food and housing?

3. What are the benefits and costs of doing away with federal standards?

4. What is the justification for overriding the preferences in the housing allowance experiment?

5. Present a new wave program that can accommodate the desires of the poor and those of the federal government.

The Annual Housing Survey conducted jointly by the Bureau of Census and HUD asks occupants to rate their housing as an excellent, good, fair, or poor place to live. A study[14] on resident satisfaction obtained ratings of poor renter households (income under $7,000) in the largest cities in the country. The ratings were based on a weighted scoring system in which excellent was given a 4, good a 3, fair a 2, and poor a 1.

The results revealed that the poor were fairly satisfied with their housing. The national average was a B− (2.65). The question immediately raised was, how realiable were the ratings? Do the subjective ratings reflect an objective reality? Do high raters have lower expectations? Do low raters have more defects or are they simply crankier?

To find out, the ratings were matched to an objective measure of the quality of the residence. In a postplumbing era, one has to go beyond the traditional question about kitchen and plumbing facilities. The quality differentials that exist relate to the reliablity of the services and the maintenance of the structure.

Maintenance of the structure was chosen as an objective check against the ratings of the occupants. The choice was dictated by two considerations. The survey went into great detail in the area of structural soundness. There were six possible defects relating to peeling paint, broken plaster, cracks in the walls, holes in the floors, leaks in the roof, and leaks in the basement. Other items, such as the reliability of the heating system, were not as important in the South as in the North.

There was an almost perfect match in forty-one cities (see Appendix B) between ratings and the objective quality standards. On a national basis, 87 percent of the units rated excellent; 78 percent of the good, 58 percent of the fair, and 29 percent of the poor had no structural flaws. The better the rating, the fewer the seriously inadequate (more than three defects) units—1.4 percent of the excellent, 3.4 percent of the good, 11 percent of the fair, and 38 percent of the poor. The subjective ratings of the poor seem as good if not better than that of the highly trained inspectors.

In fact this raises the question: Do we need checkers at all in the housing programs? We don't have someone checking shopping bags of food-stamp recipients to ensure that the purchases add up to a nutritious diet. The reason for the distinction is practical and historical. An inspector for every shopping bag would cause a consumer revolt, since it would slow down the turtle pace of supermarket checkout lines, and require a sophisticated understanding of cupboard inventory and household food consumption that seems beyond our capability. And historically, at the inception of the food-stamp program, it was obvious the problem was not an inadequate supply of food. In contrast, when the housing programs began fifty years ago more than one-third of the nation was ill-housed.

At present, the focus of housing policy has shifted to the rent burden of the poor. The policies based on affordability, however, are being carried out by programs designed for a bygone age. They are premised on the belief that unscrupulous landlords will take advantage of incompetent clients and make them pay good (government) money for bad housing. (Even the legislation authorizing the housing allowance required that the recipient of an allowance had to live in standard housing.)

The result is that many participants in programs such as the Section 8 leasing program never qualify for a subsidy. Participants tell of searching for months for an apartment in which the rent certificate can be used. There is often no problem finding an apartment within the cost range of the program. The trouble is finding a landlord willing to be subjected to the required inspection—against a twenty-page checklist. What inspector is not going to find violations? What inspector ever got into trouble for being too scrupulous? At "best," after repairs to meet the checklist, the rent goes up, which in the certificate program the government pays. As a result, because funding is limited, fewer people receive assistance. At worst, in a sea of apartments, the participant cannot get a drop from the housing-subsidy bucket.

Is there another reason for federal standards? A prudent housing official would say there is: in order to protect and preserve program funds from predatory journalists, General Accounting Office watchdogs, and Inspector General junkyard dogs. Without standards, there would be instances in which the poor household was taken advantage of, or received assistance in a unit that was grossly inadequate.

But this preoccupation with avoiding waste and abuse is counterproductive. Fewer than 2 percent of the units rated "excellent" and fewer than 4 percent of the units rated "good" were seriously inadequate. A risk that a poor person will be satisfied with a firetrap is small. The fraud and waste are trivial compared to the money squandered on inefficient housing programs. As Edward Luttwak has written with regard to our defense program:

The obsessive attention now being devoted to micromanagement is the root cause of an evil far greater than any marginal inefficiency or any thievery could possibly be. For it leads to the neglect of strategy—and of tactics. Our leaders are systematically distracted from the pursuit that should be their dominant business by a wrong-headed quest for paper efficiencies and marginal savings.[15]

Still, there was a reason to override the preferences of the poor in the case of the experimental program. If a program is designed in such a way that the participant is encouraged to choose the cheapest and most dangerous unit, the designer of such a program could be rightly criticized as being recklessly negligent if the unit did not meet a minimum housing standard. The Experimental Program housing allowance design (now doing business as Housing Voucher Program) was just such a design. The administrators set a rent based on their judgment of what decent housing costs in each community. They then set a ratio for what the poor household could afford and provided a subsidy to fill the gap between the right ratio and the right rent. In all respects this is the familiar "housing gap" model used in the Section 8 certificate program—with one large exception. The tenants received the subsidy based on housing costs but were free to spend the money on anything they desired. Given the impoverished status of most of the recipients, the temptation is strong to seek the cheapest apartment. At this juncture, the prudent official, to preserve the housing justification, must impose standards on the unit that can be selected. He must keep the participants' feet away from the fire.

How did the experimenters paint themselves into such a corner? For this we must take another look at the housing-gap approach. Its great virtue is its simplicity and logic. Its great fault is that it is based on fictions and presents the choice of either structured inflation or an income transfer masquerading as a housing program.

RIGHT RENTS AND RIGHT RATIOS

There is no such thing as a single "right rent" or single "right ratio." The idea of a single right rent (based on bedroom size) in a housing market that may contain hundreds of thousands of housing units in a diverse landscape of ethnically pure and impure neighborhoods is a brash presumption. Even if all the units had exactly the same physical and fiscal features, there would not be a single right rent. In low-income areas, a key determinant of rent is the quality of the occupant. As a study of low-income areas in Baltimore discovered:

> One finds a three track pricing policy in which the most desirable long-term tenants receive discounts; average families pay market rents; and high risk tenants pay premiums usually for the least desirable units.[16]

The practical difficulties are as great as the conceptual ones. It is in the interest of all groups in the area, both those interested in doing good and those interested in doing well, to have the government set the highest rent. In fact, local pressure for "special exceptions" to the "fair-market rent" resulted in actual rents in the Section 8 program that are above the supposed fair-market ceiling.

A right ratio is no easier to find. Sherman Maisel and Louis Winnick observed:

> Housing expenditures of American families are far too diverse to be explained by simple principles. Much of the diversity is real, i.e., inherent in consumer behavior. Choice of housing (which necessarily means choice of community and neighborhood) is a response to an extremely complex set of economic, social, and political impulses.[17]

The history of federal programs in which the right ratio has been set by gut feelings of politicians rather than logic should give one pause. The ratio of 25 percent was so sacred for a time that in one program it served as a maximum contribution and in another it served as a minimum contribution—and then all of a sudden the magic ratio jumped to 30. The respectability of the right ratio was laid to rest by one of the contractors in the housing allowance experiment:

> It is clear that the rule of thumb does not adequately describe the ratio of shelter expenditures to family income. It is also an inappro-

priate guideline for practices by . . . rental agencies and federal housing programs.[18]

The Section 8 certificate program based on a housing gap also was inherently inflationary. It turned an average rent into a floor. The amount the family paid was related to its income rather than the rent of the unit. Thus, if the right rent for a unit was set at $250, the family in an apartment that rents for $150 has no interest in objecting to a rent increase. And when the government surveys rent the following year, it finds a new and higher average.

Since one of the key missions of the housing allowance experiment was to gauge the inflationary effect of a large-scale allowance program, the Section 8 design had to be avoided. To counteract the inflationary tendency on the housing market, the experimenters eliminated the earmark for housing—the only rule was that the household receiving the money had to live in standard housing. This solution was especially attractive to the economists, since they were by training enamored of the preferences of consumers.

Unfortunately, the combination of allowing participants to pocket the money and maintaining the housing standard undercut the experiment. As John Kain noted:

> Not only did the housing requirements fail to increase the recipient's housing consumption by much, but they also seem to have adversely affected participation, especially among households in greatest need.
>
> Having induced such a small increase in demand, the supply experiment had no perceptible impact on rents. . . . The experiment's findings to date are therefore of little or no help in assessing a national housing allowance program that would use a form of earmarking to induce a significant increase in housing expenditure.[19]

There was some experimenting with a program that was earmarked for housing—a percent-of-rent formula in which the amount the tenant paid and the amount of the allowance increased if the rent went up (and the tenant's contribution and the allowance went down if the rent went down). Unfortunately, few of the participants understood the relationship. Even after two years in the program fewer than half understood that an increase in rent would require an increase in the amount they would pay, and less than one quarter understood the direction and the additional amount they would have to pay.[20] Ironically, the luminaries who looked at the formula could not see beyond the fraud issue:

> Both Henry Aaron and HUD's representatives claimed that Congress would never pass a percent of rent form of allowances because it was too susceptible to collusive fraud by tenants and landlords. . . . Neither Kain nor the others who agreed with him that another form of allowance should have been tested in the supply experiment were able to suggest alternative forms not subject to the same political drawback.[21]

They had not considered an alternative that a former Undersecretary of HUD, Richard Van Dusen, suggested that they should consider:

> [He] offers his own version of the housing allowance. . . . His claim for administrative simplicity and market discipline were persuasive to me.
>   Builders won't like . . . the program—because it is a housing allowance. Others may protest that the poor family can't be expected to bargain effectively, and that government employees must assure that the housing is standard and the rental fair. By limiting payments to rent, the program violates the theory that the poor should get money—and how they spend it is their business. Having listened to all of these arguments for four years, I'm inclined to think that any program that offends so many special interests and power blocs can't be all bad. I hope that in the housing allowance experiment now underway there may be room to try the Welfeld plan.[22]

A MORE MODEST FEDERAL ROLE

The poor come in all sizes, shapes, colors, and ages and have a dizzying variety of housing, neighborhood, and even regional preferences. Federally determined right rents and right ratios are economic myths. It is time to discard the notion that the "government knows best," that the government knows what housing is adequate or appropriate for a particular family. The one-dimensional rental formula used in present programs, which narrows the scope of consumer decision making, should be replaced by a program that widens the variety of housing options by providing a range of subsidies.

What the government *does* know is that it wants people to obtain decent housing in a suitable environment without having to sacrifice the other necessities of life. (Looked at from the other end of the spectrum, people should be able to obtain the necessities of life without having to sacrifice housing.) It does know the more rent that is paid the more likely the unit will be adequate. The program, therefore, should be structured to provide the greatest inducement for upgrading toward the point of adequate housing. As the family moves beyond adequate housing the subsidy should be phased down and out.

The subsidy a household receives should be determined by its rent-income ratio. A family unwilling to pay 20 percent of its income would receive no subsidy. The program would then provide a strong incentive for the household to spend more than 20 percent by subsidizing a large portion on the incremental rent over the 20 percent level (in the table below $18 for every increased percentage point of rent-to-income ratio) until 25 percent is reached. Between 25 and 30 percent, the federal government would pay less, the subsidy would drop to $15 for each percentage point increase. And between 30 and 35 percent the federal share would drop again to $12. The government would not share any increase in cost when the rent rises above 35 percent.

The program would enable a four-person household with an income of $6,000 to obtain an apartment with a monthly rental of $118 if it wished to pay 20 percent of its income; $233 if it wished to pay 25 percent of its income; $333 if it wished to pay 30 percent of its income; and $418 if it wished to pay 35 percent of its income.

It is important to note that there is no magical quality to the numbers. The subsidies set forth may be revised to suit political

Table 16. Possible Subsidies and Variations in the Program

Rent-to-Income Ratio	Monthly Assistance Payment
Less than 20%	$ 0
20%	18
21%	36
22%	54
23%	72
24%	90
25%	108
26%	123
27%	138
28%	153
29%	168
30%	183
31%	195
32%	207
33%	219
34%	231
35%	243
More than 35%	243

The basic subsidy is set for a 3–4-person household and varies directly with the size of the household.

Family Size Variations

Family Size	% of Monthly Assistance
1–2 persons	85%
3–4 persons	100%
5–6 persons	115%
7–8 persons	130%
9–10 persons	145%

and economic dictates. The choice of subsidy is a pragmatic one. It must satisfy two conflicting objectives: it must be high enough to give poor households a choice of decent units, and it must be low enough so that the expansion of the program to all eligible families is acceptable to taxpayers not directly benefiting from the program.

There are no free rides in this program. If a family prefers improved housing, it most prove it by bearing a portion of the additional rent. The government should be generous, but should not encourage extravagance. By providing a declining subsidy and by getting out at 35 percent, the government signals that there is more to life than housing. At the same time, it allows the family to continue spending as it pleases.

Applicants for housing assistance would get in touch with the local administering agency, where they would certify their income and family size. Applicants, if eligible, would be supplied with a rent table appropriate to their income and household size. The table would set forth the refund for different monthly rents at $1 intervals. The tenants would then shop for housing. When he returned with an executed lease, the subsidy would be determined and the monthly check would be sent to him at that address. Below is a sample table (note the refunds were calculated based on different subsidy assumptions).

The U.S. Department of Housing and Urban Development wants to help you live in good housing so we're offering you rent refunds. The rent refund is available whether you decide to live in your present apartment or move to another apartment.

If your rent includes heat and utilities, the amount of your refund is shown next to the dollar amount of your rent on the accompanying table.

If your rent does not include heat or utilities, call _____ at _____, she will tell you how much to add to obtain your rent for the purpose of finding your refund.

Tenant Name _____ Family Income ___$7,200___
Tenant Address _____ Family Size ___3___

Rent	Refund	Rent	Refund	Rent	Refund	Rent	Refund
Less than							
$ 96.00	—	159.00	45	222.00	88	285.00	127
97.00	1	160.00	46	223.00	89	286.00	127
98.00	1	161.00	46	224.00	89	287.00	128
99.00	2	162.00	47	225.00	90	288.00	128
100.00	3	163.00	48	226.00	91	289.00	129
101.00	4	164.00	49	227.00	91	290.00	129
102.00	4	165.00	49	228.00	92	291.00	130
103.00	5	166.00	50	229.00	93	292.00	130
104.00	6	167.00	51	230.00	93	293.00	130
105.00	6	168.00	51	231.00	94	294.00	131
106.00	7	169.00	52	232.00	94	295.00	131
107.00	8	170.00	53	233.00	95	296.00	132
108.00	9	171.00	54	234.00	96	297.00	132

109.00	9	172.00	54	235.00	96	298.00	133
110.00	10	173.00	55	236.00	97	299.00	133
111.00	11	174.00	56	237.00	98	300.00	134
112.00	11	175.00	56	238.00	98	301.00	134
113.00	12	176.00	57	239.00	99	302.00	135
114.00	13	177.00	58	240.00	99	303.00	135
115.00	14	178.00	59	241.00	100	304.00	135
116.00	14	179.00	59	242.00	101	305.00	136
117.00	15	180.00	60	243.00	101	306.00	136
118.00	16	181.00	61	244.00	102	307.00	137
119.00	16	182.00	61	245.00	103	308.00	137
120.00	17	183.00	62	246.00	103	309.00	138
121.00	18	184.00	63	247.00	104	310.00	138
122.00	19	185.00	64	248.00	104	311.00	139
123.00	19	186.00	64	249.00	105	312.00	139
124.00	20	187.00	65	250.00	106	313.00	140
125.00	21	188.00	66	251.00	106	314.00	140
126.00	21	189.00	66	252.00	107	315.00	140
127.00	22	190.00	67	253.00	108	316.00	141
128.00	23	191.00	68	254.00	108	317.00	141
129.00	24	192.00	69	255.00	109	318.00	142
130.00	24	193.00	69	256.00	109	319.00	142
131.00	25	194.00	70	257.00	110	320.00	143
132.00	26	195.00	71	258.00	111	321.00	143
133.00	26	196.00	71	259.00	111	322.00	144
134.00	27	197.00	72	260.00	112	323.00	144
135.00	28	198.00	73	261.00	113	324.00	145
136.00	29	199.00	74	262.00	113	325.00	145
137.00	29	200.00	74	263.00	114	326.00	145
138.00	30	201.00	75	264.00	114	327.00	146
139.00	31	202.00	76	265.00	115	328.00	146
140.00	31	203.00	76	266.00	116	329.00	147
141.00	32	204.00	77	267.00	116	330.00	147
142.00	33	205.00	78	268.00	117	331.00	148
143.00	34	206.00	78	269.00	118	332.00	148
144.00	34	207.00	79	270.00	118	333.00	149
145.00	35	208.00	79	271.00	119	334.00	149
146.00	36	209.00	80	272.00	119	335.00	150
147.00	36	210.00	81	273.00	120	336.00	150
148.00	37	211.00	81	274.00	121	337.00	150
149.00	38	212.00	82	275.00	121	338.00	151
150.00	39	213.00	83	276.00	122	339.00	151
151.00	39	214.00	83	277.00	123	340.00	152
152.00	40	215.00	84	278.00	123	341.00	152
153.00	41	216.00	84	279.00	124	342.00	153
154.00	41	217.00	85	280.00	124	343.00	153
155.00	42	218.00	86	281.00	125	344.00	154

Rent	Refund	Rent	Refund	Rent	Refund	Rent	Refund
Less than							
$156.00	43	219.00	86	282.00	125	345.00	154
157.00	44	220.00	87	283.00	126	346.00	155
158.00	44	221.00	88	284.00	126	347.00	155

Although there will always be some abuse, there are three features of the program (in addition to the animosity between tenant and landlord) that will minimize it: (1) every tenant will have a different table, (2) the tenant has to share the cost of every increase, and (3) as the rent goes up the subsidy share decreases.

The program is predicated on the use of a single table for the entire nation, so that, a three-person household with an income of $7,000 would receive the same table whether it lived in Albany, Georgia, or Albany, New York. The income limit for eligibility will, however, be different in different localities and based on the greater of the national poverty level or 50 percent the local median (widely used in present HUD programs).

Using one table for the entire country seems to defy economic sensibilities. A model of the program was put to a test in each of the 285 metropolitan areas of the nation, assuming that a household with an income equal to 50 percent of the local median rented an apartment at 80 percent of the HUD-determined fair-market rent level in the locality. In no area was the required rent to income ratio less than 18 percent (the subsidy table provided for eligibility starting at 15 percent and a maximum cap at 30 percent) and in no area greater than 27 percent. The overwhelming number of cases clustered between the rent-income ratios of 18 and 23 (See Appendix C). As a general rule, areas of high housing costs are areas of high income and areas of low housing costs are areas of low income. It may be argued that residents of Eau Claire, Wisconsin (the 18 percent area), have an easier time than the residents of Miami, Florida (the 27 percent area), at the least in the nonwinter months. In response, the flow of federal money would be directed toward the area with the highest ratios. The areas of greatest housing need would receive the greatest subsidy.

The table works at the top of the eligibility scale. However, there are many families (especially in such places as Texas, where the welfare level is under $1,700 a year for a family of four) in which some supplemental housing assistance would be needed. This could be accommodated by a high-need bonus geared for households below 50 percent of the national *poverty* level.

High Need Bonus Table

Percent of Poverty	Bonus
0–10%	20%
10–20	16
20–30	12
30–40	8
40–50	4

With the bonus, the Texas family could rent a $302 unit if it spent 35 percent of its income. (See Appendix D but again note different subsidy numbers are used.)

Is the table certificate program fair? Two standards should be applied. The first, an economic standard, is that, all things being equal, the most subsidy should go to the poorest family. Under the program if two families with incomes of $6,000 and $12,000 each were renting a $350 apartment, the former's subsidy will be more than twice as large ($158 vs. $71). The second standard is a political one—the Avis Principle. The poor should not get better housing than higher-income households unless they try harder. Under the previous example, if the two families expend the same effort, they get the same subsidy and the $12,000 family gets a better unit. At 30 percent of income the $12,000 family is able to obtain a $483 unit while the $6,000 family is limited to a $333 unit. The percentage of rent covered by the subsidy in the latter case is, nevertheless, much higher for the poorer family (55 percent vs. 38 percent).

To the uninitiated (or the overinitiated), the proposal looks very much like the percent-of-rent design. The table certificate does share a common trait with the percent-of-rent approach—the subsidy is based on actual rather than theoretical housing expenditures. But if we keep in mind the previous example, we can see the greater fairness of the table certificate. If a higher- and a lower-income person pay the same rent, the table certificate pays the poorer household a larger subsidy; under the percent-of-rent design, both households receive the same subsidy. If they expend the same effort, the table-certificate program provides the same subsidy for each but pays a higher percentage of the poorer family's rent. In contrast, the percent-of-rent formula provides the richer household twice the subsidy of the poorer household and keeps the percent of the rent the same.

The "notch" problem, whereby an extra dollar of income results in the loss of hundreds of dollars of subsidy, can be minimized but not totally eliminated in a program that gives households a choice and adheres to the Avis Principle. The solution requires a trade-off between fairness on the one hand and work incentives and program cost on the other. One solution would provide full eligibility for families with incomes up to 50 percent of the median, a 5 percent "grace" margin, and a phase-out of subsidy through a 10 percent decline for each 5 percent increase in income.

Under the approach, which would feature uniform subsidies and variable rents, competition with existing HUD programs would be based on the merits of the housing offered. This would free each program from many of the rules and restrictions that insulate it from the market. As tenants gain mobility, older projects would have to enter the marketplace. Both the public and private assisted programs can be restructured to operate under the new arrangements.

Before dealing with how the new arrangement would be applied to the present problems at the low-rent end of the private market and to public housing, a historical note. After the housing allowance experiment, HUD submitted a budget to OMB that included a 15,000-unit demonstration program of the alternative allowance scheme, which was then referred to as the Bounty program. OMB rejected it without giving any justification. The rejection got a non-bureaucratic "confidential" response that was printed in the Congressional Record:*

The denial of the . . . Housing Bounty demonstration merely proves that the technicians at OMB would rather criticize old programs than

* *Congressional Record/December 7, 1981*, S. 14646.

examine new ideas. Their argument that a "tight budget year" is the wrong time for innovative ideas shows a good deal about the OMB mentality and the intellectual level of their analysis.[23]

To paraphrase Pogo, OMB was confronted with an insurmountable opportunity.

HIGHER PRICES AND GREATER AFFORDABILITY

The analysis in Chapter 7 indicates there are two separate problems at the bottom of the housing inventory. The landlords in the low-rent sector are not only not making huge profits but, in fact, many are hanging on for dear life. Their tenants are more or less in the same position. They are carrying large housing burdens and the street looms if for any reason there is an interruption in their income.

The assistance programs by HUD do not address the two-sided nature of the problem. The rent-certificate and the rent-voucher programs are aimed at providing tenants with average housing (the fair market rent is set at the 45th percentile of rents for recent movers in the local housing market area), with rents at or near the median of the market. A comparison of the two programs found that the average nationwide rent paid by a sample of nonelderly recipients of the certificate was $431 and of the voucher, $467. The respective average subsidies were $314 and $292.[24]

This an extravagance which neither the nation nor poor people can afford. The larger the per-unit cost, the smaller the volume of the program. The extravagance is compounded when a poor non-recipient is evicted for not having the rent and is then penalized by the system that provides expensive but not decent hotel and motel rooms.

We are mistaking our housing obligation to the poor, and the poor are suffering for it. Our obligation is to provide decent housing not average housing. And in this country in the eighties, *sub-average is not substandard*.

I would suggest that the new system be initially targeted to the tenants in the lowest-rent sector of the market. That is where tenants are to be found who have the greatest need for support to help them with their rent burden and buildings whose fiscal foundations are the weakest. Although tenants would be able to take their subsidy and move elsewhere, the absence of a standard will mean that they can take the subsidy and stay in a less-than-perfect building. Forty percent of the recipients of subsidy certificates could not transform them into subsidies, since they could not find units that met the standards.[25] In New York City two out of three recipients of certificates failed to receive subsidies.[26]

If the bounty were applied in the three areas in New York City in which tenants had the highest-rent burdens, the burdens would be substantially reduced at far less cost to the government even if we were to freeze their income at a 1984 level and increase their rent by $30 a month.

Table 17. Applying the Bounty in New York City

	Old Rent	New Rent	Income	Old Burden	New Ratio	Subsidy
South Bronx	$263	$293	$6,874	47%	27.0%	$138
Northeast Manhattan	222	252	7,071	38	24.9	106
North Brooklyn	274	304	8,968	37	25.2	111

Since landlords of low-rent buildings have to be selective about their tenants—given the precarious nature of their operation—the "housing homeless," who usually became homeless because of nonpayment of rent or less than standard behavior, will usually not be welcome even if they come bearing a subsidy. They might, however, get a better reception from a landlord, who has moved away from the brink of financial disaster, especially if the program allowed for a rent increase equal to the cost of one night's lodging at a less than quality inn.

MAINSTREAMING PUBLIC HOUSING

There is even hope for public housing. But first the relationship between the three parties—HUD, the PHAs, and the tenants must be fundamentally altered. The relationship between HUD and the local authorities has to continue (subsidies are crucial), but it need not be intimate. The fount of all wisdom is not in HUD, and in the main there is competency and honesty at the local level. What sets PHAs apart from private management operations is that they serve very poor people in a system that lacks a pricing system and that has delivered required subsidies in an erratic manner.

The relationship between the authority and its tenants need also continue, but from a different point of view. The tenant needs to be viewed as a consumer who is to be offered choices, rather than as a supplicant who is to be assigned space. The relationship must be transformed from dependency to independence.

The foundation of a new system in public housing is apartment rents that reflect the condition, cost, and location of the unit rather than the size of the tenant's pocketbook. The setting of these rents is the task of the local PHA. Although the PHA would have total freedom, the rents would have to reflect the debt service and operating costs attributable to an apartment, taking into consideration such items as reserves for replacements and vacancies. Although PHAs may be a bit rusty, since in most authorities the books have been consolidated for years, the allocation of costs is not an insurmountable obstacle. Firms that manage buildings for numerous owners must and do separate costs on a building and unit basis every day. The mechanism is also self-correcting. The PHA will soon obtain signals from the market. The PHA will be facing a new breed of tenant, one marked by buying power—in possession of the previously discussed bounty certificate. (See Appendix E for the difference in impact from the concept of "vouchering out of public housing.")

The absolute need for a rational rent system is illustrated by the current paradox of housing authorities that have both a huge waiting list and a large number of vacancies. Or, as in the case of Newark, a huge waiting list and wholesale demolition of public housing units:

> Thirteen more public housing high-rises in Newark will fall some time next year. . . . When these buildings collapse, each imploded by a 5-second charge, Newark Public Housing Authority . . . will

have demolished nearly a third of its public housing units. . . . [T]he authority's waiting list, now closed, contains 11,000 names.[27]

Absurd but absolutely predictable. As Louis Winnick, using a theatrical analogy in the context of urban renewal, put it:

> It would be irrational, if not disastrous for a theatre manager to . . . offer all his seats at the same price. The likely result would be excess demand (a waiting list) for the desirable orchestra seats and vacant seats . . . in the balcony. . . . If families are offered housing at equal cost . . . there will be little reason for families to seek out the balcony seats of the city and consequently little hope for their renewal.[28]

Public housing is now living the disaster.

Could public housing be competitive, if its rents reflected the quality of the unit and tenants had a choice of taking their subsidy to private housing? Public housing managers will argue that they are at a competitive disadvantage:

> Private landlords have a competitive "edge" on public housing that it may never be able to overcome. Utility costs are frequently paid by the tenants directly in . . . privately owned low income housing. . . . Where the landlord does pay for utility costs he is free to raise rents, at least up to the point that the local market will bear. . . .
>
> Public housing incurs administrative, social services, and security expenses not imposed to the same degree on a private landlord. By virtue of our law and public accountability, we need to maintain a system of merit employment and equal opportunities . . . to maintain a system for competitive bidding on purchases . . . to negotiate with labor unions . . . to maintain a housing application office and its responsiveness to the urgent competing needs in the communities.[29]

Under the new regime, when the authority is free to raise rents and when energy ceases to be free the first disadvantage would disappear. And private owners would note some PHA advantages—

subsidized debt service, property-tax abatements, and the non-profit status operation.

In comparing the competing advantages, facts can be useful. In a sample that included 556 public housing projects, average operating expenses in 1981 dollars were $193 per month. During approximately the same period the average operating expenses in nonsubsidized private projects insured by the Federal Housing Administration were $191. If there is an advantage, it is likely to be *de minimis* on the national level.

At the local level, everything won't average out. If the long waiting lists are true indicators, most PHAs should have no difficulty in prospering under the new system. In an area where the waiting lists only represent the bargain price of public housing and in an area in which there is a housing surplus, the PHA will have to make a difficult decision: whether to retain its role as the keeper of dead-end housing or to take on the role of the gatekeeper of housing opportunity. The PHA will have an opportunity to broaden its role from that of a landlord to that of a minister of housing for low-income families—responsible for seeing that the best use is made of federal housing assistance dollars channeled into the community. Under the present system, the distinction between public and subsidized private housing is so sharp as to necessitate their being placed under separate assistant secretaries at HUD. The new system and perspective will dissolve the walls that separate public housing and its tenants from the mainstream of housing.

PHAs will have to think and compete like their private brethren, and their residents will have the luxury of choice. Portions of the public housing stock are so far gone that expensive or extensive improvements with anything but Monopoly money is not in the best interest of the poor tenant or the PHA. Luckily, the best estimate of public housing units in the latter category is approximately 10 percent of the inventory of 1.3 million units.

A modernization equation must include the locality's housing supply situation. A housing crisis can begin with a housing surplus. Rents in the private market can be driven down, but if the tenants still cannot afford the price, the apartment will be driven off the market. In such a situation, the wise strategy for the city may be the channeling of money to private tenants to enable them to afford the proper upkeep of their present private units, rather than increasing or upgrading of public housing. The best for public housing may be the enemy of the good for housing of low-income families.

Different choices will have to made at both ends of the quality spectrum. In low-quality projects, which at present may have high vacancy rates, there is a possibility of stabilization when tenants are offered lower rents. It is, however, just as likely that the granting of choice will quicken the exodus—the market's answer to whether the project is serving an economic or social purpose. The answer should be accepted. The wise businessman does not continue making Edsels after consumers have voted for a different model. And what is good for Ford is good for housing policy. Public housing policy is not grounded in buildings but in providing for the housing needs of people.

The possibility of projects emptying out requires a few words about the mechanics of the new approach. Assume a PHA receives an allocation of 1,000 certificates and 2,000 tenants want to move out of public housing. Is the PHA required to suffer 1,000 vacancies, or is the PHA's allocation to be increased to cover all the tenants who want to move? What is to prevent the program from becoming a new entitlement program immediately? The answer is an existing mechanism put to a new use—*a waiting list to move out*. Since there are only 1,000 certificates, only 1,000 tenants can move out with the certificate. They can be selected in any number of ways—length of tenure, hardship, first come–first served. The remaining 1,000 will have to wait for next year's allocation of certificates.

The other new situation will occur at the high-quality, high-subsidy end of the spectrum. There will be cases of very low-income households living in very expensive units. It is likely to occur in some of the showcase elderly projects. Raising rents cold turkey is obviously political suicide. Any increases will have to be phased in, and most likely the elderly household would be grandfathered at their existing rent.

Some authorities may not make it because of poor management. However, their problems will be divorced from the concern of the government that the poor receive good housing and the concern of the tenants that they obtain affordable shelter. For PHAs what is being offered is an opportunity to play the game on a level field, for tenants the dignity of choice.

In sum, the introduction of new programs need not be at the expense of the housing produced by prior programs. Most important, it is possible to have an allowance program that respects both the preferences of the poor and the preferences of the electorate. In the words of Paul Goodman, "What stands most in the way of solving our most important problems is the feeling of well-intentioned people that there are no alternatives; all we can do is improve the present methods." [30]

APPENDIX A

From "On the Ecology of Micromotives"
by Thomas Schelling

WE CAN WORK IT OUT

Some vivid dynamics can be generated by any reader with a half hour to spare, a roll of pennies and a roll of dimes, a tabletop, a large sheet of paper and a spirit of scientific inquiry or, lacking that spirit, a fondness for games.

Get a roll of pennies, a roll of dimes, a ruled sheet of paper divided into one-inch squares, preferably at least the size of a checkerboard (64 squares in eight rows and eight columns) and find some device for selecting squares at random.* We place dimes and pennies on some of the squares, and suppose them to represent the members of two homogeneous groups—men and women, blacks and whites, French-speaking and English-speaking, officers and enlisted men, students and faculty, surfers and swimmers, the well dressed and the poorly dressed, or any other dichotomy that is exhaustive and recognizable. We can spread them at random or put them in contrived patterns. We can use equal numbers of dimes and pennies or let one be a minority. And we stipulate various rules for individual decision.

Reprinted by permission of the author from *The Public Interest*, No. 25 (Fall 1971), pp. 81–88. © 1971 by National Affairs, Inc. Reprinted in Thomas Schelling, *Micromotives and Macrobehavior* (New York: W. W. Norton and Co., 1978, pp. 146–54.

* A table of two-digit random numbers, the digits identifying row and column, is ideal if available. There are, however, ways of using dice, coins, roulette wheels, decks of cards, spinning devices and other bits of machinery to generate equi-probable number selections to determine row and column.

For example, we could postulate that every dime wants at least half its neighbors to be dimes, every penny wants a third of its neighbors to be pennies, and any dime or penny whose immediate neighborhood does not meet these conditions gets up and moves. Then by inspection we locate the ones that are due to move, move them, keep moving them if necessary and, when everybody on the board has settled down, look to see what pattern has emerged. (If the situation never "settles down," we look to see what kind of endless turbulence or cyclical activity our hypotheses have generated.)

Define each individual's neighborhood as the square territory surrounding him. We suppose it to be the eight surrounding squares; he is the center of a 3 x 3 neighborhood. He is content or discontent with his own local neighborhood according to the mix of colors among the occupants of those eight surrounding squares, some of which may be empty. We furthermore suppose that, if he is discontent with the color of his own neighborhood, he moves to the nearest empty square that meets his minimum demands.

As to the order of moves, we can begin with the discontents nearest the center of the board and let them move first, or start in the upper left and sweep downward and to the right, or let all the dimes move first and then the pennies; but it usually turns out that the precise order is not crucial to the outcome.

Then we choose an overall ratio of pennies to dimes, the two colors being about equal or one of them being a "minority." There are two basically different ways we can distribute the dimes and the pennies. We can put them in some prescribed pattern that we want to test, or we can spread them at random. (The two ways can be combined, as will be illustrated.)

Let us start with equal numbers of dimes and pennies and suppose that the demands of both are "moderate"—that each wants something more than one-third neighbors like himself. The number of neighbors that a coin can have will be anywhere from zero to eight. We make the following specification of demands. If a person has one neighbor, he must be the same color; of two neighbors, one must be his color; of three, four or five neighbors, two must be his color; and of six, seven or eight neighbors, he wants at least three.

It is possible to form a pattern that is regularly "integrated," and in which everybody is satisfied. A simple alternating pattern does it (figure 1), on condition that we take care of the corners.

No one can move, except to a corner because there are no other vacant cells; but no one wants to move. We now mix them up a little, and in the process empty some cells to make movement feasible.

There are 60 coins on the board. We remove 20, using a table of random

```
            #  O  #  O  #  O
         #  O  #  O  #  O  #  O
         O  #  O  #  O  #  O  #
         #  O  #  O  #  O  #  O
         O  #  O  #  O  #  O  #
         #  O  #  O  #  O  #  O
         O  #  O  #  O  #  O  #
            O  #  O  #  O  #
```

Figure 1

digits; we then pick 5 empty squares at random and replace a dime or a penny with a 50/50 chance. The result is a board with 64 cells, 45 occupied and 19 blank. Forty individuals are just where they were before we removed 20 neighbors and added 5 news ones. The left side of figure 2 shows one such result, generated by exactly this process. The #'s are dimes and the O's are pennies; alternatively, the #'s speak French and the O's speak English, the #'s are black and the O's are white, the #'s are boys and the O's are girls, or whatever you please.

```
—  #  —  #  O  #  —  O        —  —  —  #  —  #  —  —
#  #  #  O  —  O  #  O        —  —  —  —  —  —  —  —  —
—  #  O  —  —  #  O  #        —  —  —  —  —  —  —  —  —
—  O  #  O  #  O  #  O        —  —  #  —  #  —  #  —
O  O  O  #  O  O  O  —        —  —  —  —  —  —  —  —  —
#  —  #  #  #  —  —  O        #  —  —  —  —  —  —  —  —
—  #  O  #  O  #  O  —        —  —  O  —  O  —  O  —
—  O  —  O  —  —  #  —        —  —  —  —  —  —  —  —  —
```

Figure 2

The right side of figure 2 identifies the individuals who are not content with their surrounding neighborhoods. Six #'s and three O's want to move; the rest are content as things stand. The pattern is still "integrated"; even the discontent are not without some neighbors like themselves, and few among the content are without neighbors of opposite color. The general pattern is not strongly segregated in appearance. One would be hard-put to block out #-neighborhoods or O-neighborhoods at this stage. (The upper left corner might be described as a #-neighborhood.) The problem is to satisfy a fraction (9 of 45) among the #'s and O's by letting them move somewhere among the 19 blank cells.

Anybody who moves leaves a blank cell that somebody can move into. Also, anybody who moves leaves behind a neighbor or two of his own color; and when he leaves a neighbor, his neighbor loses a neighbor and may become discontent. Anyone who moves gains neighbors like himself, adding a neighbor like them to their neighborhood but also adding one of opposite color to the unlike neighbors he acquires.

I cannot too strongly urge you to get the dimes and pennies and do it yourself. I can show you an outcome or two. A computer can do it for you a hundred times, testing variations in neighborhood demands, overall ratios, sizes of neighborhoods, and so forth. But there is nothing like tracing it through for yourself and seeing the thing work itself out. In an hour you can do it several times and experiment with different rules of behavior, sizes and shapes of boards, and (if you turn some of the coins heads and some tails) subgroups of dimes and pennies that make different demands on the color compositions of their neighborhoods.

CHAIN REACTION

What is instructive is the "unraveling" process. Everybody who selects a new environment affects the environments of those he leaves and those he moves among. There is a chain reaction. It may be quickly damped, with little motion, or it may go on and on and on with striking results. (The results of course are only suggestive, because few of us live in square cells on a checkerboard.)

One outcome for the situation depicted in figure 2 is shown in figure 3. It is "one outcome" because I have not explained exactly the order in which individuals moved. If the reader reproduces the experiment himself, he will get a slightly different configuration, but the general pattern will not be much different. Figure 4 is a replay from figure 2, the only difference from figure 3 being in the order of moves. It takes a few minutes to do the experiment again, and one quickly gets an impression of the kind of outcome to expect. Changing the neighborhood demands, or using twice as many dimes as pennies, will drastically affect the results; but for any given set of numbers and demands, the results are fairly stable.

All the people are content in figures 3 and 4. And they are more segre-

```
      #  #        O  #  #                    #  #  #  O              O
#  #  #  O  O  O  #  #               #  #  #  O        O     O
#  #  O  O           O  #            #  #  O              O
#  O     O        O  O  O               O        O        O     O
O  O  O  #  O  O  O                  O  O  O  #  O  O  O
   O  #  #  #  O  O  O                     #  #  #  O  O  O
      #  #  #  #                     O  #  #  #  #  #  #  #
O  O                 #               O  O           #  #  #
```

| Figure 3 | Figure 4 |

gated. This is more than just a visual impression; we can make a few comparisons. In figure 2 the O's altogether had as many O's for neighbors as they had #'s; some had more or less than the average, and 3 were discontent. For the #'s the ratio of #-neighbors to O-neighbors was 1.1, with a little colony of #'s in the upper left corner and 6 widely distributed discontents. After sorting themselves out in figure 3, the average ratio of like to unlike neighbors for #'s and O's together was 2.3, more than double their original ratio and about triple the ratio that any individual demanded. Figure 4 is even more extreme. The ratio of like to unlike neighbors is 2.8, nearly triple the starting ratio and four times the minimum demanded.

Another comparison is the number who had no opposite neighbors in figure 2. Three were in that condition before people started moving; in figure 3 there are 8 without neighbors of opposite color, and in figure 4 there are 14.

What can we conclude from an exercise like this? We may at least be able to disprove a few notions that are themselves based on reasoning no more complicated than the checkerboard. Propositions that begin, "It stands to reason that . . . ," can sometimes be discredited by exceedingly simple demonstrations that, though perhaps true, they do not exactly "stand to reason." We can at least persuade ourselves that certain mechanisms could work, and that observable aggregate phenomena could be compatible with types of "molecular movement" that do not closely resemble the aggregate outcomes that they determine.

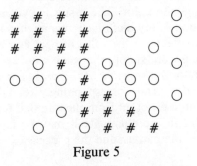

Figure 5

There may be a few surprises. What happens if we raise the demands of one color and lower the demands of the other? Figure 5 shows typical results. Here we increased by one the number of like neighbors that a # demanded and decreased by one the number that an O demanded, as compared with figures 3 and 4. By most measures, "segregation" is about the same as in figures 3 and 4. The difference is in population densities; the O's are spread out all over their territory, while the #'s are packed in tight. The reader will discover, if he actually gets those pennies and dimes and tries it for himself, that something similar would happen if the demands of the two colors were equal but one color outnumbered the other by two or three to one. The minority then tends to be noticeably more tightly packed. Perhaps from figure 5 we could conclude that if surfers mind the presence of swimmers less than swimmers mind the presence of surfers, they will become almost completely separated, but the surfers will enjoy a greater expanse of water.

Is it "segregated"?

The reader might try guessing what set of individual preferences led from figure 2 to the pattern in figure 6.

```
        #   #             #   #
    #   #   #         #   #   #
    #   #   O   O   O   #   O
        O   O   O   O   O   O   O
    O   O   O   #   O   O   O
        O   #   #   #   O   O   O
        #   #   #         O   O
        #   #
```

Figure 6

The ratio of like to unlike neighbors for all the #'s and O's together is slightly more than three to one; and there are 6 O's and 8 #'s that have no neighbors of opposite color. The result is evidently segregation; but following a suggestion of my dictionary, we might say that the process is one of *aggregation*. Because the rules of behavior ascribed both to #'s and to O's in figure 6 were simply that each would move to acquire three neighbors of like color *irrespective of the presence or absence of neighbors of opposite color*. And correspondingly for O's. As an individual motivation this is quite different from the one that formed the patterns in figures 3 and 4. But in the aggregate it may be hard to discern which motivation underlies the pattern and the process of segregated residence. And it may matter.

The first impact of a display like this on a reader may be—unless he finds it all "irrelevant"—discouragement. A moderate urge to avoid small-minority status may cause a nearly integrated pattern to unravel and highly segregated neighborhoods to form. Even a deliberately arranged viable pattern, as in figure 1, when buffeted by a little random motion, proves unstable and gives way to the separate neighborhoods of figures 3 through 6. These then prove to be fairly immune to continued random turnover.

APPENDIX B

Table 1. Ratings by Poor Residents on the Mean Number of Structural Flaws by Housing Rating

	Excellent	Good	Fair	Poor	All
Atlanta	0.23952	0.49904	0.99138	2.12903	0.83448
Chicago	0.18018	0.27663	0.87417	1.86093	0.61237
Cincinnati	0.23864	0.45185	0.92079	2.25000	0.67614
Columbus	0.17241	0.40336	1.04575	2.09677	0.66012
Kansas City	0.26316	0.71698	1.06593	2.21053	0.97802
Miami	0.14706	0.19847	0.33333	2.02326	0.48882
Milwaukee	0.23077	0.40777	0.77876	1.97727	0.61674
New Orleans	0.21277	0.36047	1.10989	2.58929	0.77966
Paterson	0.00000	0.25333	0.91228	2.61765	0.86486
Philadelphia	0.30769	0.48843	1.18362	2.25664	0.87734
Portland, Oregon	0.19048	0.54000	0.81915	1.95652	0.65152
Rochester	0.22222	0.54783	0.91753	1.85714	0.78571
San Bernardino	0.02703	0.37931	0.53333	0.80000	0.37037
San Diego	0.14141	0.26222	0.78151	1.53333	0.44820
San Francisco	0.24725	0.39490	0.70608	1.13750	0.52008
Baltimore	0.36364	0.54717	1.22581	2.63043	1.06042
Birmingham	0.27778	0.39007	0.61111	1.75000	0.61808
Cleveland	0.23913	0.38636	0.79137	2.04255	0.73626
Denver	0.23611	0.30488	0.49438	0.80000	0.36812
Honolulu	0.07018	0.16447	0.23009	1.95238	0.27988
Houston	0.14394	0.20822	0.58896	1.33333	0.49744
Indianapolis	0.15789	0.22283	0.59130	1.48700	0.45000
Louisville	0.35000	0.41872	0.73485	2.05128	0.68602
New York	0.10919	0.38194	1.06092	2.37872	0.91429
Oklahoma City	0.13725	0.16149	0.59292	1.75000	0.42210
Providence	0.21429	0.20667	0.59494	1.31579	0.36446
Sacramento	0.07143	0.21569	0.41892	0.85714	0.30962
St. Louis	0.12757	0.27580	0.75787	2.33333	0.65771
Seattle	0.19898	0.33252	0.71698	1.48387	0.52233
Buffalo	0.15385	0.34286	0.84536	1.89474	0.59733
Anaheim	0.10236	0.08955	0.28261	0.76923	0.20000
Boston	0.25921	0.53322	1.03183	2.01299	0.79628
Dallas	0.08772	0.13740	0.44954	1.34783	0.32107
Detroit	0.24028	0.40864	0.87701	2.25203	0.03481
Fort Worth	0.06818	0.09483	0.48315	0.84000	0.28467
Los Angeles	0.15132	0.17200	0.43229	1.24390	0.36609
Madison	0.05832	0.33186	0.60606	0.48387	0.42159
Minneapolis	0.18421	0.40230	0.90000	1.81250	0.62189
Phoenix	0.10526	0.16547	0.58889	1.77143	0.44860
Pittsburgh	0.14286	0.27728	0.75472	1.52632	0.54070
Washington, D.C.	0.19008	0.47222	0.98153	2.15789	0.81980

269

Table 2. Ratings by Poor Residents on Percent of Private Housing with No Structural Flaws [a]

	Excellent	Good	Fair	Poor	All
Atlanta	83.234	70.520	53.017	22.581	60.230
Chicago	87.838	83.148	55.629	29.139	69.691
Cincinnati	84.091	71.852	51.485	21.429	65.057
Columbus	86.207	73.950	51.634	22.581	66.208
Kansas City	84.211	56.604	49.451	13.158	52.015
Miami	94.118	87.023	80.000	34.884	78.275
Milwaukee	82.418	72.330	54.867	22.727	65.198
New Orleans	85.106	76.357	42.857	16.071	61.695
Paterson	100.000	84.000	63.158	17.647	67.027
Philadelphia	84.024	72.222	45.480	25.664	60.300
Portland, Oregon	87.302	71.333	60.638	30.435	68.485
Rochester	87.037	66.957	54.639	30.952	61.688
San Bernardino	97.297	80.460	71.667	60.000	80.423
San Diego	89.899	81.333	60.504	33.333	74.841
San Francisco	84.066	75.799	62.838	53.750	71.687
Baltimore	76.364	69.811	41.129	10.870	51.964
Birmingham	86.111	74.468	65.079	32.500	67.347
Cleveland	80.435	72.727	54.676	34.043	61.813
Denver	86.111	76.220	66.292	65.000	75.072
Honolulu	92.982	90.132	83.186	38.095	85.131
Houston	92.424	81.454	59.816	35.833	70.113
Indianapolis	87.719	84.783	69.565	36.585	75.819
Louisville	76.667	73.649	62.121	28.205	65.435
New York	85.135	79.167	53.361	18.723	61.324
Oklahoma City	90.196	88.199	68.142	35.714	77.904
Providence	82.143	85.333	63.291	36.842	76.506
Sacramento	92.857	85.294	74.324	57.143	80.753
St. Louis	89.712	81.614	60.827	22.619	68.071
Seattle	86.224	79.707	55.094	35.484	69.990
Buffalo	84.615	76.571	57.732	34.211	68.800
Anaheim	94.872	94.030	80.435	53.046	87.273
Boston	82.379	67.802	45.358	20.779	50.587
Dallas	94.737	88.550	71.560	43.478	80.625
Detroit	86.538	76.080	58.289	20.325	62.306
Fort Worth	93.182	92.241	65.169	56.000	80.292
Los Angeles	86.667	87.200	75.000	42.276	78.413
Madison	94.110	76.106	59.848	35.484	72.912
Minneapolis	86.842	72.414	61.667	37.500	69.154
Phoenix	94.737	88.409	72.222	31.429	78.816
Pittsburgh	85.714	81.944	62.264	36.842	71.512
Washington, D.C.	86.777	72.475	53.826	24.561	61.782

[a] Percent refers to the percentage of the sample with no structural flaws.

APPENDIX C

Bounty System in Metropolitan Area

Area	Income*	Rent**	Tenant Contribution	Subsidy	Rent/ Income
SMSA					
Albany–Schnectady–					
Troy, N.Y.	$10,600	$240	$178	$62	20.2
Binghamton, N.Y.	9,400	201	151	50	19.3
Syracuse, N.Y.	10,550	219	170	49	19.3
Utica–Rome, N.Y.	9,100	178	140	38	18.5
Albuquerque, N.M.	8,800	217	148	69	20.2
Anchorage, Alaska	15,350	380	289	91	22.6
Albany, Ga.	8,850	184	140	44	19.0
Altanta, Ga.	11,250	254	190	64	20.3
Augusta, Ga.	8,950	239	160	79	21.4
Chattanooga, Tenn.	9,000	213	151	62	20.1
Columbus, Ga.	8,350	206	141	65	20.3
Macon, Ga.	9,100	184	142	42	18.7
Savannah, Ga.	9,100	226	156	70	20.6
Baltimore, Md.	11,750	284	207	77	21.2
Washington, D.C.	14,200	292	235	57	19.8
Wilmington, Del.	11,900	278	206	72	20.8
Anniston, Ala.	7,700	162	121	41	18.8
Birmingham, Ala.	9,350	224	159	65	20.3
Columbus, Ga.	8,350	206	141	65	20.3
Florence, Ala.	8,450	217	146	71	20.7
Gadsden, Ala.	8,250	162	127	35	18.4
Huntsville, Ala.	8,750	222	151	71	20.7
Mobile, Ala.	8,550	180	135	45	19.0
Montgomery, Ala.	8,950	173	138	35	18.5
Tuscaloosa, Ala.	8,350	210	144	66	20.7
Boise, Idaho	11,450	230	184	46	19.3
Boston, Mass.	11,350	315	219	96	23.2
Brockton, Mass.	10,900	259	190	69	20.9
Fall River, Mass.	9,350	252	170	82	21.8
Fitchburg–Leominster, Mass.	10,250	246	176	70	20.6
Lawrence–Haverhill, Mass. .	10,650	278	194	84	21.9
Lowell, Mass.	10,850	268	191	77	21.1
New Bedford, Mass.	9,400	252	170	82	21.7
Pittsfield, Mass.	10,500	210	166	44	19.0
Providence, R.I.	9,900	252	175	77	21.2
Springfield, Mass.	10,100	257	179	78	21.3
Worcester, Mass.	10,750	278	195	83	21.8
Buffalo, N.Y.	10,200	222	167	55	19.7
Elmira, N.Y.	9,300	225	159	66	20.5
Rochester, N.Y.	12,150	248	197	51	19.4

* 80 Percent of Median—EMAD—July 1980
** 80 Percent of FMR—2 Bedroom Unit—March 1981

Area	Income*	Rent**	Tenant Contribution	Subsidy	Rent/ Income
SMSA					
Waco, Tex.	$ 8,650	$216	$148	$68	20.5
Colorado Springs, Colo.	9,300	229	159	70	20.6
Denver–Boulder, Colo.	11,350	292	208	84	22.0
Fort Collins, Colo.	9,550	241	167	74	21.0
Greeley, Colo.	9,450	224	160	64	20.3
Pueblo, Colo.	9,350	234	162	72	20.8
Cedar Rapids, Iowa	11,500	240	187	53	19.5
Des Moines, Iowa	11,250	256	191	65	20.3
Dubuque, Iowa	11,250	247	187	60	20.0
Omaha, Nebr.–Iowa	10,900	238	181	57	19.8
Sioux City, Nebr.–Iowa	9,750	241	169	72	20.8
Waterloo-Cedar Falls, Iowa .	11,150	206	171	35	18.4
Ann Arbor, Mich.	10,500	304	205	99	23.4
Detroit, Mich.	12,850	284	218	66	20.4
Bismarck, N.D.	8,550	237	155	82	21.7
Fargo–Moorhead, N.D.– Minn.	10,100	246	175	71	20.8
Grand Forks, N.D.–Minn. ...	9,300	237	163	74	21.0
Bay City, Mich.	10,850	239	180	59	19.9
Flint, Mich.	12,000	250	196	54	19.6
Saginaw, Mich.	11,600	239	188	51	19.4
Fresno, Calif.	8,700	246	160	86	22.0
Modesto, Calif.	8,900	250	164	86	22.1
Battle Creek, Mich.	11,150	215	174	41	18.7
Grand Rapids, Mich.	10,900	230	177	53	19.5
Jackson, Mich.	11,550	215	178	37	18.5
Kalamazoo–Portage, Mich. .	10,400	258	183	75	21.0
Lansing–East Lansing, Mich.	11,550	273	201	72	20.8
Muskegon, Mich.	9,850	201	156	45	19.0
Asheville, N.C.	8,250	192	136	56	19.7
Burlington, N.C.	9,750	221	162	59	19.9
Charlotte–Gastonia, N.C. ...	10,600	266	188	78	21.3
Fayetteville, N.C.	7,800	223	141	82	21.7
Greensboro–Winston Salem, N.C.	10,050	221	165	56	19.7
Norfolk–Virginia Beach, Va.–N.C.	9,600	280	184	96	23.1
Raleigh–Durham, N.C.	10,000	236	170	66	20.4
Wilmington, N.C.	9,050	206	149	57	19.8
Abilene, Tex.	8,100	193	134	59	19.9
San Angelo, Tex.	8,350	193	137	56	19.7
Wichita Falls, Tex.	8,900	213	150	63	20.2

Area	Income*	Rent**	Tenant Contribution	Subsidy	Rent/ Income
SMSA					
Atlantic City, N.J.	$ 8,950	$241	$161	$ 80	21.6
Philadelphia, Pa.-N.J.	11,050	282	200	82	21.7
Trenton, N.J.	11,350	247	188	59	19.9
Vineland–Millville–					
Bridgeton, N.J.	9,600	249	170	79	21.3
Wilmington, Del.-N.J.-Md. . .	11,900	278	205	73	20.7
Charleston, W.V.	9,400	242	166	76	21.2
Huntington, W.V.-Ky.-					
Ohio	8,750	227	153	74	20.9
Parkersburg, W.V.-Ohio	8,950	224	154	70	20.7
Steubenville, Ohio-W.V. ...	9,900	223	164	59	19.9
Wheeling, W.V.-Ohio	9,350	225	159	66	20.4
Davenport, Iowa-Mo./					
Nebr.-Ill.	11,600	248	191	57	19.8
Kankakee, Ill.	10,400	210	165	45	19.0
Rockford, Ill.	11,450	253	192	61	20.1
Chicago, Ill.	12,550	332	239	93	22.9
Cincinnati, Ohio-Ky.-Ind. . .	10,600	234	176	58	19.9
Dayton, Ohio	11,350	237	184	53	19.6
Hamilton–Middletown, Ohio	10,700	206	166	40	18.7
Akron, Ohio	11,400	245	188	57	19.8
Canton, Ohio	10,500	218	169	49	19.3
Cleveland, Ohio	11,950	230	187	43	18.8
Lima, Ohio	9,900	220	163	57	19.8
Lorain–Elyria, Ohio	11,800	238	189	49	19.2
Mansfield, Ohio	10,050	210	161	49	19.3
Toledo, Ohio-Mich.	11,300	218	177	41	18.8
Youngstown–Warren, Ohio..	10,950	210	170	40	18.7
Springfield, Ohio	9,600	224	161	63	20.2
Augusta, Ga.-S.C.	8,950	239	160	79	21.4
Charleston, S.C.	8,600	248	160	88	22.3
Columbia, S.C.	9,400	239	165	74	21.0
Greenville, S.C.	9,750	203	156	47	19.2
Fort Lauderdale, Fla.	10,350	350	225	125	26.0
Fort Myers–Cape Coral, Fla.	8,250	283	171	112	24.8
Miami, Fla.	10,150	354	226	128	26.7
West Palm Beach, Fla.	9,750	315	202	113	24.8
Dallas–Fort Worth, Tex.	11,100	253	189	64	20.3
Killeen–Temple, Tex.	7,500	216	135	81	21.6
Longview–Marshall, Tex. ...	8,600	177	135	42	18.8
Sherman–Denison, Tex.	9,150	187	144	43	18.9
Texarkana, Tex.-Ark.	8,250	177	131	46	19.0
Tyler, Tex.	8,800	177	137	40	18.7

Area	Income*	Rent**	Tenant Contribution	Subsidy	Rent/ Income
SMSA					
Bridgeport, Conn.	$12,050	$277	$207	$70	20.6
Bristol, Conn.	11,650	249	192	57	19.8
Danbury, Conn.	12,100	311	224	87	22.2
Hartford, Conn.	12,200	290	215	75	21.0
Meriden, Conn.	10,850	238	180	58	19.9
New Britain, Conn.	11,200	249	188	61	20.1
New Haven, Conn.	10,800	284	199	85	22.0
New London, Conn.	10,250	246	176	70	20.7
Norwalk, Conn.	14,700	319	251	68	20.5
Stamford, Conn.	16,200	335	272	63	20.2
Waterbury, Conn.	10,950	238	181	57	19.8
Billings, Mont.	9,400	270	178	92	22.7
Great Falls, Mont.	8,750	250	162	88	22.3
Honolulu, Hawaii	12,250	334	237	97	23.2
Beaumont, Tex.	10,250	212	164	48	19.2
Bryan, Tex.	8,150	212	141	71	20.7
Galveston, Tex.	10,450	238	176	62	20.2
Houston, Tex.	11,500	250	191	59	19.9
Anderson, Ind.	10,600	208	166	42	18.8
Bloomington, Ind.	9,500	226	161	65	20.3
Elkhart, Ind.	10,300	227	170	57	19.8
Evansville, Ind.-Ky.	9,400	227	160	67	20.4
Fort Wayne, Ind.	10,950	242	182	60	20.0
Gary, Ind.	11,850	226	185	41	18.7
Indianapolis, Ind.	10,910	230	177	53	19.5
Kokomo, Ind.	11,200	226	179	47	19.2
Lafayette, Ind.	10,450	237	175	62	20.1
Louisville, Ky.-Ind.	10,550	210	166	44	18.9
Muncie, Ind.	9,400	208	154	54	19.6
South Bend, Ind.	10,300	237	174	63	20.2
Terre Haute, Ind.	8,750	216	149	67	20.5
Biloxi, Miss.	7,250	204	128	76	21.1
Jackson, Miss.	9,150	234	159	75	21.0
Memphis, Tenn.-Ark.-Miss.	9,450	218	158	60	20.0
Pascagoula, Miss.	9,150	212	152	60	20.0
Gainesville, Fla.	9,050	225	155	70	20.6
Jacksonville, Fla.	9,450	236	164	72	20.8
Panama City, Fla.	7,850	225	142	83	21.8
Pensacola, Fla.	8,500	235	154	81	21.6
Tallahassee, Fla.	9,450	225	160	65	20.3

Area	Income*	Rent**	Tenant Contribution	Subsidy	Rent/ Income
SMSA					
Las Vegas, Nev.	$11,000	$273	$195	$ 78	21.3
Fayetteville, Ark.	7,600	187	127	60	20.0
Fort Smith, Ark.–Okla.	7,200	178	119	59	19.9
Little Rock, Ark.	9,450	202	152	50	19.3
Pine Bluff, Ark.	7,550	182	125	57	19.8
Clarksville, Ind.–Ky.	7,250	213	131	82	21.7
Lexington–Fayette, Ky.	9,600	236	166	70	20.7
Owensboro, Ky.	9,500	236	164	72	20.8
Bakersfield, Calif.	8,700	249	162	87	22.2
Los Angeles, Calif.	11,200	309	215	94	22.9
Oxnard, Calif.	11,450	298	211	87	22.2
Santa Barbara, Calif.	10,100	333	214	119	25.4
Amarillo, Tex.	10,000	184	151	33	18.2
El Paso, Tex.	8,650	226	151	75	21.0
Lubbock, Tex.	9,350	193	148	45	19.0
Midland, Tex.	11,000	203	168	35	18.3
Odessa, Tex.	10,050	203	159	44	19.0
St. Joseph, Mo.	8,500	170	135	45	19.0
Springfield, Mo.	8,600	187	138	49	19.3
Johnson City, Tenn.–Va. ...	9,000	218	153	65	20.3
Knoxville, Tenn.	8,750	213	148	65	20.3
Manchester, N.H.	9,600	282	185	97	23.2
Nashua, N.H.	10,800	282	198	84	22.0
Appleton–Oshkosh, Wis. ...	10,650	228	174	54	19.6
Duluth, Minn.–Wis.	9,650	243	168	75	21.0
Eau Claire, Wis.	9,550	174	144	30	18.1
Green Bay, Wis.	10,950	208	169	39	18.6
Jonesville, Wis.	9,900	216	162	54	19.6
Kenosha, Wis.	10,100	238	172	66	20.4
La Crosse, Wis.	9,200	190	145	45	19.0
Madison, Wis.	11,500	247	190	57	19.8
Milwaukee, Wis.	11,950	268	203	65	20.4
Minneapolis–St. Paul, Minn.	12,400	298	220	78	21.3
Racine, Wis.	11,600	238	187	51	19.4
Rochester, Minn.	11,550	262	196	66	20.4
St. Cloud, Minn.	8,900	254	166	88	22.3
Nashville–Davidson, Ind. ...	9,900	233	168	65	20.3

Area	Income*	Rent**	Tenant Contribution	Subsidy	Rent/ Income
SMSA					
Baton Rouge, La.	$10,100	$250	$176	$ 74	20.9
Lafayette, La.	9,100	218	154	64	20.3
Lake Charles, La.	9,150	218	155	63	20.2
New Orleans, La.	9,450	232	162	70	20.6
Nassau–Suffolk, N.Y.	13,350	364	262	102	23.7
Poughkeepsie, N.Y.	12,100	241	179	62	19.2
New York, N.Y.–N.J.	11,000	326	220	106	24.1
Allentown, Pa.–N.J.	10,450	259	184	75	21.0
Jersey City, N.J.	9,750	245	170	75	21.0
Long Branch, N.J.	11,900	291	212	79	21.4
New Brunswick, N.J.	12,600	302	224	78	21.3
Newark, N.J.	12,600	293	220	73	20.9
Paterson, N.J.	11,150	306	212	94	22.9
Lawton, Okla.	8,050	213	140	73	20.9
Oklahoma City, Okla.	9,950	217	163	54	19.6
Lincoln, Nebr.	10,150	246	175	71	20.7
Daytona Beach, Fla.	7,250	215	132	83	21.8
Melbourne–Titusville, Fla. ..	9,900	278	187	91	22.6
Orlando, Fla.	9,000	273	175	98	23.3
Harrisburg, Pa.	10,000	258	179	79	21.4
Lancaster, Pa.	10,100	243	174	69	20.6
Northeast, Pa.	8,450	200	140	60	20.0
Reading, Pa.	10,150	216	164	52	19.4
Williamsport, Pa.	9,050	171	138	33	18.2
York, Pa.	9,900	230	167	63	20.2
Phoenix, Ariz.	9,900	284	190	94	22.9
Altoona, Pa.	8,350	201	140	61	20.1
Erie, Pa.	9,300	207	152	55	19.7
Johnstown, Pa.	8,700	200	143	57	19.8
Pittsburgh, Pa.	10,050	246	174	72	20.8
Eugene, Oreg.	9,800	224	163	61	20.0
Portland, Oreg.–Wa.	11,000	260	190	70	20.7
Salem, Oreg.	9,300	266	175	91	22.6
Reno, Nev.	11,200	364	241	123	25.8
Lynchburg, Va.	9,500	255	172	83	21.8
Newport News, Va.	10,300	260	182	78	21.3
Petersburg, Va.	9,800	248	172	76	21.1
Richmond, Va.	11,200	262	193	69	20.6

Area	Income*	Rent**	Tenant Contribution	Subsidy	Rent/ Income
SMSA					
Roanoke, Va.	$10,000	$255	$177	$ 78	21.3
Sacramento, Calif.	10,300	255	180	75	21.0
Stockton, Calif.	9,700	236	167	69	20.6
Provo-Orem, Utah..........	9,150	224	156	68	20.5
Salt Lake City, Utah	10,100	241	173	68	20.5
Austin, Tex.	9,850	294	193	101	23.6
Brownsville, Tex.	5,850	228	119	109	24.4
Corpus Christi, Tex.	8,950	222	154	68	20.6
Laredo, Tex.	5,550	235	117	118	25.3
McAllen, Tex.	5,300	228	111	117	25.2
San Antonio, Tex.	9,000	251	165	86	22.0
San Diego, Calif.	9,950	308	201	107	24.2
Salinas, Calif.	9,650	299	193	106	24.1
San Francisco, Calif.	12,250	327	233	94	22.9
San Jose, Calif.	12,450	351	247	104	23.9
Santa Cruz, Calif.	9,000	308	190	118	25.3
Santa Rosa, Calif.	9,750	304	197	107	24.2
Vallejo, Calif.	10,500	283	195	88	22.3
Anaheim, Calif.	12,000	325	230	95	23.0
Riverside, Calif.	9,050	286	181	105	24.0
Seattle, Wash.	11,850	315	223	92	22.7
Tacoma, Wash.	10,250	250	177	72	20.8
Yakima, Wash.	8,550	230	152	78	21.3
Alexandria, La.	7,050	177	117	60	20.0
Monroe, La.	8,250	177	131	46	19.1
Shreveport, La.	8,650	196	141	55	19.6
Rapid City, S.D.	7,900	230	145	85	22.0
Sioux Falls, S.D.	10,000	242	172	70	20.7
Richland, Wash.	10,400	250	179	71	20.7
Spokane, Wash.	9,600	243	168	75	21.0
Champaign–Urbana, Ill.	9,850	239	170	69	20.6
Decatur, Ill.	10,900	226	176	50	19.3
Peoria, Ill.	11,950	248	195	53	19.6
St. Louis, Mo.–Ill.	10,950	250	186	64	20.3
Springfield, Ill.	10,400	226	171	55	19.7
Columbia, Mo.	10,050	216	163	53	19.5
Bradenton, Fla.	7,100	283	156	127	26.4
Lakeland, Fla.	8,350	234	151	83	21.8
Sarasota, Fla.	8,400	283	172	111	24.6

Area	Income*	Rent**	Tenant Contribution	Subsidy	Rent/ Income
SMSA					
Tampa, Fla.	$ 8,300	$252	$158	$94	22.9
Lawrence, Kans.	9,500	242	166	76	21.0
Topeka, Kans.	9,850	218	162	56	19.7
Wichita, Kans.	9,750	219	162	57	19.8
Tucson, Ariz.	9,150	262	172	90	22.5
Tulsa, Okla.	9,900	228	166	62	20.1
Bloomington–Normal, Ill. ..	10,950	216	172	44	18.9
Columbus, Ohio............	10,600	220	170	50	19.4
Enid, Okla.	8,700	187	140	47	19.3
Iowa City, Iowa............	9,900	240	170	70	20.6
Kansas City, Mo.–Kans. ...	11,100	224	177	47	19.2
Las Cruces, N.M.	6,400	182	111	71	20.8
Lewiston–Auburn, Maine ...	9,250	223	157	66	20.4
Portland, Maine	9,500	261	175	86	22.1

APPENDIX D

U.S. Department of Housing and Urban Development
Bounty Demonstration Program for Family Income of $1776 and Family Size of 3 or 4 Persons
Income Represents Maximum Welfare Benefits Provided in the State of Alabama

High Need Category 2—Bonus of 16 Percent

Rent	You Pay	Rent	You Pay	Rent	You Pay	Rent	You Pay	Rent	You Pay
$ 30	$ 30	$ 75	$ 34	$120	$ 39	$165	$ 43	$210	$ 48
$ 31	$ 30	$ 76	$ 34	$121	$ 39	$166	$ 43	$211	$ 48
$ 32	$ 30	$ 77	$ 35	$122	$ 39	$167	$ 43	$212	$ 48
$ 33	$ 30	$ 78	$ 35	$123	$ 39	$168	$ 43	$213	$ 48
$ 34	$ 30	$ 79	$ 35	$124	$ 39	$169	$ 44	$214	$ 48
$ 35	$ 31	$ 80	$ 35	$125	$ 39	$170	$ 44	$215	$ 48
$ 36	$ 31	$ 81	$ 35	$126	$ 39	$171	$ 44	$216	$ 49
$ 37	$ 31	$ 82	$ 35	$127	$ 39	$172	$ 44	$217	$ 49
$ 38	$ 31	$ 83	$ 35	$128	$ 39	$173	$ 44	$218	$ 49
$ 39	$ 31	$ 84	$ 35	$129	$ 39	$174	$ 45	$219	$ 49
$ 40	$ 31	$ 85	$ 35	$130	$ 39	$175	$ 45	$220	$ 49
$ 41	$ 31	$ 86	$ 36	$131	$ 39	$176	$ 45	$221	$ 49
$ 42	$ 31	$ 87	$ 36	$132	$ 40	$177	$ 45	$222	$ 49
$ 43	$ 31	$ 88	$ 36	$133	$ 40	$178	$ 45	$223	$ 49
$ 44	$ 31	$ 89	$ 36	$134	$ 40	$179	$ 45	$224	$ 49
$ 45	$ 31	$ 90	$ 36	$135	$ 40	$180	$ 45	$225	$ 50
$ 46	$ 31	$ 91	$ 37	$136	$ 40	$181	$ 45	$226	$ 50
$ 47	$ 31	$ 92	$ 37	$137	$ 40	$182	$ 45	$227	$ 50
$ 48	$ 31	$ 93	$ 37	$138	$ 40	$183	$ 45	$228	$ 50
$ 49	$ 32	$ 94	$ 37	$139	$ 40	$184	$ 45	$229	$ 50
$ 50	$ 32	$ 95	$ 37	$140	$ 40	$185	$ 45	$230	$ 50
$ 51	$ 32	$ 96	$ 37	$141	$ 41	$186	$ 45	$231	$ 50
$ 52	$ 32	$ 97	$ 37	$142	$ 41	$187	$ 45	$232	$ 50
$ 53	$ 32	$ 98	$ 37	$143	$ 41	$188	$ 46	$233	$ 50
$ 54	$ 32	$ 99	$ 37	$144	$ 41	$189	$ 46	$234	$ 50
$ 55	$ 32	$100	$ 37	$145	$ 41	$190	$ 46	$235	$ 50
$ 56	$ 32	$101	$ 37	$146	$ 42	$191	$ 46	$236	$ 50
$ 57	$ 32	$102	$ 37	$147	$ 42	$192	$ 46	$237	$ 50
$ 58	$ 33	$103	$ 37	$148	$ 42	$193	$ 46	$238	$ 50
$ 59	$ 33	$104	$ 37	$149	$ 42	$194	$ 46	$239	$ 50
$ 60	$ 33	$105	$ 37	$150	$ 42	$195	$ 46	$240	$ 50
$ 61	$ 33	$106	$ 37	$151	$ 42	$196	$ 46	$241	$ 50
$ 62	$ 33	$107	$ 37	$152	$ 42	$197	$ 47	$242	$ 50
$ 63	$ 34	$108	$ 37	$153	$ 42	$198	$ 47	$243	$ 50
$ 64	$ 34	$109	$ 37	$154	$ 42	$199	$ 47	$244	$ 50
$ 65	$ 34	$110	$ 37	$155	$ 42	$200	$ 47	$245	$ 50
$ 66	$ 34	$111	$ 37	$156	$ 42	$201	$ 47	$246	$ 50
$ 67	$ 34	$112	$ 37	$157	$ 42	$202	$ 48	$247	$ 50
$ 68	$ 34	$113	$ 38	$158	$ 42	$203	$ 48	$248	$ 50
$ 69	$ 34	$114	$ 38	$159	$ 42	$204	$ 48	$249	$ 50
$ 70	$ 34	$115	$ 38	$160	$ 43	$205	$ 48	$250	$ 50
$ 71	$ 34	$116	$ 38	$161	$ 43	$206	$ 48	$251	$ 50
$ 72	$ 34	$117	$ 38	$162	$ 43	$207	$ 48	$252	$ 50
$ 73	$ 34	$118	$ 39	$163	$ 43	$208	$ 48	$253	$ 51
$ 74	$ 34	$119	$ 39	$164	$ 43	$209	$ 48	$254	$ 52

For rents below $30 you pay the full rent. For rents above $252 you pay the full rent less $202.

U.S. Department of Housing and Urban Development
Bounty Demonstration Program for Family Income of $2520 and Family Size of 3 or 4 Persons
Income Represents Maximum Welfare Benefits Provided in the State of North Carolina

High Need Category 3—Bonus of 12 Percent

Rent	You Pay	Rent	You Pay	Rent	You Pay	Rent	You Pay	Rent	You Pay
$ 42	$ 42	$ 88	$ 48	$134	$ 55	$180	$ 61	$226	$ 68
$ 43	$ 42	$ 89	$ 48	$135	$ 56	$181	$ 61	$227	$ 69
$ 44	$ 42	$ 90	$ 48	$136	$ 56	$182	$ 61	$228	$ 69
$ 45	$ 42	$ 91	$ 49	$137	$ 56	$183	$ 62	$229	$ 69
$ 46	$ 43	$ 92	$ 49	$138	$ 56	$184	$ 62	$230	$ 69
$ 47	$ 43	$ 93	$ 49	$139	$ 56	$185	$ 62	$231	$ 69
$ 48	$ 43	$ 94	$ 49	$140	$ 56	$186	$ 62	$232	$ 69
$ 49	$ 43	$ 95	$ 49	$141	$ 56	$187	$ 62	$233	$ 69
$ 50	$ 43	$ 96	$ 49	$142	$ 56	$188	$ 63	$234	$ 69
$ 51	$ 43	$ 97	$ 49	$143	$ 56	$189	$ 63	$235	$ 69
$ 52	$ 44	$ 98	$ 49	$144	$ 56	$190	$ 63	$236	$ 69
$ 53	$ 44	$ 99	$ 49	$145	$ 56	$191	$ 63	$237	$ 70
$ 54	$ 44	$100	$ 50	$146	$ 56	$192	$ 64	$238	$ 70
$ 55	$ 44	$101	$ 50	$147	$ 56	$193	$ 64	$239	$ 70
$ 56	$ 44	$102	$ 50	$148	$ 57	$194	$ 64	$240	$ 70
$ 57	$ 44	$103	$ 50	$149	$ 57	$195	$ 64	$241	$ 70
$ 58	$ 44	$104	$ 51	$150	$ 57	$196	$ 64	$242	$ 70
$ 59	$ 44	$105	$ 51	$151	$ 57	$197	$ 64	$243	$ 70
$ 60	$ 44	$106	$ 51	$152	$ 57	$198	$ 65	$244	$ 70
$ 61	$ 44	$107	$ 51	$153	$ 57	$199	$ 65	$245	$ 70
$ 62	$ 45	$108	$ 51	$154	$ 58	$200	$ 65	$246	$ 71
$ 63	$ 45	$109	$ 51	$155	$ 58	$201	$ 65	$247	$ 71
$ 64	$ 45	$110	$ 52	$156	$ 58	$202	$ 65	$248	$ 71
$ 65	$ 45	$111	$ 52	$157	$ 58	$203	$ 65	$249	$ 71
$ 66	$ 45	$112	$ 52	$158	$ 58	$204	$ 65	$250	$ 71
$ 67	$ 45	$113	$ 52	$159	$ 59	$205	$ 65	$251	$ 71
$ 68	$ 45	$114	$ 52	$160	$ 59	$206	$ 65	$252	$ 71
$ 69	$ 45	$115	$ 52	$161	$ 59	$207	$ 65	$253	$ 71
$ 70	$ 45	$116	$ 52	$162	$ 59	$208	$ 66	$254	$ 71
$ 71	$ 46	$117	$ 52	$163	$ 59	$209	$ 66	$255	$ 71
$ 72	$ 46	$118	$ 52	$164	$ 60	$210	$ 66	$256	$ 71
$ 73	$ 46	$119	$ 53	$165	$ 60	$211	$ 66	$257	$ 71
$ 74	$ 46	$120	$ 53	$166	$ 60	$212	$ 66	$258	$ 71
$ 75	$ 47	$121	$ 53	$167	$ 60	$213	$ 66	$259	$ 71
$ 76	$ 47	$122	$ 53	$168	$ 60	$214	$ 66	$260	$ 71
$ 77	$ 47	$123	$ 53	$169	$ 60	$215	$ 66	$261	$ 71
$ 78	$ 47	$124	$ 53	$170	$ 60	$216	$ 66	$262	$ 71
$ 79	$ 47	$125	$ 54	$171	$ 60	$217	$ 67	$263	$ 71
$ 80	$ 47	$126	$ 54	$172	$ 60	$218	$ 67	$264	$ 71
$ 81	$ 48	$127	$ 54	$173	$ 60	$219	$ 67	$265	$ 71
$ 82	$ 48	$128	$ 54	$174	$ 60	$220	$ 67	$266	$ 71
$ 83	$ 48	$129	$ 54	$175	$ 60	$221	$ 68	$267	$ 71
$ 84	$ 48	$130	$ 55	$176	$ 60	$222	$ 68	$268	$ 72
$ 85	$ 48	$131	$ 55	$177	$ 61	$223	$ 68	$269	$ 73
$ 86	$ 48	$132	$ 55	$178	$ 61	$224	$ 68	$270	$ 74
$ 87	$ 48	$133	$ 55	$179	$ 61	$225	$ 68	$271	$ 75

For rents below $42 you pay the full rent. For rents above $267 you pay the full rent less $196.

U.S. Department of Housing and Urban Development
Bounty Demonstration Program for Family Income of $4188 and Family Size of 3 or 4 Persons
Income Represents Maximum Welfare Benefits Provided in the State of Oklahoma

High Need Category 5—Bonus of 4 Percent

Rent	You Pay	Rent	You Pay	Rent	You Pay	Rent	You Pay	Rent	You Pay
$ 70	$ 70	$116	$ 80	$162	$ 90	$208	$100	$254	$110
$ 71	$ 70	$117	$ 80	$163	$ 90	$209	$100	$255	$110
$ 72	$ 70	$118	$ 80	$164	$ 90	$210	$101	$256	$110
$ 73	$ 71	$119	$ 80	$165	$ 90	$211	$101	$257	$110
$ 74	$ 71	$120	$ 80	$166	$ 91	$212	$101	$258	$111
$ 75	$ 71	$121	$ 81	$167	$ 91	$213	$101	$259	$111
$ 76	$ 71	$122	$ 81	$168	$ 91	$214	$101	$260	$111
$ 77	$ 72	$123	$ 81	$169	$ 92	$215	$101	$261	$111
$ 78	$ 72	$124	$ 81	$170	$ 92	$216	$101	$262	$112
$ 79	$ 72	$125	$ 82	$171	$ 92	$217	$102	$263	$112
$ 80	$ 72	$126	$ 82	$172	$ 92	$218	$102	$264	$112
$ 81	$ 72	$127	$ 82	$173	$ 93	$219	$102	$265	$113
$ 82	$ 73	$128	$ 82	$174	$ 93	$220	$102	$266	$113
$ 83	$ 73	$129	$ 82	$175	$ 93	$221	$103	$267	$113
$ 84	$ 73	$130	$ 83	$176	$ 93	$222	$103	$268	$113
$ 85	$ 73	$131	$ 83	$177	$ 93	$223	$103	$269	$114
$ 86	$ 73	$132	$ 83	$178	$ 94	$224	$103	$270	$114
$ 87	$ 73	$133	$ 83	$179	$ 94	$225	$103	$271	$114
$ 88	$ 73	$134	$ 84	$180	$ 94	$226	$104	$272	$114
$ 89	$ 74	$135	$ 84	$181	$ 94	$227	$104	$273	$114
$ 90	$ 74	$136	$ 84	$182	$ 94	$228	$104	$274	$115
$ 91	$ 74	$137	$ 85	$183	$ 94	$229	$104	$275	$115
$ 92	$ 74	$138	$ 85	$184	$ 94	$230	$105	$276	$115
$ 93	$ 75	$139	$ 85	$185	$ 95	$231	$105	$277	$115
$ 94	$ 75	$140	$ 85	$186	$ 95	$232	$105	$278	$115
$ 95	$ 75	$141	$ 86	$187	$ 95	$233	$106	$279	$115
$ 96	$ 75	$142	$ 86	$188	$ 95	$234	$106	$280	$115
$ 97	$ 75	$143	$ 86	$189	$ 96	$235	$106	$281	$116
$ 98	$ 76	$144	$ 86	$190	$ 96	$236	$106	$282	$116
$ 99	$ 76	$145	$ 86	$191	$ 96	$237	$107	$283	$116
$100	$ 76	$146	$ 87	$192	$ 96	$238	$107	$284	$116
$101	$ 76	$147	$ 87	$193	$ 96	$239	$107	$285	$117
$102	$ 77	$148	$ 87	$194	$ 97	$240	$107	$286	$117
$103	$ 77	$149	$ 87	$195	$ 97	$241	$107	$287	$117
$104	$ 77	$150	$ 87	$196	$ 97	$242	$108	$288	$117
$105	$ 78	$151	$ 87	$197	$ 97	$243	$108	$289	$117
$106	$ 78	$152	$ 87	$198	$ 98	$244	$108	$290	$118
$107	$ 78	$153	$ 88	$199	$ 98	$245	$108	$291	$118
$108	$ 78	$154	$ 88	$200	$ 98	$246	$108	$292	$118
$109	$ 78	$155	$ 88	$201	$ 99	$247	$108	$293	$118
$110	$ 79	$156	$ 88	$202	$ 99	$248	$108	$294	$119
$111	$ 79	$157	$ 89	$203	$ 99	$249	$109	$295	$120
$112	$ 79	$158	$ 89	$204	$ 99	$250	$109	$296	$121
$113	$ 79	$159	$ 89	$205	$100	$251	$109	$297	$122
$114	$ 80	$160	$ 89	$206	$100	$252	$109	$298	$123
$115	$ 80	$161	$ 89	$207	$100	$253	$110	$299	$124

For rents below $70 you pay the full rent. For rents above $294 you pay the full rent less $175.

U.S. Department of Housing and Urban Development
Bounty Demonstration Program for Family Income of $1692 and Family Size of 3 or 4 Persons
Income Represents Maximum Welfare Benefits Provided in the State of Texas

High Need Category 2—Bonus of 16 Percent

Rent	You Pay	Rent	You Pay	Rent	You Pay	Rent	You Pay	Rent	You Pay
$ 28	$ 28	$ 73	$ 32	$118	$ 38	$163	$ 41	$208	$ 46
$ 29	$ 28	$ 74	$ 32	$119	$ 38	$164	$ 41	$209	$ 46
$ 30	$ 28	$ 75	$ 33	$120	$ 38	$165	$ 41	$210	$ 46
$ 31	$ 28	$ 76	$ 33	$121	$ 38	$166	$ 41	$211	$ 46
$ 32	$ 28	$ 77	$ 33	$122	$ 38	$167	$ 42	$212	$ 46
$ 33	$ 29	$ 78	$ 33	$123	$ 38	$168	$ 42	$213	$ 46
$ 34	$ 29	$ 79	$ 33	$124	$ 38	$169	$ 42	$214	$ 47
$ 35	$ 29	$ 80	$ 33	$125	$ 38	$170	$ 42	$215	$ 47
$ 36	$ 29	$ 81	$ 33	$126	$ 38	$171	$ 42	$216	$ 47
$ 37	$ 29	$ 82	$ 33	$127	$ 38	$172	$ 43	$217	$ 47
$ 38	$ 29	$ 83	$ 33	$128	$ 38	$173	$ 43	$218	$ 47
$ 39	$ 29	$ 84	$ 34	$129	$ 38	$174	$ 43	$219	$ 47
$ 40	$ 29	$ 85	$ 34	$130	$ 38	$175	$ 43	$220	$ 47
$ 41	$ 29	$ 86	$ 34	$131	$ 38	$176	$ 43	$221	$ 47
$ 42	$ 29	$ 87	$ 34	$132	$ 38	$177	$ 43	$222	$ 47
$ 43	$ 29	$ 88	$ 34	$133	$ 38	$178	$ 43	$223	$ 48
$ 44	$ 29	$ 89	$ 35	$134	$ 38	$179	$ 43	$224	$ 48
$ 45	$ 29	$ 90	$ 35	$135	$ 38	$180	$ 43	$225	$ 48
$ 46	$ 29	$ 91	$ 35	$136	$ 38	$181	$ 43	$226	$ 48
$ 47	$ 30	$ 92	$ 35	$137	$ 38	$182	$ 43	$227	$ 48
$ 48	$ 30	$ 93	$ 35	$138	$ 38	$183	$ 43	$228	$ 48
$ 49	$ 30	$ 94	$ 35	$139	$ 39	$184	$ 43	$229	$ 48
$ 50	$ 30	$ 95	$ 35	$140	$ 39	$185	$ 43	$230	$ 48
$ 51	$ 30	$ 96	$ 35	$141	$ 39	$186	$ 44	$231	$ 48
$ 52	$ 30	$ 97	$ 35	$142	$ 39	$187	$ 44	$232	$ 48
$ 53	$ 30	$ 98	$ 35	$143	$ 39	$188	$ 44	$233	$ 48
$ 54	$ 30	$ 99	$ 35	$144	$ 40	$189	$ 44	$234	$ 48
$ 55	$ 30	$100	$ 35	$145	$ 40	$190	$ 44	$235	$ 48
$ 56	$ 31	$101	$ 35	$146	$ 40	$191	$ 44	$236	$ 48
$ 57	$ 31	$102	$ 35	$147	$ 40	$192	$ 44	$237	$ 48
$ 58	$ 31	$103	$ 36	$148	$ 40	$193	$ 44	$238	$ 48
$ 59	$ 31	$104	$ 36	$149	$ 40	$194	$ 44	$239	$ 48
$ 60	$ 31	$105	$ 36	$150	$ 40	$195	$ 45	$240	$ 48
$ 61	$ 32	$106	$ 36	$151	$ 40	$196	$ 45	$241	$ 48
$ 62	$ 32	$107	$ 36	$152	$ 40	$197	$ 45	$242	$ 48
$ 63	$ 32	$108	$ 36	$153	$ 40	$198	$ 45	$243	$ 48
$ 64	$ 32	$109	$ 36	$154	$ 40	$199	$ 45	$244	$ 48
$ 65	$ 32	$110	$ 36	$155	$ 40	$200	$ 46	$245	$ 48
$ 66	$ 32	$111	$ 36	$156	$ 40	$201	$ 46	$246	$ 48
$ 67	$ 32	$112	$ 37	$157	$ 40	$202	$ 46	$247	$ 48
$ 68	$ 32	$113	$ 37	$158	$ 41	$203	$ 46	$248	$ 48
$ 69	$ 32	$114	$ 37	$159	$ 41	$204	$ 46	$249	$ 48
$ 70	$ 32	$115	$ 37	$160	$ 41	$205	$ 46	$250	$ 48
$ 71	$ 32	$116	$ 37	$161	$ 41	$206	$ 46	$251	$ 49
$ 72	$ 32	$117	$ 38	$162	$ 41	$207	$ 46	$252	$ 50

For rents below $28 you pay the full rent. For rents above $250 you pay the full rent less $202.

APPENDIX E

PRIVATIZING OR MAINSTREAMING PUBLIC HOUSING

The most popular solution to the public housing problem in recent years has been to "privatize" it by giving each tenant a housing voucher. Under a housing voucher system, the government sets a standard in a locality ($350 a month) and a standard of what a tenant should pay (30 percent of income) and pays the tenant the difference. In the case of a family with an income of $6,000, the family's contribution would be $150, and the amount of the subsidy would equal $200. If the tenant can find a cheaper unit than the standard it would pocket the difference. If the tenant cannot find a unit under $350, the difference must come out of pocket.

In the typical case, the voucher places the PHA in a Procrustean bed. An authority will have units of different quality that would rent at different prices. Assume three categories of units—$250, $350, $450—and three families with incomes of $6,000. If a voucher is used: the family that chooses a $250 unit need only expend $50 and in effect $100 leaks from the housing subsidy bucket; in the $350 case there is a perfect fit; in the $450 case the family would have to pay $250 out of its pocket and face a rent burden of 50 percent of its income. The federal government has spent $600 and the PHA has received only $500 in benefits and a virtually unrentable unit.

In contrast, under the bounty or table certificate program, the family in the $250 unit would spend $129.25 (approximately 26 percent of its income) and receive a subsidy of $120.75; the family in the $350 unit would spend $155 (31 percent of its income) and receive a subsidy of

$195. The family that chose the $450 unit would pay $207 (41.4 percent of its income) and receive the maximum subsidy of $243. The total amount expended by the federal government would be $558.75 ($41.75 less than in the voucher), the PHA would receive $558.75 ($58.75 more than in the voucher), and the tenant's subsidy would be related to *its* housing expenditure.

Voucher System At Different Rentals

	$250	$350	$450
Subsidy	$200	200	200
Tenant Payment	50	150	250
Rent/Income Ratio	10%	30%	50%

Table Certificate At Different Rentals

	$250	$350	$450
Subsidy	$120.75	195	243
Tenant Payment	129.25	155	207
Rent/Income Ratio	26%	31%	41.4%

NOTES
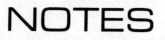

INTRODUCTION

1. Elazar, Daniel J., "Are We a Nation of Cities," 50.
2. Cooper, Clare, "The House as Symbol of the Self," 135.

CHAPTER I

1. Kelly, Burnham, *The Prefabrication of Houses*, 7–14.
2. Stevenson, Katherine Cole, and H. Ward Jandl, *Houses by Mail*, 19.
3. Kelly, *op. cit*, 14.
4. Dahlberg, Bror, "New Homes for Everyone."
5. Booz, Allen & Hamilton, *Survey of Lustron Corporation for Reconstruction Finance Corporation*, 149.
6. *Building the American City*, 437.
7. Census, *Construction Reports, Housing Starts, June 1987*, Table S-1.
8. *Ibid.*, 11.
9. Census Construction Report, *Characteristics of New Housing: 1986*.
10. Census/HUD, *Annual Housing Survey: 1983, General Housing Characteristics*, Tables A 2–4.
11. Herbers, John, *The New Heartland*, 118.
12. Census/HUD, *Annual Housing Survey: 1983, op. cit.*, Table A-3.
13. HUD, *Sixth Report to Congress on the Manufactured Housing Program*, III, 23.
14. *Ibid.*, 24.
15. Technology + Economics, *Economic Benefit-Cost and Risk Analysis of the Results of Mobile Home Research*, 2 (HUD: 1980).

16. McGraw-Hill Information Systems, "Study of Comparative Time & Cost for Building Five Selected Types of Low-Cost Housing," 1.
17. Mayer, Martin, *The Builders,* 230.
18. Eichler, Ned, *The Merchant Builders,* 67–68.
19. *Ibid.*
20. Owen, David, "The Walls Around Us," 75–78.
21. Ball, Robert, "Employment Created by Construction Expenditures," Table 2.
22. Johnson, Ralph, "Housing Technology and Housing Costs," 60.
23. National Association of Home Builders (NAHB), *Housing America —The Challenges Ahead—Long Range Planning Report,* 86.
24. The President's Committee on Urban Housing, *A Decent Home,* 115.
25. Wasserman, Richard, "Levitt's Comments," 69.
26. Ahluwalia, Gopal, "What Do Builders Do," 5.
27. Ahluwalia, Gopal, "Residential Construction Industry," 12.
28. NAHB, *op. cit.,* 111.

CHAPTER II

1. Bonner, Yelena, "Americans Don't Want War," 1, 5.
2. Wolf, Peter, *Land in America: Its Value, Use and Control,* 24–25.
3. Fallows, James, "The Rice Plot," 22.
4. Gottmann, Jean, *Megalopolis,* 347
5. Cited in Winnick, Louis, *Rental Housing: Opportunities for Private Investment,* 81.
6. *Ibid,* 83.
7. *Federal Role in Urban Affairs, Hearings of the U.S. Senate Comm. on Government Operations, 89th Cong., 2nd Sess., Appendix to Part 1,* 41–42.
8. Schlivek, Louis, *Man in the Metropolis,* 31.
9. Winnick, *op. cit.,* 56.
10. Fitzwilliams, Jeanette, "Size Distribution of Income 1963," cited in Task Force on Economic Growth, *First Report: The Concept of Poverty,* 2.
11. Winnick, *op. cit.,* 54.
12. Gans, Herbert, *The Levittowners,* Chapter 2.
13. Riley, H., "Housing Costs and Family Income," 70.
14. Daun, Ake, "Setbacks and Advances in the Swedish Housing Market."
15. Census, *Household and Family Characteristics: March 1983,* 9.

CHAPTER III

1. Merrett, S., *The Right to Rent—A feasibility study.*
2. Downs, Anthony, *Rental Housing in the 1980s,* 3–4.

3. Winnick, Louis, *Rental Housing: Opportunities for Private Investment,* 113.
4. Starr, Roger, "The End of Rental Housing," 31–32.
5. Winnick, *op. cit.,* 21–23.
6. See generally, Winnick, *ibid.,* 121–30.
7. Housing and Home Finance Agency (HHFA), *Housing in the United States . . . a Graphic Presentation,* 36–37.
8. Winnick, *op. cit.,* 156–57.
9. HHFA, *Eleventh Annual Report 1957,* 62.
10. Winnick, *op. cit.,* 157.
11. HHFA, *op. cit.,* 62.
12. Winnick, *op. cit.,* 143.
13. Taubman, Paul, "Housing and Income Tax Subsidies," 983.
14. Quoted in M. Schlefer, "Study of Legislative History of the Rapid Depreciation Provision," E, 1053.
15. Touche Ross, *Study of Tax Considerations in Multi-Family Housing Investments,* 18.
16. Baskin & Winchester, "FHA Middle Income Housing: Some Tax Aspects," 81.
17. HUD, *The Conversion of Rental Housing to Condominiums and Co-operatives, A National Study of Scope, Causes and Impacts,* viii.
18. Census/HUD, *Annual Housing Survey: 1983, General Housing Characteristics,* Table A-2.

CHAPTER IV

1. Lampard, Eric, "The Urbanizing World," 6.
2. *Encyclopedia Judaica, Vol. 9,* 1366–67.
3. Hoyt, Homer, "The Function of the Ancient and Modern City," 263.
4. Lampard, *op. cit.,* 5.
5. Handlin, Oscar, "The Social System," 13.
6. See "Report of the Comm. on Hsng. and Regional Planning to Gov. Alfred E. Smith (1926) in Sussman, ed., *Planning the Fourth Migration: The Neglected Vision of the Regional Planning Assoc. of America,* 146 (M.I.T. Press: 1976).
7. Quoted in *ibid.*
8. "Report," *op. cit.* 66.
9. Patton, Phil, *Open Road,* 55.
10. Vernon, Raymond, *The Myth and Reality of Our Urban Problems.*
11. Warner, Sam, Jr., *Streetcar Suburbs,* 34.
12. Cited in Winnick, Louis, "Facts and Fictions in Urban Renewal" in Wheaton, William et al., eds., *Urban Housing,* 4.
13. Quoted in Berry, Brian, and Quentin Guillard, *The Changing Shape of Metropolitan America,* 11–12.

14. Vernon, *op. cit.,* 18.
15. Bruce-Briggs, B., "Mass Transportation and Minority Transportation," 43–45.
16. Vernon, *op. cit.,* 25–31.
17. *Ibid.*
18. *Ibid.*
19. Starr, Roger, *The Rise and Fall of New York City,* 209.
20. *Ibid.*
21. Vernon, *op. cit.,* 60–71.
22. See generally Patton, *op. cit.*
23. *Ibid.*
24. Blumenfeld, Hans, "Metropolis Extended," 346.
25. Lockwood, Charles, and Christopher B. Leinberger, "Los Angeles Comes of Age," 31.
26. *Washington Post,* July 30, 1987, B 7.
27. Gale, Dennis, *Neighborhood Revitalization and the Post-Industrial City,* 77–79
28. Goleman, Daniel, "The Problems of Autonomy for Children in High-Rises," C1.
29. Kowinski, William, "Endless Summer in the World's Biggest Shopping Wonderland," 35.
30. Lewis, Roger, "Shaping the City," F-6.
31. Kowinski, *op. cit.,* 35.
32. *Industrial Location Policy, Hrgs. Ad Hoc Subcomm. of H.R. Comm. on Banking and Currency, 91st Cong., 2nd Sess. Part 3,* 332 (1970).
33. Blumenfeld, *op. cit.,* 347.
34. *Genesis,* Chapter I, v. 7; Chapter II, v. 3.
35. *Ibid.,* Chapter II, v. 3–25.
36. Blumenfeld, *Metropolis . . . and Beyond,* 65 (John Wiley: 1979).
37. Blumenfeld, "Metropolis Extended," *op. cit.,* 347–48.
38. Gans, Herbert, *Levittowners,* 409–10.
39. Elazar, Daniel, *Building Cities in America,* 268–69.

CHAPTER V

1. Census, *Provisional Estimates of Social, Economic and Housing Characteristics—1980,* Table P-3.
2. See *President's Report on National Growth—1972,* 16.
3. *Ibid.*
4. *Ibid.*
5. Robinson, I., "Blacks Move Back to the South."
6. Quoted in Lemann, Nicholas, "The Origins of the Underclass," 39.
7. Frieden, Bernard, *The Future of Old Neighborhoods,* 12–17.
8. Robinson, *op. cit.,* 42–43.

9. Gans, Herbert, *Levittowners,* 35.
10. *California,* January 1986.
11. See "California: After 19 Million, What?"
12. Kasarda, John, et al., "The South Is Still Rising," 33.
13. Robey, Bryant, *The American People,* 69–70 (E. P. Dutton: 1985).
14. Drucker, Peter, "The Changed World Economy."
15. *Ibid.*
16. Ackerman, Louise, "Reebok: Tennis' Billion Dollar Superstar," 46.
17. "Marketing Firm Slices U.S. Into 240,000 Parts to Spur Client's Sales," *Wall Street Journal,* November 3, 1986, 1.
18. Quinn, Sally, "The Demise of the Washington Hostess," 30.
19. Source unknown.
20. Noyelle, Thierry, and Thomas Stanback, *The Economic Transformation of American Cities.*
21. "Glutted Markets; A Global Overcapacity Hurts Many Industries; No Easy Cure Is Seen," *Wall Street Journal,* March 9, 1987, 1.
22. Belkin, L. "Glum News for U.S. Apparel," B1.
23. Census, *State Population and Household Estimates, With Age, Sex and Components of Change: 1981–1986,* 3 (September 1987).
24. Lemann, *op. cit.*

CHAPTER VI

1. HUD, Office of Policy Research and Development, *How Well Are We Housed? . . . Blacks,* 3.
2. Census/HUD, *Annual Housing Survey, General Housing Characteristics,* Table A-7.
3. Ardagh, John, "How the French Got a New Start," 55, 58.
4. See generally Hirsch, Arnold, "The Causes of Racial Segregation: A Historical Perspective," 56–74.
5. Hirsch, *ibid.,* 63.
6. Abrams, Charles, *The City as the Frontier,* 61.
7. Hirsch, *op. cit.,* 70.
8. Wye, Christopher, "The New Deal and the Negro Community: Toward a Broader Conceptualization," 623.
10. Pettigrew, Thomas, "Attitudes on Race and Housing: A Social-Psychological View," 59–60.
11. Clark, William, "Residential Segregation in American Cities," 35.
12. Gans, Herbert, *Levittowners,* 377–83.
13. Clark, *op. cit.,* 34.
14. Schelling, Thomas, "On the Ecology of Micromotives," 61, 82.
15. Clark, *op. cit.,* 38–39.
16. Granat, D., et al., "Blacks and Whites in Washington—How Separate? How Equal?" 168, 169.

17. Clark, *op. cit.*, 39–40.
18. Welfeld, Irving, "The Courts and Desegregated Housing," 123.
19. Welfeld, Irving, "The Limits of Good Intentions," 25.
20. Sanning, John, "Death Styles," 54, 95.
21. *Building the American City, A Report to the Congress and the President of the United States,* 130 (1968).
22. Flournoy, Craig, "Still Separate and Unequal, 24.
23. Welfeld, Irving, "Exercises in Irrelevance: Federal Enforcement of Fair Housing in Federally Subsidized Housing," 221.
24. Starr, Roger, "New York City: Aftermath of the Civil Rights Revolution," 3, 4.
25. Carter et al., *Equality,* xx.

CHAPTER VII

1. Comptroller General, *Rental Housing: A National Problem That Needs Immediate Action, Report to Congress.*
2. Birkle, Baltas, Deputy Director, General Accounting Office, "Statement," 78–79.
3. Lowry, Ira, "Rental Housing in the 1970s: Searching for the Crisis," 25–26.
4. Ozanne, Larry, "Double Vision in the Rental Housing Market and a Prescription for Correcting It," 45.
5. Downs, Anthony, *Rental Housing in the 1980s,* 32.
6. *Ibid.*
7. Arthur D. Little, Inc., *The Owners of New York's Rental Housing: A Profile.*
8. Downs, Anthony, *op. cit.*
9. de Leeuw, Frank, "A Synthesis of Views on Rental Housing," 63.
10. Census/HUD, *Annual Housing Survey, 1980,* Part A, 1.
11. *Ibid.,* 5.
12. Downs, *op. cit.,* 31.
13. Lea, Michael, *Rental Housing, Condition and Outlook,* 45, 48.
14. Census, *Current Housing Reports, Housing Vacancies, Third Quarter, 1987.*
15. Census, *Household and Family Characteristics: March 1985,* 1–4 (Sept., 1986).
16. *Ibid.*
17. Census/HUD, *Annual Housing Survey/1983, Part I, General Housing Characteristics.*
18. Brown, H. James, and James Yinger, *Home Ownership and Housing Affordability in the United States: 1963–1985,* 9.
19. Arthur D. Little, Inc., *op. cit.,* 6.
20. Stegman, Michael A., *Housing in New York: Study of a City, 1984,* 4.

21. *Ibid.*, 23.
22. "Homeless People, Peopleless Homes," 19.
23. Stegman, *op. cit.*, 143.
24. Stegman, Michael, *The Dynamics of Rental Housing in New York City* (1982).
25. Arthur D. Little, Inc., *op. cit.*, 2–20.
26. Arthur D. Little, Inc., *op. cit.*, 3.
27. Arthur D. Little, Inc., *op. cit.*, 8–9.
28. Arthur D. Little, Inc., *op. cit.*, 18.
29. Stegman, *Housing in New York,* 183.

CHAPTER VIII

1. 80 *Congressional Record,* 4924.
2. Sec. 3213, H.R. 5300, 99th Cong. 2nd Sess.
3. Cited in McDonnell, T. *The Wagner Housing Act,* 42.
4. *Congressional Record* (June 16, 1936), 9558.
5. McDonnell, *op. cit.*, 235–36.
6. 81 *Congressional Record,* 9241.
7. *Ibid.*, 9249.
8. *U.S.* v. *Certain Lands,* 9 F, Supp. 137 (W.D. Kentucky), aff'd 78 F. 2d 684 (6th Circuit), *dismissed* 294 U.S. 735 (1935), 297 U.S. 726 (1936).
9. 81 *Congressional Record,* 9241.
10. Cited in Abner Silverman, "Users Needs and Social Services," 584.
11. U.S., HHFA, Public Housing Administration, "Report of a Special Committee on Reserves for Low-Rent Report (March 19, 1948)" (Unpublished).
12. Cited in 95 *Congressional Record,* 8135.
13. HHFA, *The Housing Situation,* 5. (1949).
14. Kristof, Frank, *Urban Housing Needs Through the 1980s: An Analysis and Projection,* 9 (The National Commission on Urban Problems Research Report No. 10, 1968).
15. *House Report No. 590, 81st Cong., 1st Sess.,* 23. (1949).
16. 95 *Congressional Record,* 4609, 4838, 8132, 8147. (1949).
17. *Ibid.*, 5618.
18. Bell, Robert, *The Culture of Policy Deliberations,* 142.
19. 95 *Congressional Record,* 4811.
20. *Ibid.*, 8133.
21. *Ibid.*, 5618.
22. Bauer, Catherine, "The Dreary Deadlock of Public Housing," 138.
23. Rapkin, Chester, "Rent-Income Ratio," 12 (1957).
24. "Urban Design Symposium," 98.
25. Wolfe, Tom, *From Bauhaus to Our House,* 61–62.
26. *Ibid.*, 73.

27. HHFA, *Views on Public Housing,* Appendix II (March 1960).
28. McMurray, J. P., *Ways and Means of Providing Housing for Families Unable to Afford Rentals or Mortgage Payments Necessary for Adequate Private Rentals* (National Association of Home Builders, 1960).
29. Burstein, Joseph, "New Techniques in Public Housing," 528.
30. Welfeld, Irving, "Rent Supplements and the Subsidy Dilemma," 465, 467.
31. *Ibid.*
32. *Senate Report on Housing and Urban Development Act of 1968* (Report No. 1123), 184.
33. U.S., HUD, *HUD Statistical Yearbook,* 166.
34. *Hearings on HUD-Space-Science-Veterans Appropriations for 1973, Part 3, before a Subcommittee of the H.R. Approp. Comm., 92nd Cong., 2nd Sess.,* 1364.

CHAPTER IX

1. Abrams, Charles, "The Subsidy and Housing," 131, 138.
2. *The President's Advisory Committee on Government Housing Policies and Programs* (Eisenhower Report), 323–30.
3. *Ibid.*
4. Cited in *ibid.* 328.
5. 95 *Congressional Record,* 4837–38.
6. *Eisenhower Report,* op. cit., 263.
7. The Report of the President's Committee on Urban Housing, *A Decent Home,* 47.
8. *Ibid.,* 71.
9. Cited in Welfeld, Irving, "That Housing Problem," *Public Interest, Spring 1972,* 90.
10. *Welfare—The Political Economy of Welfare Reform in the United States,* 141–42 (Hoover Institution: 1978).
11. Tobin, James, "On Limiting the Domain of Inequality," 263.
12. Scott, Roger, "Avarice, Altruism and Second Party Preferences," 17.
13. Bell, Robert, *The Culture of Policy Deliberation,* 176.
14. Silverman, Abner, "User Needs and Social Services," 598.
15. GAO, *Serving A Broader Economic Range of Families in Public Housing Could Reduce Operating Subsidies,* 3 (1979).
16. GAO, *op. cit.,* 30.
17. HUD, *Alternative Operating Subsidy Systems for the Public Housing Program,* 272 (May, 1982).

Chapter X

1. Florida, Richard, "The Origins of Financial Deregulation . . . ," 52, 57.
2. Gramley, Lyle, "Short-Term Cycles in Housing Production: An Overview of the Problem and Possible Solutions," 14.
3. NAHB, *Housing America—The Challenge Ahead*, 53.
4. Florida, Richard, "Overview," xiii.
5. U.S. Savings and Loan League, *Homeownership: Coping with Inflation* (1980).
6. Carron, Andrew, "The Rescue of the Thrift Industry," 212.
7. Nash, Nathaniel, "400 Thrift Units Called Unsound," D4
8. Rosen, Kenneth, M. D. Youngblood, Judy Hustick, Robert Hopkins, and Jennifer Stepan, *Housing and Mortgage Market Review,* February 1987, 10.

Chapter XI

1. "Builders' Plight Growing Worse as Home Construction Grinds to a Halt," 264.
2. Frieden, Bernard, "The New Housing-Cost Problem," 70.
3. Sternlieb, George, "Preface," 2.
4. Frieden, *op. cit.,* 73.
5. Mayer, Neil, "Homeownership: The Changing Relationships of Costs and Incomes and Possible Federal Roles," 28.
6. Sternlieb, *op. cit.,* 3–5.
7. *Government Regulations and Government Cost,* 6
8. *Ibid.,* Part 1.
9. Grigsby, William, and Morton Baratz, "Residential Investment: Too Much or Too Little," 33–34.
10. Weicher, John, "The Controversy Over Housing Affordability, Reply," 369–70.
11. Weicher, John, "The Affordability of New Homes," 214.
12. Weicher, John, "The Paradox of Housing Costs," Op-Ed.
13. *Savings and Loan News, November 1981.*
14. Cited in NAHB, *Housing America—The Challenge Ahead* (1985), 20.
15. *Homeownership: The American Dream Adrift* (1982), 5.
16. Quoted in Harney, Kenneth, "The Nation's Housing, Study Finds Drop in Home Ownership," E3.
17. *Ibid.*
18. Galbraith, John, *The Great Crash,* 6.
19. NAHB, *op. cit.,* 21.
20. NAHB, *op. cit.,* 22.

21. Brown, H. James, and John Yinger, *Home Ownership and Housing Affordability in the United States: 1963–1985,* 9.
22. NAHB, *op. cit.,* 23.
23. Rosen, et al., *Housing and Mortgage Market Review,* 4.
24. U.S. League of Savings Institutions, *Homeownership: A Decade of Change,* 3.
25. Rosen, Kenneth, and Janet Spratlin, *The Impact of Tax Reform on the Mortgage Market,* 3.
26. Chambers, Daniel N., and Douglas B. Diamond, "Homeownership: Who's Ahead, Who's Behind," 8.

CHAPTER XII

1. Kristol, Irving, "Ideology and Supply-Side Economics," 48.
2. Lawton, M. Powell, "Housing Problems of Community Resident Elderly."
3. Baker, S., and M. Parry, *Housing for Sale to the Elderly—What Do People Want? How Big Is the Market?,* 14.
4. Marans, Robert, and Mary E. Colton, "U.S. Rental Housing Practices Affecting Families with Children."
5. Census/HUD, *Annual Housing Survey: 1983 Part C, Financial Characteristics of the Housing Inventory,* Table A2.
6. Census/HUD, *Annual Housing Survey: 1983 Part A, General Housing Characteristics,* Table A4.
7. Welfeld, Irving, "Our Graying Suburbs: Solving an Unusual Housing Problem," 54.
8. Census, *Current Population Reports, Consumer Income, Money Income of Households, Families and Persons in the U.S.: 1983,* Table 10 (1983).
9. Lawton, M. Powell, Elaine Brody, and Patricia Turner-Massey, "The Relationship of Environmental Factors to Changes in Well-Being," 137.
10. Mostoller, Michael, "A Single Room: Housing for the Low-Income Single Person," 191.
11. Demery, Thomas, HUD Assistant Secretary for Housing, "Testimony," 13.
12. "Conference Discussion," in Bradbury, Katherine, and Anthony Downs, *Do Housing Allowances Work?* 383.
13. "Housing Allowances: An Experiment That Worked," *Public Interest,* Spring 1980, 35.
14. Welfeld, Irving, and Joseph Carmel, "A New Wave Housing Program: Respecting the Intelligence of the Poor," 1984, 293.
15. Luttwak, Edward, "Why We Need More Waste, Fraud, and Mismanagement in the Pentagon."

16. Stegman, Michael, *Housing Investment in the Inner City.*
17. Maisel, Sherman, and Louis Winnick, *Family Housing Expenditures: Elusive Laws and Intrusive Variances.*
18. Lane, Terry, *What Families Spend for Housing—The Origins and Uses of the "Rule of Thumb."*
19. Kain, John, "A Universal Housing Allowance Program," 365.
20. Friedman, Joseph, and Daniel Weinberg, *The Demand for Rental Housing: Evidence from a Percent of Rent Housing Allowance,* 140–42.
21. "Conference Discussion," *op. cit.,* 393.
22. Van Dusen, Richard, "Books in Review: *America's Housing Problem: An Approach to a Solution by Irving H. Welfeld,"* I-2.
23. *Congressional Record,* December 7, 1981, S. 14646.
24. Kennedy, Stephen, and Meryl Finkel, *Report of First Year Findings for the Freestanding Housing Voucher Demonstration Program,* 82.
25. *Ibid.,* 3.
26. *Ibid.,* 163.
27. "Why Is Newark Razing a Third of Its Units?" 6.
28. Winnick, Louis, "Facts and Fictions in Urban Renewal."
29. Letter dated January 14, 1982, to author from the Commissioner of the Baltimore Department of Housing and Community Development.
30. "An Interview with Paul Goodman," 63.

BIBLIOGRAPHY

Abrams, Charles. *The City as the Frontier* (Harper & Row: 1965).
———. "The Subsidy and Housing," *Journal of Land and Public Utility Economics* 22 (1946).
———. "Preface" in Carter, Robert, Dorothy Kenyon, Peter Marcuse, and Loren Miller, *Equality* (Pantheon: 1965).
———. "Urban Design Symposium," *Progressive Architecture,* August 1956.
Ackerman, Louise. "Reebok: Tennis' Billion-Dollar Superstar," *Tennis,* December 1987.
Ahluwalia, Gopol. "What Do Builders Do," *Housing Economics,* December 1987 (National Association of Home Builders).
———. "Residential Construction Industry," *Housing Economics,* November 1987.
Anderson, Martin. *Welfare—The Political Economy of Welfare Reform in the United States* (Hoover Institution: 1978).
Architectural Record. *When Better Homes Are Built* (F. W. Dodge: 1943).
Ardagh, John. "How the French Got a New Start," *The Wilson Quarterly,* New Years, 1986.
Arthur D. Little, Inc. *The Owners of New York's Rental Housing: A Profile* (Rent Stabilization of New York City: 1985).
Baker, S., and M. Parry. *Housing for Sale to the Elderly—What Do People Want? How Big Is the Market?* (The Housing Research Foundation: 1985).
Ball, Robert. "Employment Created by Construction Expenditures," *Monthly Labor Review,* December 1981.

Baskin, Sheldon, and Walter Winchester. "FHA Middle Income Housing: Some Tax Aspects," *Massachusetts CPA Review,* October–November 1966.

Bauer, Catherine. "Dreary Deadlock of Public Housing," *Architectural Forum,* No. 5 (1956).

Belkin, L.. "Glum News for U.S. Apparel," *New York Times,* September 26, 1986.

Bell, Robert. *The Culture of Policy Deliberations* (Rutgers University Press: 1985).

Berry, Brian. "Testimony," *Hearings of House Ad Hoc Subcommittee on Industrial Location Policy, 91st Cong. 2nd Sess., Part 3* (1970).

———, and Quentin Gillard. *The Changing Shape of Metropolitan America* (Ballinger: 1960).

Bettmann, Otto L. *The Good Old Days—They Were Terrible!* (Random House: 1974).

Birkle, Baltas. "Statement," *Rental Housing, Problems and Solutions Part II, Hearings Before the Subcommittee on Housing and Urban Affairs, 96th Cong. 2d Sess.* (1980).

Blumenfeld, Hans, *Metropolis . . . and Beyond* (John Wiley: 1979).

———, "Metropolis Extended," *American Planners Assoc. Journal,* Summer 1986.

Bonner, Yelena. "Americans Don't Want War," Outlook Section, *Washington Post,* May 18, 1986.

Booz, Allen & Hamilton. *Survey of Lustron Corporation for Reconstruction Finance Corporation* (1949).

Bradbury, Katherine, and Anthony Downs. "Conference Discussion," in Bradbury and Downs, eds., *Do Housing Allowances Work?* (Brookings Studies on Social Experimentation: 1981).

Brown, H. James, and John Yinger. *Home Ownership and Housing Affordability in the United States: 1963–1985* (Joint Center for Housing Studies of M.I.T. and Harvard: 1986).

Bruce-Briggs, B. "Mass Transportation and Minority Transportation," *The Public Interest,* Summer 1975.

Burstein, Joseph. "New Techniques in Public Housing," 32 *Law and Contemporary Problems* (1967).

"California: After 19 Million, What?" *Population Bulletin,* June 1966.

Carron, Andrew, "The Rescue of the Thrift Industry," in Florida, ed.

Clark, William. "Residential Segregation in American Cities," in *Issues in Housing Discrimination, A Consultation/Hearing of the U.S. Commission on Civil Rights—November 1985.*

Comptroller General. *Rental Housing: A National Problem That Needs Immediate Action, Report to Congress* (GAO: 1979).

———. *Serving a Broader Range of Families in Public Housing Could Reduce Operating Subsidies* (GAO: 1979).

Congressional Record. Vol. 80, 81, 95, December 7, 1981.

Cooper, Clare, "The House as Symbol of the Self," in Lang, Jon, et al., eds., *Designing for Human Behavior* (Dowden, Hutchinson & Ross Inc.: 1974).

Dahlberg, Bror. "New Homes for Everyone," *This Week,* January 30, 1944.

Daun, Ake. "Setbacks and Advances in the Swedish Housing Market," *Current Sweden Series,* May 19, 1985 (Stockholm: Swedish Institute).

de Leeuw, Frank. "Synthesis of Views on Rental Housing" in Weicher et al.

Demery, Thomas, Assistant Secretary for Housing. "Testimony," *U.S. Senate Subcommittee on Housing & Urban Affairs Hearings on Declining Supply of Low and Moderate Income Rental Housing,* 13 (June 5, 1987).

Downs, Anthony. *Rental Housing in the 1980s* (Brookings: 1983).

Drucker, Peter. "The Changed World Economy," *Foreign Affairs,* Spring 1987.

Eichler, Ned. *The Merchant Builder* (M.I.T. Press: 1982).

Elazar, Daniel J. "Are We a Nation of Cities," *The Public Interest, Summer 1966.*

———. *Building Cities in America* (Hamilton Press: 1987).

Encyclopedia Judaica (Keter: 1978).

Fallows, James. "The Rice Plot," *The Atlantic,* January 1987.

Fefferman, Hilbert. *Federal Role in Urban Affairs, Hearings of the U.S. Senate Commission on Government Operations, 89th Cong. 2nd Sess. Appendix to Part 1.* (1966).

Fitzwilliams, Jeanette. "Size Distribution of Income 1963," cited in Task Force on Economic Growth, *First Report: The Concept of Poverty* (U.S. Chamber of Commerce: 1965).

Florida, Richard. "The Origins of Financial Deregulation," in Florida, ed., *Housing and the Financial Markets* (Rutgers Center for Urban Policy Research: 1986).

Flournoy, Craig. "Still Separate and Unequal," *New Perspectives,* Summer 1985.

Frieden, Bernard. *The Future of Old Neighborhoods* (M.I.T.–Harvard Joint Center: 1964).

———. "The New Housing-Cost Problem," *Public Interest,* Fall 1977.

———. "Housing Allowances: An Experiment That Worked," *Public Interest,* Spring 1980.

Friedman, Joseph, and Daniel Weinberg. *The Demand for Rental Housing: Evidence from a Percent of Rent Housing Allowance* (Abt Associates: 1980).

Gale, Dennis. *Neighborhood Revitalization in the Postindustrial City* (Lexington: 1984).

Gans, Herbert. *The Levittowners* (Pantheon: 1967).

Gates, Paul. *Landlords and Tenants on the Prairie Frontier* (Cornell University Press: 1973).

Goleman, Daniel. "The Problems of Autonomy for Children in High-Rises," *New York Times,* September 10, 1987.

Goodman, Paul. "An interview with," *Harvard Review,* Fall 1964.

Gottmann, Jean. *Megalopolis* (The Twentieth Century Fund: 1961).

Gramley, Lyle. "Short-Term Cycles in Housing Production: An Overview of the Problem and Possible Solutions," in Federal Reserve Staff Study, *Ways to Moderate Fluctuations in Housing Construction,* 14 (1972).

Granat et al. "Blacks and Whites in Washington—How Separate? How Equal?" *Washingtonian,* October 1986.

Grigsby, William, and Morton Baratz. "Residential Investment: Too Much or Too Little" (Research Report No. 7, University of Pennsylvania: 1978).

Hall, Peter. "The Urban Culture and the Suburban Culture: A New Look at an Old Paper," in Agnew, John, et al., ed., *The City in Cultural Context* (Allen and Unwin: 1984).

Handlin, Oscar. "The Social System," *Daedalus,* Winter 1961.

Harney, Kenneth. "Study Finds Drop in Homeownership," *Washington Post,* August 13, 1983.

Hearings on HUD, Space, Science, Veterans Appropriations for 1973, Part 3 Before a Subcommittee of the H.R. Committee on Appropriations, 92nd Cong., 2nd Sess.

Hirsch, Arnold. "The Causes of Residential Segregation: A Historical Perspective," in *Issues in Housing Discrimination, A Consultation/Hearing of the U.S.; Commission on Civil Rights, November 1985.*

Hoyt, Homer. "The Function of the Ancient and Modern City," *Land Economics,* August 1962, 262.

Johnson, Ralph. "Housing Technology and Housing Costs," in The President's Committee on Urban Housing, *Technical Studies,* Vol. II (1968). [Technical Studies]

Kahn, Herman. Source Unknown.

Kain, John. "A Universal Housing Allowance Program," in Bradbury et al.

Kelly, Burnham. *The Prefabrication of Houses* (M.I.T. Technology Press & John Wiley: 1951).

Kennedy, Stephen, and Meryl Finkel. *Report of First Year Findings for the Freestanding Housing Voucher Demonstration* (PDR/HUD: 1987).

Kowinski, William Severini. "Endless Summer at the World's Biggest Shopping Wonderland," *Smithsonian,* December 1986.

Kristof, Frank. *Urban Housing Needs Through the 1980s: An Analysis and Projection* (The National Commission on Urban Problems Research Report No. 10, 1968).

Lampard, Eric. "The Urbanizing World," in Dyos H. J., and Michael Wolf, eds. *The Victorian City* (Routledge & Kegan Paul: 1973).

Lane, Terry. *What Families Spend for Housing: The Origins and Uses of the "Rule of Thumb"* (Abt Associates: 1977).

Lawton, M. Powell, Elaine Brody, and Patricia Turner-Massey. "The Relationship of Environmental Factors to Changes in Well-Being," *The Gerontologist,* April 1978.

Lea, Michael. *Rental Housing: Housing Condition and Outlook* (HUD: 1981).

Leibowitz, Nehama. *Studies in Shemot [Exodus] Part 2* (Jerusalem: World Zionist Organization, 1976).

Lemann, Nicholas. "The Origins of the Underclass," *The Atlantic,* June 1986.

Lewis, Roger. "Shaping the City," *Washington Post,* August 2, 1986.

Lockwood, Charles, and Christopher B. Leinberger. "Los Angeles Comes of Age," *The Atlantic,* January 1988.

Lowry, Ira. "Rental Housing in the 1970s: Searching for the Crisis," in Weicher et al.

Luttwak, Edward. "Why We Need More Waste, Fraud, and Mismanagement in the Pentagon," *Commentary,* February 1982.

Maisel, Sherman, and Louis Winnick. *Family Housing Expenditures: Elusive Laws and Intrusive Variances* (University of California–Berkeley Real Estate Research Program: 1960).

Marans, Robert, and Mary Ellen Colton. "U.S. Rental Housing Market Practices Affecting Families and Children: Hard Times for Youth," in van Vliet, William et al., *Housing Needs and Policy Approaches* (Duke University Press: 1985).

Mayer, Martin. *The Builders* (Norton: 1978).

Mayer, Neil. *Homeownership: The Changing Relationships of Costs and Incomes and Possible Federal Roles* (Congressional Budget Office: 1977).

McDonnell, Timothy. *The Wagner Housing Act* (Chicago: Loyola University Press: 1957).

McGraw-Hill Information Systems. "A Study of Comparative Time and Cost for Building Five Selected Types of Low-Cost Housing," in The President's Committee on Urban Housing, *Technical Studies,* Vol. II.

McMurray, J. P. *Ways and Means of Providing Housing for Families Unable to Afford Rentals or Mortgage Payments* (National Association of Home Builders: 1960).

Merrett, Stephen. *The Right to Rent—A feasibility study* (Greater London Housing Council: 1985).

Morton, Henry. "Soviet Life: The Housing Game," *Wilson Quarterly,* Autumn 1985.

Moses et al. *TANAKH* [Jewish Bible] (English Translation - Jewish Publication Society: 1976).

Mostoller, Michael. "A Single Room: Housing for the Low-Income Single Person," in Birch, Eugenie Lander, ed., *The Unsheltered Woman* (Rutgers Center for Urban Policy Research: 1985).

National Association of Home Builders. *Housing America—The Challenge Ahead* (1985).

National Commission on Urban Problems (Douglas Commission). *Building The American City, Report to the Congress and the President of the United States* (1968).

Noyelle, Thierry, and Thomas Stanbach. *The Economic Transformation of American Cities* (Rowman and Allanheld: 1984).

Owen, David. "The Walls Around Us," *The Atlantic,* May 1987.

Ozanne, Larry. "Double Vision in the Rental Market and a Prescription for Correcting It," in Weicher et al.

Patton, Phil. *Open Road: A Celebration of the American Highway* (Simon and Schuster: 1986).

Pettigrew, Thomas. "Attitude on Race and Housing, A Social-Psychological View," in National Academy of Science, *Segregation in Residential Areas* (1973).

The President's Advisory Committee on Housing Policies and Programs. *A Report to the President* [Eisenhower] (1963).

The President's Committee on Urban Housing (Kaiser Comm.). *A Decent Home* [Johnson] (1968).

President's Report on National Growth 1972 [Nixon] (1972).

Quinn, Sally. "The Decline of the Washington Hostess," *The Washington Post Magazine,* December 13, 1987.

"Report of the Commission of Housing and Regional Planning to Governor Alfred E. Smith" (1926) in Sussman, ed. *Planning the Fourth Migration: The Neglected Vision of the Regional Planning Association of America* (M.I.T. Press: 1976).

The Report of the President's Commission on Housing [Reagan] (1982).

Riley, H. "Housing Costs and Family Income," *Study of Mortgage Credit, Hearings of U.S. Senate Subcommittee on Housing, 85th Congress (1959).*

Robey, Bryant. *The American People* (E. P. Dutton: 1985).

Robinson, I. "Blacks Move Back to the South," *American Demographics,* June 1986.

Rosen, Kenneth, and Janet Spratlin. *The Impact of Tax Reform on the Mortgage Market* (Salomon Brothers: December 1986).

Rosen, Kenneth, M. D. Youngblood, Judy Hustick, Robert E. Hoskins, and Jennifer Stepans, *Housing and Mortgage Market Review* (Salomon Brothers: February 1987).

Rutgers University Center for Urban Policy Research. *Government Regulations and Housing Costs* (Smith Richardson Foundation: 1977).

Sansing, John. "Death Styles," *Washingtonian*, August 1973.

Schelling, Thomas. "The Ecology of Micromotives," *The Public Interest*, Fall 1971.

Schlefer, Marion. "Study of Legislative History of the Rapid Depreciation Provision," in *Congressional Record*, March 1, 1974.

Schlivek, Louis. *Man in the Metropolis* (Doubleday: 1965).

Scott, Roger. "Avarice, Altruism and Second Party Preferences," *The Quarterly Journal of Economics*, February 1972.

Silverman, Abner. "Users' Needs and Social Services," in *Papers Submitted to Subcommittee on Housing Panels, House Committee on Banking and Currency, 92nd Cong. 1st Sess.* (1971).

Starr, Roger. "The End of Rental Housing," *The Public Interest*, Fall 1979.

———. "New York City: Aftermath of the Civil Rights Revolution," *New Perspectives*, Spring 1985.

———. *The Rise and Fall of New York City* (Basic Books: 1985).

Stegman, Michael. *Housing in New York: Study of a City, 1984* (Rutgers Center for Urban Policy Research: 1985).

———. *The Dynamics of Rental Housing in New York City* (Rutgers Center for Urban Policy Research: 1982).

———. *Housing Investment in the Inner City* (M.I.T. Press: 1972).

Stein, Clarence. "Dinosaur City," in Sussman, ed., *Planning the Fourth Migration: The Neglected Vision of the Regional Planning Association of America* (M.I.T. Press: 1976).

Sternlieb, George. "Preface," Rutgers University Center for Policy Research.

Stevenson, Katherine Cole, and H. Ward Jandl. *Houses by Mail* (Preservation Press: 1986).

Taubman, Paul. "Housing and Income Tax Subsidies," *National Housing Policy Review Housing in the Seventies Working Papers, 2* (HUD: 1976).

Technology + Economics. *Economic Benefit-Cost and Risk Analysis of the Results of Mobile Home Research* (HUD: 1980).

Tobin, James. "On Limiting the Domain of Inequality," *Journal of Law and Economics*, October 1970.

Touche Ross. *Study of Tax Considerations of Multi-family Housing Investments* (HUD: 1972).

Tucker, William. "Homeless People, Peopleless Homes," *American Spectator*, February 1987.

U.S. Census. *Census of Housing: 1940.*
———. *Construction Report, Characteristics of New Housing:* 1986 (G.P.O.: 1987).
———. *Construction Report, Housing Starts: June, 1987* (G.P.O.).
———. *Geographical Mobility: 1985* (G.P.O.: 1987).
———. *Household and Family Characteristics: March 1983.*
———. *Household and Family Characteristics: March 1985* (G.P.O.: 1986).
———. *Industry Series, Single-Family Housing Construction: 1982* (G.P.O.: 1983).
———. *Provisional Estimates of Social, Economic and Housing Characteristics: 1980.* (G.P.O.).
———. *State Population and Household Characteristics, With Age and Components of Change: 1981–1986* (G.P.O.: 1987).
U.S. Census/HUD. *Annual Housing Survey: 1980, General Housing Characteristics* (G.P.O.: 1982).
———. *Annual Housing Survey: 1983, General Housing Characteristics* (G.P.O.: 1984).
———. *Annual Housing Survey: 1983, Financial Characteristics* (G.P.O.: 1985).
U.S., Housing and Home Finance Agency. *Eleventh Annual Report* (G.P.O.: 1957).
———. *Housing in the United States . . . a Graphic Presentation* (G.P.O.: 1956).
———. *The Housing Situation* (G.P.O.: 1949).
———. *Views of Public Housing* (March 1960).
U.S., HUD. Alternative Operating Subsidy Systems for the Public Housing Program.
———. *How Well Are We Housed? . . . Blacks* (G.P.O.: 1979).
———. *Measuring Racial Discrimination in American Housing Markets* (G.P.O.: 1979).
———. *Sixth Report to Congress on the Manufactured House Program* (1984).
———. *The Conversion of Rental Housing to Condominiums and Cooperatives, A National Study of Scope, Causes and Impacts,* (G.P.O.: 1980).
U.S. League of Savings and Loan Associations. *Homeownership: Realizing the American Dream* (1978).
———. *Homeownership: Coping with Inflation* (1980).
———. *Homeownership: The American Dream Adrift* (1984).
U.S. League of Savings Institutions: *Homeownership: A Decade of Change* (1988).
Van Dusen, Richard. "Books in Review," *Housing and Development Reporter,* May 1, 1974.

Vernon, Raymond. *Myths and Realities of Our Urban Problems* (Joint Center of M.I.T. and Harvard: 1962).

Warner, Sam, Jr. *Streetcar Suburbs* (Harvard and M.I.T. Press: 1962).

Wasserman, Richard. "Levitt's Comments," in The President's Committee on Urban Housing, *Technical Studies,* Vol. II.

Weicher, John. "The Affordability of New Homes," *American Real Estate and Urban Economics,* Summer 1977.

———. "Reply," *Ibid., Fall 1977.*

———. "The Paradox of Housing Costs," *Wall Street Journal,* October 26, 1977.

Weicher, John, Kevin Villani, and Elizabeth Roistacher, eds. *Rental Housing: Is There a Crisis?* (Washington, D.C.: Urban Institute, 1981).

Welfeld, Irving. "American Housing Policy: Perverse Programs by Prudent People," *The Public Interest,* Summer 1977.

———. "Exercises in Irrelevance: Federal Enforcement of Fair Housing in Federally Subsidized Housing," in *Issues in Housing Discrimination . . . op. cit.*

———. "Our Graying Suburbs: Solving an Unusual Housing Problem," *Public Interest,* Fall 1986.

———. "The Limits of Good Intentions," *New Perspectives,* Summer 1985.

———. "That 'Housing Problem'—The American vs. the European Experience," *The Public Interest,* Spring 1972.

———. "Rent Supplements and the Subsidy Dilemma," *Law and Contemporary Problems, Housing Part II,* Summer 1967.

———, and Joseph Carmel. "A New Wave Housing Program: Respecting the Intelligence of the Poor," *Journal of Urban Law and Policy,* June 1984.

"Why Is Newark Razing a Third of Its Units?" *Housing Affairs Letter,* December 11, 1987.

Winnick, Louis. *American Housing and Its Uses* (Wiley: 1957).

———. *Rental Housing: Opportunities for Private Investment* (McGraw-Hill: 1958).

———. "Facts and Fictions in Urban Renewal," in Wheaton, William, Grace Milgram, and Margy Meyerson, eds., *Urban Housing* (Free Press: 1966).

Wolf, Peter. *Land in America—Its Value, Use and Control* (Pantheon: 1982).

Wolfe, Tom. *From Bauhaus to Our House,* (Farrar Strauss Giroux: 1981).

Wye, Christopher. "The New Deal and the Negro Community: Toward a Broader Conceptualization," *The Journal of American History,* December 1972.

INDEX

ABOUT THE
AUTHOR

Irving Welfeld is a senior analyst in the Department of Housing and Urban Development and was formerly an attorney in the Department's Office of the General Counsel. He has also served as a house counsel for a private real estate developer and been on the staff of the Boston Redevelopment Authority. The author is a graduate of Brooklyn College and Harvard Law School, and has done graduate work in City Planning at MIT. Mr. Welfeld has been admitted to the bar of New York, Massachusetts, and the District of Columbia. He has taught at the University of Maryland and lectured at Yale Law School, the University of Southern California Law School, the University of California, Berkeley, and the University of Pennsylvania, and has served as a consultant to the U.S. Civil Rights Commission. He is the author of monographs that have been published by the government and by the American Enterprise Institute, and of a score of articles that have appeared in law and housing journals and *The Public Interest*. The views expressed in this book are solely those of the author.